4-

The Charter Game

ROSS NORGROVE

The Charter Game

How to Make Money Sailing Your Own Boat

International Marine Publishing Company   CAMDEN, MAINE

Copyright © 1978
by International Marine Publishing Company
Library of Congress Catalog Card Number 78-55784
International Standard Book Number 0-87742-092-0
Typeset by Foam House Composition, North Chichester, New Hampshire
Printed by The Alpine Press, South Braintree, Massachusetts
Bound by The New Hampshire Bindery, Concord, New Hampshire

Second Printing, 1980

Published by International Marine Publishing Company
21 Elm Street, Camden, Maine 04843

Contents

Acknowledgments

During the writing of this book, various friends, family, old shipmates, fellow charter skippers, charter brokers—some of whom only heard via the "coconut grapevine" that I was about to tell it all—offered unstintingly to send information, photos, anything that would help present a true picture of the "game."

I would like to sincerely thank the following:

My wife, Minine, on whom the romance, adventure, and hard work of cruising and chartering has never palled. Also Dave and Roz Ferneding, Stuart and Emily Riddell, Dorothy Butler, Bob Wheeler, Hank Milstrey, Jo Bliss, Evelyn Whitney, Fergie Walker, Bob Jill, Bob and Dorothy Smith, Louis and Claude Czukelter, Ridge and Deta Ridgeway, Shelley and Jane De Ridder, Colin White, Bruce and Dawn Berriman, Barry and Faith Sexton, Bill and Betty Bray, Carl and Jeanne Moesly.

Preface

The chartering of ships is no longer confined to governments or shipping companies. More and more people, imbued with a desire to get away from it all, are chartering boats to sail them from island to island or bay to bay in their vacation time. As each year goes by, the thrill of a cruise aboard a well-found vessel that is their own private yacht for the term of the charter attracts increasing numbers of people.

This book is for the person who would cater to the game; whose desire is to cruise aboard his own boat and be in business while he is doing it—working at his vocation. Chartering, being paid to take people sailing or cruising, can be one of the world's most rewarding occupations if you know what to prepare for and how to go about it.

In the following pages, I will endeavor to describe the tactics (most of them learned through trial and error) that I adopted, for the benefit of the reader who might some day feel the urge to down tools, turn his back on the office, and do as I did—pursue my hobby and make it pay.

To buy a boat and use her in the charter trade is to work within one of the last bastions of individualism, and the game attracts all types. I've met carpenters, fishermen, an ex-county judge, a lumberjack, a barber, an aeronautical engineer, electricians, an ex-Air Force fighter pilot, a stockbroker, a plumber, an insurance salesman—all charter skippers. The list goes on and on, and we all have one thing in common—the desire for a life in the open air and sunshine, away from a hustling, bustling world.

Often a cruising yacht, in the course of a world voyage, will do a few charters to build up the cruising "kitty." These temporary stopovers can go on for months, or even years. There are those who buy a boat and charter a few weeks a year to augment a small income, annuity, or service pension. There is also the yachtsman who buys a boat and has her sailed to the West Indies by a crew who charter her, thus enabling him to gain a certain amount of tax shelter on the ship's expenses, while at the same time using her himself for pleasure at various times.

Then there are those who just drift into it, find the life is to their liking, and, realizing that at long last they have found their forte, stay on and work at it happily year after year, standing on their own deck, independent, answering to no man. . . .

To show how to do it, what type of vessel is most suited, how she should be equipped, how to stock her, how to attract business, how much to charge—in fact, every aspect of the charter game necessary to the person who would successfully "have his cake and eat it too"—is the purpose of this book.

The Charter Game

Chapter One

The Customers You Serve

It is not unusual in this world for people to change their occupation, to pander to some inner urge that has been telling them to get out of the rut or furrow they have been following—often successfully, albeit unhappily—for years. It is not uncommon to find an erstwhile accountant working as a car salesman (I happen to know one); or a meteorologist cheerfully buying a kit of tools and starting at the bottom in the carpentry trade; or a house painter studying to be an electronics technician; or anyone, for that matter, having the burning ambition to become, of all things, a charter-boat captain.

The desire for change is not always motivated by monetary gain. The former orthopedic surgeon, besmeared from stem to stern with antifouling paint, and lying on his back underneath the old tub he was painting (hauled out on a West Indies beach), couldn't have been doing it for money—at least not when I saw him. Or the retired Rear Admiral who was working a little shipyard . . . he just didn't need the dough; I know he didn't.

Most of us, however, prefer to make a buck at whatever we do, whether or not we are obliged to do so. If we make a change, it is not only a great satisfaction to be doing what we have yearned to do for years, it is also nice to be able to keep the wolf a respectable distance from the door at the same time. All of which brings me to mention (and I'll spend the rest of this book hammering the point home) that for the guy (or girl) who would be his own boss; who is prepared to apply himself and accept a certain amount of responsibility; whose mind reels at the thought of white sails, blue skies, and tropic lagoons—there is much to be said for the charter game.

Before I go any further, I must point out that although I am dealing mainly with auxiliary sailing vessels in this book, most of what is written would apply equally to a motor yacht being used for charter purposes (more of this and other types of craft used in chartering later on).

I know of no charter-boat skipper who ever became a millionaire. But then having a lot of money isn't everything. In fact, on the many occasions I've watched a real, live millionaire leave our ship after a cruise and go home to work hard so that he could come back in a year's time and do the same thing (which we would be doing with frequent rests in his absence), I've more than once wondered just who was the wealthier. . . .

But while my own entry into the chartering trade was not inspired by any starry-eyed vision of monetary riches to come (all I wanted was a life afloat with the ship paying her way and keeping us comfortable at the same time) I have, over the years, been forced to the conclusion that, believe it or not, or, more specifically, plan it or not—if you run your ship as she should be run and do your modest best, you'll have all the business you can handle. This means that in addition to having fun you'll make money. Yes, it's amazing—but true.

Remuneration in the charter game can come in other ways, too. In addition to the obvious satisfaction of keeping one's head above water in a field of one's own choosing, there is the compensation derived from meeting people from many walks of life who, if they've been shown a good time, come back year after year. This, as well as being good for business, can also sometimes lead to lasting friendships—such as the one between Bob and myself.

Owner of a 39-foot Concordia yawl, Bob and his wife came aboard our schooner with friends (two other couples), and during the charter cruise, he announced he was entering the Newport-Bermuda race the following year. After a few cocktail sessions, during which I confessed to not having been in an ocean race for a few years, and Bob declared it was high time I got away from the comfortable sailing of the tropics for a short spell, it was agreed that I would join him and his crew in Newport, Rhode Island, in 14 months' time. We didn't win the Bermuda race, but we tried, and we haven't seen each other for a few years now, but we'll always be friends—good ones.

Referrals and repeats (people returning year after year) can make up a large proportion of a successful charter boat's clientele after a few years in the game. The longer you are chartering, the more of them you get, and you meet like old friends.

When people go away together on a boat for a week or two, they get to know each other more quickly and more intimately than if they were staying at a resort or hotel where, for instance, they may only occasionally see the manager or person in charge—and seldom if ever meet the cook. Aboard the average charter boat, which is rarely less than 35 feet in length or more than one hundred, they are in close contact with both, and any effort to duplicate the remote, clinically correct atmosphere usually prevailing between hotel staff and guests (and which almost never thaws) is seldom even attempted. The nature of the chartering life itself encourages informality, and it is more usual for the skipper to dispense with the "captain" bit and get down to first names with the guests as soon as they board the vessel—before the hoisting of a sail, or even a drink!

White Squall II *leaving Gorda Sound in the British Virgin Islands with a charter party on board.*

THE CHARTER GAME

There is no such thing as a typical charter guest. Aboard our 70-foot schooner *White Squall II*, the "age range" of guests who have been aboard for cruises for a week or more is from three months to 78 years. We've had people of all shapes and sizes and from many walks of life. The rich and the not-so-rich—ones who have had to save for their cruise and those who haven't. But if they differ in age, sex, or affluence, most have one thing in common—their cruise has been well planned in advance and is no sudden whim.

The people most likely to be disillusioned with a charter cruise are those who, already on vacation, board a vessel on impulse and sail off for a week or so. I've seen several such cruises go sour—not because of the ship or the way she was run, but because of people who didn't know what they wanted and who, once away, were totally unsuited to cruising.

It is usual for a group planning a cruise on a charter boat to deliberate for months before choosing a vessel. They may be coming because some friend has been on a charter trip and has recommended they try it (this often happens); or in response to literature from a charter broker; or in answer to your own advertising. But plan it they do—often a year or more in advance. This, as much as anything else—almost as much as your own preparation, attention to detail, and ability to give them a good time when on board—helps to ensure their compatibility and the overall success of the cruise.

We have frequently been asked by people contemplating chartering for a living, and often by guests themselves, if some of the people we've had aboard have been hard to get along with, or, as one inquirer put it, "God-damn obnoxious." To this I can in all honesty say, "No." Again, the time that elapses between the first inquiry, the correspondence, the deposit (often six months in advance), is, I feel, the mitigating factor. The not-really-interested or halfhearted inquirers fall by the wayside, leaving only the genuinely interested group or family to complete the arrangements. Ultimately, after many letters of what and what not to bring, and of how to get there, they arrive bright-eyed and eager on the day stated in the charter contract.

They have talked of their cruise through long winter evenings, they have shelved their business obligations to snatch this precious week or 10 days. In many cases they have relatives or friends caring for their children; they have almost invariably come a long way. One thing we can be certain of: it has taken an awful lot of planning.

I've never met the group yet that, after all this effort, wanted anything but a good time and was not prepared to cooperate in every way to get it. If our ship is clean and well stocked, and if we ourselves are efficient, such a group provides the only catalyst necessary to guarantee a cruise enjoyed by all hands and the cook.

Some of our best cruises have been when we've had a family aboard for a

ABOVE: Heart of Edna *in light airs on her 2,000-mile island-hopping charter run. (Photo by John Nicholls) LEFT: Calm weather in the Mediterranean.* Elizabeth, *40-foot auxiliary ketch off Athens. She carries seven charter guests. (Photo by Emily Riddell)*

week or so. Kids love to swim, and the warm, clear water of the tropics, topped off with sparkling white beaches, draws them like flies to a honeypot. We have never had the younger members of a charter party complain of boredom either—quite the contrary, in fact. Give a normal kid a vacation in tropical waters, good food, and a well-run yacht to sail him from island to island, and he's eating right out of your hand. Come to think of it, his parents aren't immune to that kind of treatment either!

Within my experience, most guests, after having been aboard a few days, become almost as proud of the ship as we are ourselves.

An example of this pride manifested itself one day when I was standing on the beach of Great Harbor, at the British Virgin island of Jost Van Dyke.

A round dozen yachts were lying at anchor in the bay, but I had eyes only for ours. I was thinking how well she looked, when a voice alongside me said, "Looks a picture out there, doesn't she?"

Gratified beyond measure, I turned to see a middle-aged couple, obviously charter guests off one of the other boats, gazing out into the anchorage.

"Yes," I agreed. "She's a wonderful ship!"

"Sails like a witch," said the man. And his wife chimed in, "The cockpit's comfortable, too. We slept out there in the open on deck cushions last night!"

They were not talking about my 70-footer at all. They were talking about *their* boat—the 35-footer anchored up ahead.

Another time when I saw pride and loyalty displayed was during a charter cruise of the Grenadines.

We had picked up a party in Martinique and over a period of two weeks cruised down the islands to Grenada. One morning, shortly after leaving the island of Carriacou for the run down to Halifax Harbor, Grenada, a sail was sighted ahead.

Our gang, 11 days aboard now and loyal to the core, confidently predicted that we would overtake her—no trouble at all. The sail got smaller and smaller in the distance and finally disappeared over the horizon ahead.

Our party then decided that, "She must have her engine going. They should be ashamed of themselves—using a motor in beautiful weather like this!"

Two days later, we arrived at St. George's, Grenada, and found that our opposition had been the *Panda*, a 128-foot schooner and one of the fastest things afloat in the Caribbean! This didn't faze our team at all. I remember one of the girls in the party saying to her sister, "I'm sure she had her motor going—she'd never have beaten us if she hadn't."

The age of the people in a charter party usually dictates the type of trip we embark upon (energetic or otherwise). In general, an older group is more prone to enjoy a "softer" cruise than a younger party in, say, their thirties.

ABOVE: Sinbad Severn, *65-foot ketch, a busy charter boat at anchor off Ithaca, Greece. BELOW: All types of vessels are used as charter boats. The 60-foot brigantine* Centurion *carries six guests in the Mediterranean. (Photos by Emily Riddell)*

THE CHARTER GAME

ABOVE: Myhaven at Passalimani Harbor, Piraeus, Greece. Eight charter guests. (Photo by Emily Riddell) BELOW: Trimaran Shangri-la—six charter guests and an electric organ! (Photo by Dave Ferneding)

Just because they may prefer sightseeing from on deck instead of racing ashore and galloping to the top of the nearest mountain, or choose to paddle along the edge of a beach instead of diving their heads off on a submerged reef, it doesn't mean they are not enjoying themselves.

A lot of our older groups, in addition to getting pleasure from sailing quietly from bay to bay, like to fossick around the rocks or along the foreshore. There is a little bit of beachcomber in most of us, it seems. I have often noticed that when we have landed a party on a remote beach, the first thing they do is to search along the high-water mark for anything of interest that may be washed up. I remember an exceptionally well-heeled guest's exclamations of delight over a Japanese fish float he discovered on one such occasion. He probably could have bought the factory that made it (and never missed the money), but the finding of that glass ball, intact in its tight-fitting net cover, delighted him as nothing else at that time could have done.

It was with such a party that my wife, Minine, found an ancient Carib "midden," complete with tools and pottery, on Guana Island, in the British Virgin Islands. We had anchored there to comply with the wishes of one of our guests, whose brother was a member of the club that owns this pearl of an island. The eight of us went ashore in the dinghy, and while Sam and Joan walked up the steep hill to the club, the rest of us started the serious business of beachcombing and fossicking.

The beach yielded nothing, so we strolled inland. We were a few hundred feet in, on a low, grassy area, when Minine, Virgin Island-born and a dedicated amateur archaeologist, suddenly kneeled down and stared fixedly ahead. Then a little to the left, then right.

"It's a midden!" she said.

"A what? A which?" Archaeology is not my bag.

"A midden—an old Carib or Arawak Indian campsite."

"How can you tell?" asked Charlie, one of the guests.

"Those hummocks—see that one over there?" she pointed. "There, there's another, just past it—they're man-made!"

The three women, Anne, Sally, and Minine, prowled around the low, barely discernible mounds.

The first thing they found was the top of an earthenware jar with a design scratched on it. It was sticking out of the edge of one of the mounds. One of the girls found an axehead. There was also a round tool about five inches long with a cutting edge at one end, and much pottery.

We left it all and told several club members on the beach about our discovery, but we couldn't interest a soul. Our charter party, however, was enthralled with the find, and there was no bay we anchored in during the rest of the charter that did not have its shoreline thoroughly examined.

THE CHARTER GAME

Some people go to a lot of trouble to get aboard . . . such as Bob, who broke a leg shortly before joining us. He even went for an occasional swim during the cruise, by taping a large plastic bag over the plaster cast. Then there was Mary-Ellen, who dislocated a knee two days before joining the ship with her husband and another couple in St. Thomas, Virgin Islands. She and Dick came back with their four children three years later.

On another occasion, a grown-up family—mother, father, two sons and their wives—joined us for a one-week charter. The only difference between them and any other adult family was that George (one of the sons) had lost his right arm barely four months before coming aboard. He had lost it on Lake Erie when a big power cruiser had churned right over the top of him and the Sailfish he was becalmed in. George's triumph over adversity, his guts and fortitude, made me ashamed that I had ever complained about anything. He participated in every activity during the charter—skin diving, hikes ashore, even washing his own clothes.

Then there was the ex-private detective with his fund of stories. Jim came aboard with his wife and two other couples and kept us goggle-eyed with tales, such as the one when, as a young "private eye," he was practicing "quick-draw McGraw" in a warehouse he had been given the job of guarding. His gun fired, putting a bullet through 24 television sets. . . .

We have even had the "genuine article"—a real, live sheriff who, complete with his lawyer brother and the prison doctor, plus wives, came away for a trip.

A lot of people who charter boats are enthusiastic photographers, and we have received many fine pictures from our guests. Some go to great lengths to get good photos: climbing to the top of trees or hills, standing off in the dinghy with camera "at the ready" as we leave a bay under sail, or lying out on the bowsprit in a fresh breeze are just a few of the tactics adopted to secure worthwhile shots.

Some get good photos, some just miss—as in the case of Henry, who, after taking a careful panoramic shot of the western end of Tortola, had just laid his movie camera down when a whale (it had to be 40 or 50 feet long) rose vertically out of the water for almost its full length, then crashed over on its back with an enormous splash, right in the center of the area he had filmed a few seconds before. Henry spent the rest of the trip camera in hand, but it never happened again.

It has become increasingly popular, in some parts of the world, for conventions to be held on charter boats. It is quite usual in this case for boats to be chartered in a group. For example, the Y.P.O. (Young Presidents Organization) chartered 14 of us at one time. It was a well-known insurance company on another occasion.

They frequently have their meetings ashore at some resort (either in the

RIGHT: Kunella *off Athens. Semi-planing hull; six charter guests. (Photo by Emily Riddell) BELOW: Small bare-boat motor cruiser. (Photo by Dave Ferneding)*

afternoons or evenings by prearrangement), or it might be aboard ship. On one occasion we lashed together two boats (*Flyaway* and *White Squall II*) in the bight at Norman Island (British Virgins), and over 70 people clambered aboard for their meeting.

One of the most memorable charters we have had was a group from Mexico City—three couples, all of whom spoke flawless English. They were a delight to have on a charter cruise; they appeared to be conversant with the principles of sailing; they shared the wheel watches with one another. We had never had it so good. On leaving, they extracted a promise from us that on our next vacation (yes, charter crews have vacations too), we would swing by Mexico City and do some small-boat sailing with them on a lake some one hundred miles out of town.

This we did, and I have never been so thoroughly beaten by anyone in my life as I was by Ivor in the 14-foot class of sailboat they race. It was only later, over margaritas (ahh!) in their yacht club, that we discovered he was the champion of Mexico.

Although we carry snorkeling equipment aboard, and most charter guests use it, we have never catered exclusively to diving parties, in spite of occasional requests to do so. This is usually a matter of personal preference on the part of the charter skipper. Some boats—often fast power-cruisers with large compressors aboard for recharging bottles—cater exclusively to scuba divers (*see* Chapter 5).

Charter yacht Parandah *in St. Thomas, Virgin Islands* . . .

Often a group of people will charter two or more boats for a cruise, and sail together from bay to bay. We have been on such charters many times.

Most guests like to participate in the running of the ship—taking the wheel, furling sails, and the like—and I have always encouraged them to do so. I feel, however, that it is important right at the start of a charter cruise for guests to realize that they are aboard a well-found ship, that the crew running the vessel is efficient and capable of handling their craft without help. If, after seeing you get underway without fuss or bother, they want to "bear a hand," then fine. I prefer to welcome their involvement. Some charter guests, of course, are expert yachtsmen.

Chartering a "crewed" boat is usually very popular with the women in a party. Women in general like a vacation where they don't do the cooking. After feeding a family and running a home all year, many of them prefer to leave the culinary chores to someone else and relax when their vacation comes along. That fact alone should assure a good future for the well-run and well-crewed charter yacht.

While most guests prefer a cruise that has the accent on comfort, there is the occasional party that prefers a more rugged deep-sea trip. There exists the charter guest who will join a sailing vessel on various stages of a world voyage. By advertising intelligently and by presenting faithfully the type and size of vessel you have and the kind of charter cruises you intend to do (or are doing), it is possible to get exactly the type of guest you want.

Within my experience, people who charter a boat for their vacation are

. . . . and a change of scene, in a harbor on Cephalonia, Ionian Sea, Greece. (Photos opposite and above by Dave Ferneding)

not the same ones who would take a trip on a cruise ship or go touring with a group. There are exceptions, of course, but by and large, people who get the chartering "bug"—the satisfaction of "owning" a yacht complete with crew for one or two weeks and being able to go where they please (within the limits of the charter agreement)—keep on doing exactly that in their vacation time.

It is common for a party to charter in the Greek islands one year and in the West Indies the next. One well-heeled quartet (two couples) chartered in the Mediterranean, then the Galápagos Islands, and, finally, came away with us in the Virgin Islands, all in one year.

Chartering a boat is about the only solution for people who prefer a vacation afloat and who like to participate while having some say in where their ship goes without having the responsibility of ownership. As an additional bonus, since they make up their own group before embarking, there is far less chance of their being stuck with a "sour apple." On a cruise ship, you take "potluck" on who your shipmates are going to be.

The customers we serve go to a lot of trouble to find us, to choose us, to fly to whatever corner of the world we may be working in, to sail aboard our boats, and to share our experiences for a short time before they fly back to the life from which we have escaped. They have not blindly followed the well-worn road leading to the usual "tours." Anyone can do that. They have chosen us. I like to think they are special—special enough to make the whole game worthwhile.

Chapter Two

The Choice of Chartering Areas

To own a vessel and charter her successfully can be a remunerative occupation and a rewarding experience. A number of factors, however, influence this prospect. In attempting to touch upon as many facets of the game as is reasonably possible, it is time to point out that the choice of a suitable area for chartering is as important to the overall picture of success as anything else covered in this book.

TOURIST ACCESS

We will start with tourist access, since it is no use sailing away to some beautiful, remote island group expecting to charter if people cannot get there. You'll go broke waiting for them to find you. Often, the more isolated (and desirable) a place is, the more difficult it is for people to reach. Ideally, a jet strip should be handy, or not more than a short, small-plane trip away from where the charter boat embarks or lands her people. If access is a big deal—if a lot of hopping from one plane to another is necessary to arrive at the ship—it will discourage many would-be guests. In most cases, however, they are prepared to take a jet, a small plane, and possibly a taxi to reach their designated point of departure.

WEATHER

The more reliable the weather in a charter boat's area of operation, the more confidently she can book ahead. People who are prepared to pay top dollar for their charter cruise, and who commonly book six months or a year in advance, expect, not unreasonably, to enjoy good weather. To be able to book ahead with confidence, to *know* that the weather will be good when your people arrive on board, is the ideal to aim for when selecting a region suitable for charter work.

I consider that the weather, in whatever region of the world an aspiring charter-boat operator decides to work, should allow chartering for a minimum of six months, and preferably nine. For anything less than six months, he might make enough money to keep his head above water, but it won't be for any great distance.

The West Indies is a good example of the ideal area. Here, it is possible to work virtually all year in a warm, equable climate, with time taken off only for routine maintenance, or to dodge a hurricane. In some places, no chartering is done in the worst hurricane months, this being the time the ship receives her annual overhaul.

Every day can't be a "brochure day," we know, and an odd rainy one will not worry the average charter guest, but let the rain pelt down for four or five days out of the precious seven he has planned to enjoy in the sun, and he'll feel he's been gypped.

So choose the area you intend to work in with care. A satisfied, suntanned charter guest, arriving home after a memorable cruise aboard your ship and the envy of all his friends, is as good an advertisement as you are ever likely to get.

SHELTERED WATERS

Chartering within the confines of an island group, or along a coastline protected by offlying islands with sheltered bays, is preferred over an ocean passage by most charter guests. Most people come away to sail, swim, sunbathe, and relax. If the cruise is rough enough to make them seasick, you won't get them back. And the tale they tell their friends when they get home means that you won't get them either. So you miss out on two counts. Some groups, not necessarily older people, prefer a cruise in quiet waters.

Study the prevailing winds in your chosen region. Is the area known for its wind changes? Does it make more sense to operate a motorboat because of the climate? Or a sailboat? Can you cater to those who desire a cruise in smooth waters? Are the usual conditions moderate? Are they rough? Hot and humid? Cold? Wet? Is there good alternative shelter to be had if the wind decides to blow from a direction opposite to that usually prevailing? Are the anchorages secure? Are there plenty of them? Are they too deep? Or too shallow? Does the rise and fall (range) of tide make it difficult to land parties at low water? Are there strong tidal currents?

Is it safe for swimming, snorkeling, diving, water skiing? This depends in most cases on whether the ship is working in a warm or temperate zone. Some guests, when on a boat chartering among tropic islands, spend a lot of time in the water. Many live in a bathing suit for almost the whole trip.

The opposite applies, of course, in a colder region, where a well-covered-in motor vessel can make an ideal charter boat.

To investigate an area for suitability, study the nautical charts for islands, interesting coastline, anchorages, depth of water, topography. Study wind charts for strength, direction, and reliability of wind, plus currents. Pilot books provide general and meteorological information for all seasons. Tide tables are important. Study any local small-boat guide that is available.

In addition, read every available paper, pamphlet, book, or tourist brochure relating to the area.

ACCESS TO STORES, FRESH WATER, AND ICE

People who hire a charter boat for their vacation will eat. And how they eat! Although most seem to have been on some sort of diet before coming aboard, all it takes is a bit of sailing in a clean sea breeze, away from the cares of home and office, for a large percentage of them to throw off restraint and develop into trenchermen (or women).

We must be able to stock our ship with first-class provisions—meat, vegetables, fresh fruit, etc.—and for this it is necessary to have access to stores with a comprehensive range of products, ideally at the embarkation point. If this is not possible, and side trips between charters are required to stock up with fresh food, attention should be given to the ship's refrigeration and freezer capacity, if any (see Chapter 3).

It is often possible to purchase fresh goods at various ports or settlements on a charter boat's route. This will depend on the area and also on the length of the charter, but it is a point worth investigating when studying the suitability of any region for chartering.

Access to potable, "safe" water to fill the ship's tanks is a must. It has been my experience that most busy ports with stores capable of supplying a charter boat's needs have a potable water supply. However, don't count on it. When checking out an area, ask around about the water. Read up on it in the Pilot. If the water can't be trusted, the Pilot will usually tell you. If you are at all doubtful, use chlorine and install filters (*see* Chapter 3).

The same applies to ice. Unless you have equipment aboard capable of making all the ice you need for drinks, the area you charter in must have an icehouse that can supply you. Happily, most ports have one. But remember: Ice is only as "safe" as the water used to make it.

SLIPWAYS, ENGINEERING AND ELECTRICAL SHOPS

I have long been convinced that the only "maintenance-free" ship is the one in a painting or a bottle, though I will readily concede that some hull materials are more maintenance-free than others. However, the ship (that works for a living) has yet to be built that doesn't have to haul every year for antifouling, zinc replacement, or just annual inspection.

A charter boat (as will be seen in the next chapter) carries a lot of equipment. It seems that the longer we stay afloat, the more we load aboard; and it all must be maintained. While the prudent charter captain will try to anticipate breakdowns of generators or pumps (such as engine cooling, condenser, toilet, or shower, to name but a few) by carrying spare parts, it is nice to know that an engineering shop is not too far away from the scene of operations.

A marine railway, with its attendant facilities of carpenter's, engineer's, and electrician's shops, is something to look around for and note down before sailing off to charter in any part of the world.

If the area a boat works exposes her to government inspection, the dates she must haul, or be lifted clear of the water, will be specifically stated. In this case, there doubtless will be other vessels plying the same waters, so a slipway will be available.

Often, however—and especially when working in a remote island group— it is up to the charter skipper himself to decide how often he takes his boat clear of the water for antifouling.

In some areas, the rise and fall of tide makes it possible for a boat owner to lean his vessel against a wharf, or pilings especially provided for this purpose, and, as the water recedes, to scrub her off. He can then paint the bottom with antifouling at low water, the rising tide floats her off, and the whole job is accomplished with a minimum of fuss.

Some monohulls carry "legs" with them that, when bolted or lashed, one on each side of the vessel, enable her to stand upright as the tide ebbs. This avoids a search for a jetty or pilings to lean against.

I once saw a charter boat in Academy Bay, Galápagos Islands, accomplish a scrub-off and paint in a manner that I doubt I'd be brave enough to try. Julian brought his 42-foot cutter into the shallow, inner bay at the top of a spring tide. A line was run from the masthead to a tree on the starboard side. From the same point on the mast, another went out to port to an anchor. And that was all. He scrubbed her off in the approved manner, and low water saw him painting industriously away under his 10-ton craft without a care in the world. A heart like a lion, that boy!

An illustration of how easily a twin-keel vessel can be scrubbed and painted was displayed by the 40-foot-long, 5-foot-draft sloop *Magic Dragon*, when we were anchored together behind Wandingi Island in the Fijis. Shelley and Jane anchored their vessel fore and aft over a nearby sandspit, and as the tide receded, they jumped into the tepid water and scrubbed her off. With the ship sitting steady on her twin keels, they painted her below as safe as, or safer than, in any shipyard. High tide saw her being warped back into deep water. The whole thing had been a breeze.

Such operations are only possible, of course, when the range of tide exceeds the draft of the ship. When the *Magic Dragon* was chartering in the Virgin Islands (where the rise and fall is less than one foot in the neaps, and not two feet in the springs), she was taken out of the water for antifouling every year like the rest of us.

LAUNDRY

A busy charter boat needs facilities ashore to handle ship's laundry—sheets, blankets, pillowcases, towels, etc.—so when investigating an area, bear this in mind. If no commercial laundry is available, it is usually possible to find someone who will do it. Check on prices.

Twin-keel charter boat Magic Dragon *sits on the hard for a scrub and bottom paint in Nieuport, Belgium. (Photo by Shelley De Ridder)*

COMMUNICATIONS

Any area where a charter boat "sets up shop" must have a dependable mail service. Brokers or prospective charterers must be able to contact you, and vice versa. Ideally, a cable and telephone service should also be available. The more reliable the communications system, the better chance you have of booking charters and, as a result, of succeeding in the game.

Some areas have a shore-based radio marine operator who will "patch" you into the regular telephone network. This is an ideal situation and can be of great assistance to the charter captain in confirming bookings. It is also a convenience appreciated by the charter guest wanting to contact home or business (*see* Chapter 3).

Chartering a "crewed boat" has changed very little in the past 20 years. The major difference between now and then is that more people and more boats are doing it in more parts of the world.

A charter boat capable of ocean passages does not always stay working the one area. She can, and sometimes does, change her base of operations. This is popular with crews looking for a change of scene, as well as being an attraction for the guest desiring a different locale for his next charter.

It is not uncommon for a charter boat to sail to another region after the "season" is over in the area she has been working. Thus, for example, a vessel employed in the Mediterranean in the summer (May–October) may sail to the West Indies for the lucrative winter business (November through April).

There can be a variety of reasons behind either a temporary or a permanent move. It may be that a group that has been aboard for one or two cruises wants to charter the ship in another area, and because you've had an enjoyable time with them, or because it pays, or both, you agree to do it.

One party boarded us in St. Thomas for a 10-day jaunt around the Virgins and asked if we would pick them up the next year at the island of Guadeloupe for a two-week charter. We already had all the business we could handle, but we couldn't resist it—their charter had been a ball from start to finish. So pick them up we did—three couples, off the beach at Deshayes Bay, Guadeloupe—a year later. Only folk like George and Polly could dream up such an unusual embarkation point—and the trip was one to remember. *We* should have paid *them*.

Another reason charter boats sometimes change their area of operation goes back to the basic reason for why we are floating, living, working on our boats. It is the desire to be free, to be independent, to do our thing wherever, whenever we want to. So we head off over the horizon in search of new territory to ply our trade, the only excuse for doing so being that we have "itchy feet." And if we've done a good job in the area we are leaving, some of our ex-charter guests will follow.

We had this experience when a party of ex-charterers flew to Cartagena, Colombia, to board us and, after cruising the San Blas Islands, debarked in Panama. As I write this, our old friends Louis and Claude are engaged on a two-week charter of the San Blas in their 41-foot sloop *Dragon*. Their party, which had previously chartered them in the Virgins, flew in from Washington, D.C.

To select an area for chartering, buy yourself a chart of the world. If you are a warm weather person (like me), draw a pencil line across the chart at 25 degrees North latitude, and the same below the equator at 25 degrees South. Pick the island group or country you would like to work in—also the language. Find out if such an operation is possible; will local authorities in the region of your choice give you permission to charter? If they will, it can be to their advantage. Charter boats are often responsible for a lot of money coming to an area.

If your preference is for a more temperate region, examine the chart. There is, after all, the whole world to look at.

It is impossible to list every place in the world where a living can be made chartering, if only for the reason that local attitudes can alter. Sometimes, all it takes is a change of government or the installation of an airstrip to open up a remote area perfectly suited to chartering.

Some countries (notably Pacific island groups) have made it almost impossible for vessels not registered with them to work at chartering within their boundaries by charging a large import tax on the ship. In some places it is as high as 60 percent. This can be bypassed by picking up charterers in one group (this is a party prepared to do an ocean passage), and, in the same manner as a cruise ship, sailing to another group or country. We have often chartered in this manner.

A vessel in the course of a world voyage, or on a cruise taking in several island groups or countries, can also follow this procedure. I have a friend who took four charter guests from San Diego to the Marquesas Islands on the first leg of his Pacific cruise. One of the areas in which we have done it is between Panama and the Galápagos Islands.

Another friend (he was booked almost a year ahead for the charter) picked up his party at Lautoka in the Fiji Islands, where there are full facilities for provisioning and where a jet airport at Nandi lies 20 minutes away by taxi. He island-hopped off the wind for two thousand miles, through the New Caledonia, New Hebrides, and Solomon Island groups to Port Moresby, New Guinea, where his party flew out. He wrote me that the profit from this three-month charter paid half the total expenses of his three-year circumnavigation.

The West Indies area is unique in that the islands (countries) are close together, in some cases only a few miles apart, and it is possible to sail with guests aboard from country to country, much of the time in sheltered waters. Some West Indies island groups now charge a tax on vessels chartering within their boundaries. This can be an amount from less than a dollar per head per cruising day for boats picking up locally, to almost three times that fee for ships bringing people from a foreign port. Or it can be in the form of a flat charge per charter for the entire vessel and her people. At the time of writing, a charge of $20 per boat is levied in St. Vincent on every charter boat taking a party through the Grenadines.

It would seem that charter boats can bring a lot of money to a region. In both the U.S. and British Virgin Islands, vessels flying the flags of many countries can be seen working. As a result, chartering is a multimillion-dollar business.

We spent in excess of $20,000 a year there, provisioning and maintaining *White Squall II*. And we are just one boat. Take 50 or 60 crewed vessels, plus hundreds of bareboats. . . . In addition, charter guests pour in and spend money ashore. Most stay in a hotel, either at the beginning or at the end of their charter cruise, and they all leave money behind in taxis, restaurants, nightclubs, bars, shops, native markets, and glass-bottom-boat rides.

Luck, as well as planning where to go, can take a hand in deciding the area a ship works. One couple with their young daughter were cruising the New Guinea area in their 35-foot cutter and just happened to anchor at Bougainville Island, where there are big copper workings. They started "day chartering"—taking 12 or 14 of the well-paid workers for a sail, giving them lunch, a few drinks, a swim, and then sailing them home. They did extremely well, and in the end (after almost a year) had to leave to get a rest.

I have just heard from Chanti and Rae who, with their young family of five aboard their 60-foot ferrocement brigantine *Veranima*, called at Rabaul on their way from Truk Island to the New Hebrides. They were chartered for a circumnavigation of the island of New Britain by Americans at the missile-tracking station in Rabaul. At one point, he writes, they were seven miles up a river on the island. All hands—wife, kids, charter guests—had a memorable four-week cruise.

In the selection of a chartering area, or a base of operations, the points covered in this chapter will, I hope, be used as a guide by the owner of a yacht intended for use "in the game."

Chapter Three

Choosing
and Equipping the Ship

Our object in chartering is to take a group of people sailing for a week or two, to give them a good cruise with as much comfort as possible, to serve them fine food, to send them home happy, and to enjoy ourselves at the same time.

Remember, however, that a charter boat is a commercial vessel justifying her existence by working for a living, like a trawler or a freighter. The only difference is that her cargo, often the most delicate of all to handle, walks aboard and walks ashore. Running a charter boat is also, in my estimation, the most satisfying of seagoing occupations—and I've tried a number of the others.

A charter boat, in addition to providing her passengers with recreation and enjoyment and occupying a necessary niche in the ranks of ships that ply the seas for commercial purposes, often doubles as a permanent home for her crew. So let's fit her out as comfortably as possible. This is where we are going to live!

So we need a ship with a certain amount of room, and while almost any type of sailing craft can be used, some are naturally more suitable than others. Our vessel does not need to be a giant nor have the lines of a cup defender, but she must be comfortable and have ample locker space for stores, ship's equipment, ice, clothes, etc. I know of a cutter and a yawl, both under 35 feet, that are eminently successful because they fulfill these require-ments, whereas a 12-meter of my acquaintance couldn't make a living. Gear and equipment, too, need not be of the "gold-plated" variety; the basic requirements are those of strength and dependability. Let's not forget that galvanized turnbuckles went around the Horn hundreds of times before the first bronze job poked its nose anywhere near Cape "Stiff." So did galvanized rigging!

Rig is not too important and can vary from personal preference to what is available. An old-fashioned gaff-rigged hooker that looks more like a blockade-runner than a yacht can sometimes draw more inquiries from pro-spective charter guests than a sleek, modern, teak-trimmed beauty that has just stepped down from the stage of the New York or Earl's Court boat show.

Some boats are built specifically for chartering and even have cabins that are identical so that no charter guest can feel he is shortchanged. By and large, however, the average charter boat is a cruising vessel, bought by an owner or owners who have a yen to own a ship they can cruise in, live aboard, and make a living with at the same time. If you belong in this latter category (and most would-be charter skippers do), then my advice is: After you have decided on a region you would prefer to live and charter in, and have found out if local legislation will let you do it, then look around for a boat that will suit the weather and conditions prevailing in that area.

The ship you decide upon does not have to be new—far from it. In fact, age does not seem to be one of the factors by which a charter boat's potential success (or failure) can be assessed. But she must be strong, seaworthy, and roomy enough to accommodate her passengers and crew comfortably.

The depth of a person's pocket, more than anything else, will dictate the boat's size, and here I feel compelled to insert a word of warning to the eager beaver who would rush off and, with the best intentions in the world, sink his life savings (and possibly a lot more besides) in a glittering ship that is "down by the head" with push-button contraptions and labor-saving devices. I happen to occupy a place in the front line of those who prefer to do things by the easiest route, but I have, along with most other charter skippers, learned the hard way that many of these gadgets just cannot stand up to day-in, day-out use aboard a commercial vessel. For a charter boat is nothing more or less than that—a workboat. She may also, however, be the apple of your eye, your queen of queens, and if you're wise and wish her to perform faithfully for you year after year, you'll learn to love her for it and treat her accordingly. It is whispered that the reason boats are referred to as "she" is that the rigging costs more than the hull, and although I feel in this age of women's lib that I am on dangerous ground here, I feel bound to suggest that, when purchasing the finery for your floating lady's wardrobe, you shouldn't go overboard on flimsy, "gossamer type" gear. She won't thank you for it in the long run.

So, almost any type or size of vessel, as long as she is basically sound, will do. But before taking the plunge and buying a boat for chartering, consider just where you plan to use her, for the charter locality can be a determining factor in dictating just what type of vessel is bought. It is virtually impossible to generalize and state with confidence that any one size or design is perfect for all regions. For instance, in areas such as the Bahamas and parts of Florida, the shallower the vessel (four feet or less), the better. Arrive in such a place with a ship drawing nine or ten feet and you just won't be able to compete—too many desirable anchorages will be closed to you because of your draft.

On the other hand, try beating back from Bora-Bora to Tahiti with charter guests aboard in a shallow-centerboard 30- or 40-footer; while you will make it, you'd be far more comfortable (and, more important, so would your guests) in a larger vessel with a deeper draft.

Personal preference, as well as availability and destination, can also play an important part in your choice. A person whose ambition has always been to own a cutter will in most cases be happier aboard a craft with this rig than any other; a man who has always wanted a ketch will search for his vessel with this in mind. Then there is the aspiring charter captain whose preference runs more toward a motorsailer than an auxiliary. However, it is seldom possible to buy the ship of your dreams. Availability and price—usually the latter—may make it necessary to compromise or take an alternative, and here we can draw consolation from the fact that, provided the vessel is suitable for the area selected, rig is of secondary importance. I've seen many types—from a Chesapeake bugeye to a trimaran to a brigantine—make a success of it.

As mentioned earlier, a vessel does not have to be a giant to succeed. For instance, in our 70-foot schooner *White Squall II*, we did 26 weeks of charter in our second year out of the port of St. Thomas in the Virgin Islands, and this was top—at least I thought it was until I got talking to John, a friend of mine who owned the *Anacapa*, a 34-foot Crocker-designed yawl working out of the same port. He did 27 weeks that year.

So size doesn't matter too much; small vessels can often (even when in competition with bigger boats) do extremely well. Naturally, a big boat can charge more than a small one; she has to, because maintenance, replacement of gear, costs of haulouts, etc. (if she is to be kept in first-class condition), are, I consider, in direct proportion to her displacement. Routine expenses on a 50-tonner are five times those of a 10-tonner, so in choosing a boat for chartering, it is well to bear in mind that too-easily-forgotten fact.

Another important point to think about is just how many people you are prepared to cater to on board. I believe that when a couple is running a ship—doing all the sail drill, cooking, cleaning up, anchoring, running dinghy excursions, and so on—then a maximum of six charter guests is plenty. Any more than six and you need a crew. It depends again, of course, on the individual and how hard he wants to work. I have a friend who is running a 42-foot ketch in the West Indies singlehanded; he takes as many as four guests and does all the chores himself! More usual is the 50-foot ketch *Glen-Mac*, run in the Virgin Islands by old friends Dave and Rozzy; they take up to six guests in comfort and share the work.

Proceed with care, then, when choosing your ship for the great chartering adventure. The average charter skipper usually ends up with a boat that is a combination of what he can afford and what he thinks can yield him a reasonable living. Shop around, and once your selection is made and a price agreed upon, have your choice inspected by a qualified surveyor before taking the final step.

EQUIPMENT

Most well-found cruising boats can be used for chartering, some with only small alterations, such as bunk allocation and a few extra items of equipment (additional lifejackets, towels, bed linen, etc.). But, as nothing smacks more of freedom and nonconformity than a life afloat, we find inevitably that most ships are outfitted differently. Often a vessel that at first sight may seem ideal for chartering will fail to measure up when a survey of her accoutrements and gear is taken. This chapter concerns the equipment I consider desirable to have aboard a charter vessel expected to succeed "in the game."

THE ENGINE

The boat must have an engine. I say must and I mean exactly that, though I can hear faintly the agonized howl of one or two "purists" in the distance. An engine there has to be, and a reliable one too, for the following reasons:

(1) When you're becalmed on the last day of the cruise, 10 miles away from your port of debarkation where your charter guests have a plane to catch, you have to be able to get there, and without any ifs, ands, or maybes.

(2) If your party wants to putter from bay to bay around some beautiful island in the shade of the ship's awnings and so avoid the sun for a change, it's nice to be able to do so. You'll probably get them back next year if you can oblige; if you cannot, you may never see them again.

25

(3) Electricity. Having an engine also means that an alternator or generator can keep your batteries topped up, so that the big wheel you have aboard can use your radio to call his stockbroker, or the lonely heart can call his girlfriend who, on hearing of the wonderful time her hero is having out on the briny, marries the guy on his return and insists on their both coming away the following year (I've actually had this happen).

Most auxiliary engines found on vessels employed in the charter trade are diesels. Occasionally a gasoline motor will be seen on one of the smaller boats, but as the years pass, the availability of small, lightweight diesels has meant that weight—once the main reason a gasoline engine was chosen instead of a diesel—is no longer the consideration it was. Diesel fuel is safer to handle and to carry than gasoline, and in most parts of the world it is cheaper. A concentration of gasoline as low as one-and-a-quarter percent can be exploded by a slight spark, and the result is impressive. Gasoline fumes are heavier than air, and if they are allowed to settle in the bilge of a boat, she can become a floating bomb; in fact, half of a small cup of gasoline can create enough explosive vapor to destroy a good-size vessel. If there is the slightest whiff of gasoline aboard a ship, the only safe rule is to find out why (the source of the trouble may be a leaky filter, fuel pump, pipe coupling tank—there can be a variety of reasons) and remedy the cause, which includes thoroughly ventilating the ship, before starting the engine.

While the safety factor and low operating cost of a diesel engine over its gasoline equivalent are the main reasons for its popularity, it must be remembered that any engine is only as good as its original installation, coupled with the care and maintenance it receives over the years, will allow it to be.

Keep your engine clean; give it frequent oil changes (I do it twice as often as the makers recommend); have at least three filters between the fuel pump and your main diesel supply; change the elements regularly. Let her warm up at low revs before opening her up and, after a long, hard run, let her tick over out of gear for a short time to lower the temperature before shutting her down. All this will pay over the long haul. On engines that are freshwater-cooled, check your header tank frequently; keep an eye on through-hulls, seacocks, seawater strainers, and stuffing box. And give her air. Every engine room or engine compartment should be well ventilated; there should be a drip tray under the engine, and the bilge below this should be kept clean. In short, look after your engine and it will look after you.

The following story illustrates just one of the many reasons why a charter boat should have a dependable propulsion unit aboard her.

We were anchored in a still, beautiful bay at the island of St. John in the Virgin Islands on the last night of an eight-day charter with a family aboard—mother, father, and three daughters—when the father woke me at about four in the morning with the news that his wife had a severe stomach pain. I had a short talk with her, then fired up the engine and in a glassy calm steamed full speed to St. Thomas, where I managed to get a doctor down to the ship almost immediately; the trip had taken an hour and a half. She had appendicitis, and two days later she was operated on in New York.

ON DECK

Have your decks as clear as possible and your gear topside as simple as you can make it. Simple and efficient is the standard to aim for; avoid the row of plastic jerry cans carrying extra water, fuel, etc., that we often see along the decks of most cruising boats when away on a trip. Not only is it desirable for the sake of appearances to have the decks uncluttered, but you're going to need all the space you can get when your guests decide to lie around and soak up the sun.

The deck, as well as being a necessary structural part of the ship, must be tight. It is far better to have a few spoonfuls leaking into the bilge than through the deck and onto the tip of a charter guest's nose as he lies in his bunk. Track down and deal with any deck leak—and this includes a drip through hatches, vents, or skylights—as soon as it is noticed. For not only is a deck leak annoying, it can also, in time, stain expensive coverings, cushions, or clothes. At their best, deck leaks are a nuisance; at their worst, they are dangerous, such as when an accumulation of water gets into radio equipment or behind a ship's electrical panel.

Be on the alert. Give any suspicious hatch, coaming, or porthole the hose test and, having isolated the spot, deal with it. This almost always means drying the area first; some fiberglassing may then be needed, or deck compound, or a new gasket. No two leaks will be the same, you can bet on that! So, let me repeat: find any deck leak and fix it as soon as possible.

The amount of space on deck available for lounging or sunbathing usually depends on the size of the ship, and also on whether she has a flush deck or a trunk cabin. Make the best of what you have. Cockpit cushions, deck chairs (on larger vessels), splash-proof mattresses—as many as you can sensibly have—are all part of the scene on the deck of a charter boat operating in a warm climate. Commonly, people spend almost the whole cruise on deck, so make them comfortable. Permanent deck cushions should have snap fastenings or tie-downs such as Velcro tape to hold them in place, while temporary mattresses, brought on deck to lounge or sleep upon, should at least be well wedged inside cockpit coamings; if on an open deck, they should be lashed down to prevent a sudden squall from blowing them over the side.

LIFELINES

A charter boat should have strong lifelines running through solid stanchions all the way around her. Again, there are many types. The important thing is to make sure they are rugged enough to withstand the weight of someone sliding or falling against them when the ship is heeled in a breeze. To achieve this kind of strength, they have to be well designed. The foot of a stanchion should be bolted through the deck; screws are not strong enough for this job. On ships with a rugged toerail, such as *White Squall I*, I had stanchion feet cast out of bronze that bolted through both deck and rail. Into these were fitted hardwood stanchions that I varnished. They have, at the time of writing, been there nearly 30 years and have known many charter parties and thousands of miles of ocean. For the first eight years I owned *White Squall II*, she had waist-high galvanized stanchions that passed through the two-inch teak caprail on top of the bulwarks, and then continued on down 14 inches to locate in fittings fastened to the deck (see photo). I replaced these with stanchions made of stainless steel tube when at anchor in Papeari Bay, Tahiti, and I can still feel the satisfaction of a pleasant job accomplished in beautiful and fragrant surroundings. Whatever type of stanchions you settle on, make sure that in addition to being solidly fastened, they are no less than

Stanchion, White Squall II. *(Photo by Ross Norgrove)*

Pelican hook, White Squall II. *(Photo by Ross Norgrove)*

30 inches high. They also have to be kid-catchers, which means that the wires cannot be too far apart. We get a lot of families in the charter game.

If the vessel is being outfitted to comply with the safety requirements laid down by government regulations, such as those of the United States Coast Guard or the British Board of Trade, which have definite rules for craft carrying passengers for hire, the distance between stanchions, and also their height, will be stipulated. But since the average charter boat sailing among tropic islands seldom comes under the influence of either of these august bodies, the onus is usually placed upon the captain himself to ensure that the "fence" around his ship is safe beyond any doubt, and that the stanchions are a sensible distance apart. This, in my estimation, should not exceed five feet.

Wire lifelines, which should be plastic coated (it's kinder to bare legs), can be fastened to a strong tubular "pulpit" forward and, after leading through holes in the stanchions, be tautened with small turnbuckles to a similar fixture aft. Both the forward "pulpit" and its stern counterpart (which in some parts of the world glories in the title of "pushpit") should be as securely bolted down as the stanchions; once they are thus secured, they are worthwhile additions to the deck safety hardware of any vessel.

On most boats the lifelines are broken by a "gate" where the boarding ladder attaches to the hull. This is usually a short piece of lifeline shackled to the top of one stanchion and fastened to the next (which in this case is only two or three feet away) by a pelican hook (see photo), which can be released quickly for the convenience of boarders and refastened just as quickly.

RIGGING

In this age of racing around the buoys or across the ocean with the most sophisticated gear available, a humble charter-boat captain (such as me) runs the same risk as an old music-hall act at a pop concert when he comes on strong for galvanized standing rigging and turnbuckles, instead of stainless steel and bronze. However, that's the way it is, and I have my reasons.

Now this is not a campaign against stainless-steel wire—far from it; it is just a personal belief, based on my own experience with both types of rigging. When I first launched my 33-foot yawl *White Squall* in 1949, I outfitted her with stainless-steel rigging, and over the next 14 years—in fact, right up until the time I sold her in the West Indies—I seemed continually to be replacing stays that had splintered or "spragged." In my experience, stainless-steel rigging gives little or no warning before it parts.

If you are happy with your stainless rigging, then stick with it, but me, I'm a "galvanized" man. If you treat galvanized rigging once a year, it will last a

Galvanized rigging and turnbuckles "blacked down" on White Squall II. *(Photo by Ross Norgrove)*

good 20 years or more. Once a year we choose a secluded bay. Then we run a strong line that is made fast aft on the ship, outboard of all stanchions and rigging, and bend it on to the anchor cable with a rolling hitch. The next move is to slack away on the cable and bridle the vessel off; side on to the wind; then go aloft in a bosun's chair and, with a little roller brush, paint the lee rigging. I use a mixture of one-third fish oil to two-thirds black paint and invariably find that, with the wind blowing athwart the ship, any drops of paint are carried away to leeward.

After one side is done, heave on the anchor cable (or warp) until you reach the rolling hitch, run the line back along the other side of the ship, bridle her off again, and repeat the procedure. This whole operation—on a 70-foot schooner with a lot of rigging—takes one day a year.

And now for galvanized turnbuckles (or bottle-screws). The time-honored method of dealing with these was to fill the barrel and coat the screwed ends with a mixture of white lead and tallow which, as the barrel was turned and the rigging "set up," lubricated the threads. The excess mixture displaced by the screw entering the barrel was squeezed out of the two small holes located halfway down it. The exposed threaded ends above and below the barrel were then "wormed" with spunyarn, and "parceled" with canvas. This ensured that the whole thing was protected inside and out for years to come. In fact, I remember, as a youth, going aboard the wreck of the four-masted barque *Rewa* (on the New Zealand coast), 15 years after she was stranded, and still being able to unscrew, by hand, the barrel of a huge turnbuckle that had been filled with white lead and tallow maybe 20 years before.

Aboard *White Squall II*, we use a good-quality underwater grease, such as Lubriplate or one of the graphites, inside the barrels of galvanized turnbuckles. The same grease goes on the threads outside. Then, instead of the old-time worming and parceling, we cover them with a double layer of friction tape. Our turnbuckles get the same paint treatment as the rigging.

When purchasing or outfitting a sailing charter boat, give her rig (and rigging) a lot of thought and attention. If you can find any way to simplify your rig, then do so, for even when chartering in the "out" islands away from the rat race, time is still money, and the less effort or manpower needed to get the sails up and the ship underway, the less it will cost in the long run. For instance, when I first purchased my schooner, she was gaff-rigged on the foremast, and I had to carry a crew member for the sole purpose of helping me set up the throat and peak halyards. So I sent the gaff ashore, gave the foresail to a West Indian fisherman (he thought all his birthdays had come at once), and made a stays'l schooner out of her. With a roller-furling jib, we then had a rig that, on our 60-tonner, my wife and I could set in minutes.

SAILS

Since you cannot expect your charter boat to thank you for "gossamer type" gear, you can safely exclude from her wardrobe any sails that could be placed in that category. A strong, good-setting suit of working sails is generally considered sufficient aboard a ship employed in the charter trade. If any "extra" is carried, it is usually only a genoa jib. The reason for this is that, in general, charter boats are run with as small a crew as possible—usually skipper and mate—and there is a limit to what they can handle. A vessel with too many in the crew will not only have a hard time showing a profit, she won't have any room left for charter guests. So our crew is kept to a minimum, which means that even though guests may participate in the steering and sailing, the crew aboard must be capable of doing it all themselves. This usually means no "extras."

It is common for the sails of a busy charter boat to stay on the booms and come off only for repairs, the painting of the spars, or replacement. So, to avoid damage to furled sails from continued exposure to bright sunlight (or anything else that could cause their deterioration), you should have good-fitting sail covers and use them when in port for any period longer than a few days. A roller-furling jib can be effectively shielded from the sun when rolled up by having a 12- to 14-inch-wide strip of sail cover material sewn down the leech and along the foot on the side that will be exposed when the jib is furled. The result is perfect protection for your rolled-up jib.

Look after your sails—a charter boat's ensemble can cost a lot of money to replace, and if you can't sail, you're out of business. Guard against a slack lee backstay or topping lift that might chafe sailcloth or stitching. Be careful how you rig a sunshade or awning in a bay: even the slight movement (caused by the wind) of an awning chafing across a roll of your mainsail can quickly account for more damage than months of sailing. Chafe is one of our greatest enemies; I've seen a sports jacket, carelessly left to swing free in a locker for two weeks at sea, emerge with the ends of the coat hanger poking through the sleeves at the shoulder seams. Although this was regarded as an enormous joke by all aboard (it was after an ocean race) except the owner of the coat, it demonstrates what chafe can do. If not guarded against, it can ruin sails more quickly than tropic sun or sailing.

For centuries, crews on sailing ships dealt with chafe by making "bag-o-wrinkle" out of old halyards or sheets; they wound lengths of it down an offending stay or lift that was in a position to produce wear on a sail. "Baggywrinkle" (as it is also called) is pretty tough in itself, and while the plywood-like quality of old sailing ships' flax or jute canvas made baggy-wrinkle seem "soft," the same cannot be said for most present-day sails. While the modern synthetic material used in the average sailing vessel's wardrobe nowadays can last much longer than its old counterpart, and not

LEFT: Crewed charter boat Dragon furls her jib in a Tahitian lagoon. The wide tabling down the leech and along the foot protects the rolled-up sail from the sun. RIGHT: Nearly furled. (Photos by Louis Czukelter)

shrink or lose its shape as readily, on the debit side is the fact that the stitching, which stands proud of the surface of the material, can be chafed very easily, even by baggywrinkle. Baggywrinkle, festooned about the rigging of a vessel, can look sailorly and smack of "deep sea and all that," but in addition to producing its own problem of chafe, it also collects particles of dust or dirt in the air, and if left up there long enough, each clump of it can, after a rain shower, assume all the properties of a dirty mop waiting to stain your sails after you've hoisted them. I prefer to leave baggywrinkle in the last century, or to painters of spectacular sailing ship scenes, or to men who put little ship models in bottles, or to the other guy.

Chafe—such as that caused by the lee side of a mainsail rubbing against rigging or spreaders when the sail is eased—can be dealt with by carefully marking the chafe areas, such as the end of the spreader, or the line down the sail made by an aft shroud, etc., and having sailcloth sewed onto the sail itself over these places to take the chafe. For the busy sailing charter boat that uses her gear constantly, attention to details such as this can really pay.

ANCHORS AND ANCHORING

Tying a line onto an anchor and throwing it over the side is a practice that has no place in this book—or in any other book, for that matter. But since we have seen it happen from time to time, I feel bound to lay down, in the strongest terms possible, that this will not do for a charter boat.

It is common practice for the average yachtsman (who in most cases does a bit of racing and sailing on weekends and a two- or three-week cruise each year) to anchor on a nylon warp with three or more fathoms of chain between the end of the warp and his anchor. Now while vessels have sailed around the world with such a rig, I question its suitability in the chartering game. A charter-boat captain must be prepared to accept responsibility for the safety of his guests, and while this does not mean that every time we take a group away we expect to be flirting with death or having hairbreadth escapes from disaster, it does mean that we must make every effort to ensure that our ship and her people are safe *all the time.*

It goes without saying that the boy who doesn't have a length of chain between his anchor and his warp is heading for trouble; chain should be used here because: (a) its weight helps to keep the shank of the anchor more nearly parallel to the seabed (thus helping increase its holding power) and (b) chafe from a rocky bottom, which can in time cut a warp through, is taken by the chain with no harm done.

For safety and continuity, I strongly advocate chain all the way. If you're anchoring in five fathoms (to take a common depth), let go your anchor, veer

25 or 30 fathoms, kick her astern to dig it in, and you have every right to expect to hold.

The advantage of using all chain is that its catenary (or curve) from the bow of the ship to the sea bottom and so on along to the anchor acts, by reason of its weight alone, as a big spring when the vessel on the surface is forced to leeward by the action of wind, sea, current, or any other circumstance. When properly anchored in this way, the holding power of the anchor is not extended; in many instances, the strain on it is minimal, and it is always less than if the ship were riding to warp with only a short piece of chain between the warp and the anchor. Another case for "all chain" is the risk of the anchor warp chafing through on a large coral head or rock.

Even the practice of using a piece of chain (the usual accepted length is between two and four fathoms) between the warp and the anchor does not nullify this chafing possibility, especially in the tropics, where coral heads with sharp outcrops and edges can rear up 20 feet or more from the bottom. Many is the time I've heard the grinding of our chain on a big "head" when the vessel has swung. It doesn't damage the chain (quite the contrary, in fact, and we've torn chunks off many coral heads), but it would play havoc with a warp. Also, chain will self-stow when it is fed down through a spalding (naval) pipe to a locker below decks, whereas a warp must be coiled down, lashed on deck, or stowed below, all of which takes time and effort.

The merits of various anchors, their holding power-to-weight ratio, reliability, and ease of handling are discussed wherever seamen meet. It is a fascinating subject. I prefer the CQR (plow) anchor largely because of its versatility (it cannot foul as the ship swings), and I have found the 150-pound size ideal for our vessel of 60 tons. I have a friend who, after years of chartering in the Bahamas, tells me that the Danforth is the only anchor for that area, and we have enjoyed some long evenings over a cooperative rum bottle arguing the respective virtues of both types, each of us having emerged from the debate satisfied that he had the best anchor.

The lesson here is that more than one type of anchor should be carried for a ship to be considered well found, for it cannot be said that any single design is ideal for use on all bottoms and in all circumstances. Some prefer the fisherman type, which has a lot going for it on a rocky bottom, but its exposed fluke can foul as the ship swings with wind and tide. However, a fisherman is a worthwhile addition to the ground-holding equipment of any charter boat, although in the following instances it will be seen that the CQR proved beyond any doubt that it was the ideal anchor at particular times and under certain circumstances. Every anchor has its day.

Some years ago I was anchored in my 10-ton yawl off the Balboa Yacht Club in the Canal Zone, after coming down the coast from San Diego. Tides are over 12 feet there, and with the ship swinging at every change, it is a good test for any anchor. After 10 days or so, a mooring became vacant close by us, and I mentioned this to the mooring master that night while attending a function ashore at the club, asking at the same time if I might use it.

"Use it?" he said. "Certainly, go right ahead, but I thought you were already on a mooring. You must have a mighty anchor to hold against the tide we get here!"

I told him that we were laying to a 35-pound CQR and 25 fathoms of ⅜-inch chain. This sparked a great discussion on anchors.

In Tahiti, aboard *White Squall II*, we dropped a 200-pound Danforth, and while I kicked the vessel astern, Minine stood by the brake on the windlass, paying out cable. By the time we had a couple of good lines set up to the quay astern, we had 45 fathoms of ⅝-inch-diameter chain out and I had every expectation that this was sufficient to hold us. So while Minine turned the hydraulic power on to the windlass to tighten the cable, I stood in the bows of the ship ready to signal her as it came taut. It never did; just as the anchor appeared to take hold and the chain seemed to tighten, it would drag again. We hove it right home in the end, let go aft, steamed clear, dropped the CQR, and with over 40 fathoms out on it and our stern lines ashore, held with no further trouble.

On my 10-ton, 33-foot yawl, I carried a 35-pound CQR, a 60-pound fisherman, and a small Northill anchor as a kedge. Shackled to the CQR was 40 fathoms of ⅜-inch-diameter, tested galvanized chain. For use with the fisherman or the Northill, we carried a further 10 fathoms of ⅜-inch chain and 40 fathoms of ⅝-inch-diameter nylon warp.

A little more on the windlass and she'll be home—our 200-pound, "just-in-case" Danforth. (Photo by Ross Norgrove)

THE CHARTER GAME

On *White Squall II* (60 tons, 70 feet), we carry a 150-pound CQR, a 200-pound Danforth, an 85-pound Danforth, and a 35-pound folding stainless-steel Northill. The anchor we lay to 90 percent of the time is our CQR, and it has never let us down. Even in Hurricane Bebe (120 mph) in Suva, Fiji, we budged not an inch. Shackled to it is 60 fathoms of ⅝-inch-diameter galvanized chain, and for the big Danforth, which stows in our port hawsepipe, there is a further 45 fathoms of the same chain. For our kedge, or for use as a towline, we carry 50 fathoms of one-inch-diameter nylon.

I like that little Northill; with the stock at right angles to the flukes at the crown of the anchor, it is a demon to get aboard without scratching up the hull, but the size of the flukes, their angle, and their design, make it a good piece of equipment. It could foul as easily as a fisherman with a change of wind or tide, but on the rare occasions that we use it for a kedge to haul the ship's stern around to a swell so that we pitch instead of roll, it holds as well as an anchor three times its weight.

Have a good look at the ground tackle when you're buying a ship or fitting her out as a charter boat; there is good equipment available today, so there is no excuse for having inadequate gear aboard. Remember that a vessel can, in circumstances such as a sudden wind change, become very vulnerable when at anchor, and the more successful you are, the more you'll be dropping that hook. So when buying an anchor (or two), it is always better to err on the heavy side, regardless of design. You'll be glad you did when you're lying in a bay halfway through a cruise with a full charter party aboard and it comes on to blow.

Now and again in our travels, we inevitably anchor in places where the holding is bad, such as the steeply shelving west side of Montserrat in the West Indies, or James Bay on the Galápagos island of San Salvador, but such places are exceptional. By and large, providing your ground tackle is adequate for the size and weight of your vessel, if you anchor correctly, you'll hold.

On the odd occasion when I've had reason to suspect the dependability of the holding ground under us, I have used our "anchor alarm." The sounding lead (ours weighs seven pounds) is dropped over the bow after we've anchored, and then the line itself (after it is given about 20 feet of slack) is led along the deck, down through a hatch or skylight to the galley, where it is fastened to a pot or can on the countertop, table, or any place that a pull on the line will cause it to swing off and make a noise. This arrangement is not foolproof—I get plenty of false alarms (as when the ship swings with a change of wind or tide)—but I'm never too proud to use it. One thing I do know is that if for some reason we ever drag our anchor, that pot or can will let me know.

I did not start this book with the intention of its becoming a cruising manual—it is written for the aspiring charter captain—but I feel that this section would be incomplete without some reference to anchorage selection, with our guests' comfort and safety in mind. There is often quite a difference between an anchorage we would be prepared to accept as reasonable when cruising, and what our guests expect when on charter.

Plan your overnight anchorages well in advance whenever possible. If your chartering area is blessed with a multiplicity of anchorages, then have an alternative in mind in case circumstance, such as a change of weather, indicates that your first choice could be improved upon. If you have no alternative, then so be it. But often, it even helps to anchor in a different part of the bay, cove, or harbor than you originally intended.

Do your homework well before starting a charter. Make sure that when you are actually out on a cruise with a party aboard, you will be able to anchor each night in as sheltered a haven as the area provides. An ideal anchorage should have a good holding bottom, such as mud or a combination of sand and mud. It should be sheltered, so that a swell will not come into the bay and cause the ship to roll. Depth preference can vary with the size of vessel. The depth of water that might be acceptable for a chartering trimaran would not, of course, be suitable for a vessel with "long legs," such as *White Squall II* with her eight-and-a-half-foot draft, so no single rule applies. My preference is for anchorages with depths of not less than three fathoms and not more than 10.

If you have chosen your ground tackle with care, if your windlass is adequate and your ship, once anchored, has room to swing 360 degrees clear of all dangers with plenty of scope out, then even if the bay of your choice does not in all instances measure up as perfect, you should still be safe—and comfortable.

THE WINDLASS

On a 10,000-ton ship, a man flicks a switch and tons of studded link chain are effortlessly hauled up through the hawsepipe, over the windlass to the chain locker below. An anchor, again weighing tons, is torn free of the seabed and lifted to settle neatly into place, its shank in the hawse, its flukes against the hull. And the person responsible for this mammoth feat has done nothing more energetic than flick a switch.

On a 10-tonner, a man stands on the foredeck, feet apart, back bowed, hauling on the anchor line or chain, yelling instructions to his mate in the cockpit—usually his wife or girlfriend—to steer "this way."

A wild wave of a hand, momentarily released from its muscle-cracking job, indicates the direction.

"No, that way . . . more, dammit . . . hold it!"

He heaves mightily, hand over hand, and up comes a 40-pound pick to be lifted aboard.

We haven't been able to hear what his mate has been saying because either the flapping of the mainsail or the sound of the engine exhaust has drowned out the sound of her words. But her lips have been moving and, come to think of it, her face looks a little red. Never mind—they'll be talking to each other again in an hour or so.

The moral of this tender little tale is that you should make sure you have a good winch or windlass on the foredeck to handle your cable, no matter what size of ship you settle on. For the man on a small boat to be pulling his insides out while his counterpart on a freighter only exercises a finger doesn't make sense, but very often that's the way it is. If we humans can lift a thing, even if it breaks our backs or gives us a hernia, then lift it we will. But, once we are confronted with something that no member of *Homo sapiens* (no matter how powerful) can budge, then we usually make it so easy by mechanical means that the frailest member of our kind can do it with hardly any effort at all.

If there is one thing we get a lot of practice at when on charter, it is anchoring. I estimate that in 10 years we anchored nearly 3,000 times, so a good rig to handle ground tackle is essential. So have your gaze firmly fixed on her anchoring gear when you're choosing your dream ship to take chartering. If she has no windlass, then install one; if her windlass is inadequate, then figure on replacing it—you'll be glad you did before your first charter is even halfway through.

Ideally, a windlass should be powered mechanically and, as an alternative in case of a power failure, by hand. *Carlotta*, a 100-foot heavily built schooner, has enough room for a separate engine on her foredeck to drive her windlass. *Maverick*, a big Brixham trawler "headboat," has an electric motor driving hers (power is supplied by a bank of batteries giving 110-volt D.C. that are kept charged by a separate generator). *Poseidon*, a 55-foot cutter, uses a drum on her foredeck that winds the cable around it and keeps it stowed there, like a big fishing reel. (This system is popular with Canadian West Coast fishermen.) Power is supplied mechanically from the main engine via a system of belts, rods, and bearings. *White Squall II* has a windlass powered by a hydraulic pump driven off the main engine. The pump sends the oil through tubing to a little motor (hardly any bigger than a beer can) mounted under the foredeck, from which the worm gear of the windlass is driven via sprockets and chain.

LEFT: Electric or hand windlass, Masada. CENTER: Windlass on Poseidon. All the cable is carried on deck and takes up no room below. Mechanically powered by a system of rods, sprockets, and chains from the engine room. BOTTOM: Hydraulic or hand windlass, White Squall II. (Photos by Ross Norgrove)

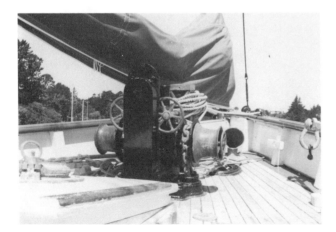

THE CHARTER GAME

I changed to hydraulic power after the electric motor that originally drove the windlass burned out in the middle of a charter at the Iles des Saintes in the West Indies. (These things never happen in your home port.) We completed that cruise and a few more besides by using manpower (Norwegian steam) to crank the windlass, and this made such a believer out of me that I almost "broke a leg," as the saying goes, in my hurry to convert to hydraulic. In 13 years, the system has never missed a beat.

The main drawback of a lot of small-boat hand-crank windlasses (especially the ones with a long handle that you stand and rock backwards and forwards) is that they do not haul the chain in fast enough; as a result, they lie unused while some hirsute character ends up heaving it in hand over hand. Now, while this is fine—and let me be the last to knock our boy showing his muscles—it should not be necessary, and when you are chartering your ship, you need your energies for things other than pully-haully strongman exhibitions on the foredeck.

Your windlass (hand or power) should be capable of hauling a minimum of 25 feet a minute. I had a small, British-made, hand-operated job on my 33-foot yawl and it could bring in 30 feet of ⅜-inch chain a minute. This was very satisfactory. On *White Squall II* the speed our chain comes in is in direct relation to engine revs, as the hydraulic pump is driven by two "V" belts from an "Albina" double-pulley clutch installed on the front of the motor itself. Usually we haul our cable at around 25 or 30 feet a minute, unless a rocky bottom makes it more prudent (the chain may have fouled on something) to lower engine revs and heave in slowly.

"Norwegian steam" windlass on the Dorcas. *(Photo by Ross Norgrove)*

Electric or hand (top-operated) capstan for the small charter boat or cruiser. Electric motor below decks gives a 3,000-pound pull. (Photo by Carl Moesly)

THE GALLEY

The next subject in order of importance is the galley, and since more work takes place there than in any other part of the vessel, it deserves more than a passing mention. A ship, like an army, travels on the stomachs of her people; and since a hungry crew is an unhappy one, the area where gastronomical miracles are to be performed needs to be planned with understanding, foresight, and care. It goes without saying that a small boat can't have the same size galley as a big one, but she will not be carrying as many people, so she does not need it. Even so, before using a ship for chartering, make sure that you have squeezed every square inch of space possible out of her for your galley. You're going to need it.

A charter boat's galley, in addition to having a stove and sink, should have as much bench space as possible. Most meals are cooked at anchor, and space for the cook to prepare her (or his) meals is important. Work in as much bench (or countertop) space as you can. Sometimes a small temporary shelf hinged onto a bulkhead will give the extra room needed to lay out the plates, make the salad, or carve the roast. You can be sure that extra care taken in planning a galley will be appreciated by the artist using it.

Locker space, and the sensible use of it, requires a certain amount of ingenuity, too. There is nothing better than having plates, pots, pans, cups, etc., immediately at hand; or all the condiments within easy reach; or canned stores, flour, bread, vegetables, etc., handily placed. In utilizing locker space intelligently, it is necessary to compromise on most vessels and get your priorities in order—for instance, it is obviously wrong to have a large bag of potatoes that would last three weeks taking up all the room in a galley vegetable locker when we are only on a one-week charter. The usual rule is: "Stow only enough in galley lockers for the present cruise."

Have cooking utensils, bulkhead can-opener, and cutlery close together; cups and plates of various sizes go in their own well-designed pigeonholes. "A place for everything and everything in its place" applies as much in a galley as anywhere else in the ship. Galley equipment should be durable—it gets a lot of use. Our pots, pans, mixing bowls, whistling kettle, trays, etc., are stainless steel, while our cups, plates, and serving dishes are Corning Ware, which I have come to regard as almost indestructible. Cocktail glasses are double-wall insulated plastic.

Wineglasses are our one weakness. I just cannot subscribe to the idea of drinking a chilled Rhine wine or a Beaujolais out of a cup or a plastic glass, so our crystal (although its mortality rate is high) remains aboard.

I like a good household-size sink (minimum 18 inches by 12 inches by 6 inches) in the galley of a charter boat. Every dish that is dirtied must be washed, and this chore is a whole lot easier if the sink is of a workable size. Some operators prefer double sinks, and if you have the room for them and still have plenty of counter space left over, by all means install them. In some boats so equipped, the dishes are washed with salt water in one sink and rinsed off with fresh water in the other.

I have yet to meet the charter captain who hasn't at some time ended up in the galley himself, whether he's planned it that way or not! Some (like me) enjoy it. Others don't. But, like it or not, if you're going to have a crack at the charter game, figure on doing some galley duty now and again. So, when laying out or redesigning this very important place on the ship, apply yourself wholeheartedly to the job. There's every chance you're going to get to know it first hand.

THE STOVE

The first requirement of the all-important stove is the same as for the vessel herself: it has to be safe. It also must be functional, have an oven, and be easy to use. The types of stoves used in charter boats are many and varied, which is as much due to preference, what is available, or what is recommended by people "in the game" as to anything else. Your choice may also be influenced by rules and regulations, depending on what part of the world you're working in. A U.S. Federal law prohibits the use of liquid petroleum (LP) gas (butane, propane, etc.) in "vessels carrying passengers for hire," into which category a charter boat falls when working out of a U.S. port. Coast Guard regulations again state, in effect, that if the owner of a pleasure boat enters into a prearranged plan or agreement with some of his guests or friends so that they all contribute a share of the expenses for a weekend away or a cruise, then this is a case of carrying passengers for hire, which means that the operator would have to be licensed and the ship equipped in accordance with the requirements for those carrying passengers for hire. And this means no butane.

As alternatives to LP gas for cooking, alcohol, kerosene, and electricity are recommended, and we will deal with each of these in turn.

Alcohol is clean, easy to light, and, in the case of a flareup or fire, can quickly be put out with water. However, in out-of-the-way places alcohol is usually impossible to procure, which means that large quantities would have to be carried aboard—not a very desirable practice. Alcohol is also very slow; compared to other fuels, it does not give as hot a flame.

A kerosene pressure stove with an oven and top burners can give years of service; while there is no guarantee that it's trouble-free (you'll have your moments), the fuel can be purchased anywhere. In fact, on one occasion after a warning by the local Coast Guard in St. Thomas that LP gas was not to be used in charter boats, I converted our butane stove into a pressure kerosene job. I made a pressure tank out of an old gas cylinder, put a valve and a gauge on it, and installed two Primus burners in the oven and four more (one in each of the spaces formerly occupied by gas burners) on the top. When I first fired it up, I thought I had invented a new type of flame thrower. That stove had a will of its own, and I never really did tame it. Neither did my wife who, after her first few burns and hairbreadth escapes, would watch warily from a safe distance as I lit the monster and gingerly coaxed it into life. However, I was obeying the law. Even if the stove had burned us both to a crisp, we could have passed through the Pearly Gates secure in the knowledge that all was not lost—we were legal!

There are, however, some good pressure kerosene stoves available now, of both American and British manufacture. The best I have ever seen was aboard an American yacht in the Fiji Islands. The owner bought it in New Zealand, and it was a solid stainless-steel, gimballed job, well insulated, with a temperature gauge and a glass inspection plate in the oven door.

Electricity is clean and, for the person using the stove, is less trouble than anything else. But its popularity can end right there. An electric stove means that whenever it is in use, a generator (and a powerful one, too) must be hammering away somewhere in the ship, supplying the power. Just when you're anchored in a tranquil cove and all hands are settling back for a congenial cocktail hour away from the hustle, bustle, and noise of civilization, you have to fire up the infernal generator because the chef wants to cook dinner. It doesn't matter how much you muffle it, there'll still be a big sigh of relief aboard every boat in the bay (including your own) when you eventually stop it. Incidentally, the way to really go over big with your floating neighbors is to crank up your power plant at six a.m. for an early-morning cup of coffee—it's a surefire recipe for finding out who your friends are.

But apart from the strain that owning an electric stove puts on a man's popularity, there is the maintenance necessary on the generator. To constantly produce enough electricity to keep a stove going gives this little demon a lot of work, which means that he's going to need care and attention.

An electric stove is okay for the vessel that spends most of her life tied up to a dock with an umbilical cord plugged in; the generator is then used only when away on the weekends or on a cruise, and this doesn't happen too often. A charter boat, however, must be a self-contained unit, in most cases only going alongside, say, once a week to take on fuel, water, and stores. So our busy power plant, which doesn't get too much rest, may decide to object and finally, in disgust, break down. And let's not kid ourselves that this will happen in our home port, where there are qualified engineers and electricians; there is not one chance in a hundred of that. No, the generator will quit in the middle of a roast dinner, in the middle of the ocean—or 50 miles at least from the nearest machine shop. You can bet your boots on that.

We have always used a butane stove except when chartering in U.S. waters, where we use pressure kerosene. A butane installation can be safe (in my opinion, the safest of all) if the following points are observed: (1) The bottles containing the fuel are always kept on deck. (2) A master "on-off" valve is placed alongside the stove (some stoves have this valve built into them, so that the unit can only be used when it is turned on). As soon as any cooking is finished, this valve is turned off. (3) An "excess-flow valve" is installed between the regulator and the bottle on deck. (This is a little gadget that, in the unlikely event of a break in the tubing between the pipeline and

Kerosene refrigerator and butane stove, White Squall II. *(Photo by Ross Norgrove)*

the stove, shuts off the gas immediately.) (4) The ship and her bilges are kept well ventilated. (5) Only one, or at the most two people aboard (who must be thoroughly conversant with the unit) are allowed to use it.

The last of these rules applies to most stoves. In fact, I remember prowling around a stove fitted into the galley of the 60-foot ketch *Thane* when we were both anchored at Virgin Gorda. It was a gleaming, white-enameled, no-wick, non-pressure kerosene job, supposed to be "just the latest." But for the life of me, I couldn't see how it worked, or how to light it. So I asked Pete (the skipper) to show me. It turned out he couldn't either—not at first, that is, and not without much fiddling, fussing, match-striking, and muttering. Finally, with a sudden "pop," one of the back burners mysteriously ignited. The stove was probably a good one, but I left the ship knowing that even if it was supposed to be safe, it was not for me. I would never be clever enough to master such an advanced piece of machinery.

There is something to be said for the drip-feed diesel stove, but only in a cold climate. They are dependable and also (if installed and tended carefully) very safe. We used one in the 85-foot ex-halibut schooner *Sitka* some years ago, when fishing for albacore off the West Coast of the United States and Mexico, and found it very dependable. The principle of this stove is very simple. A drip of diesel, which is regulated by a little valve, drops onto a truncated metal cone situated in a small "cup" (usually iron or steel) to one side and about a foot below the heavy metal top of the stove. The suction (caused by a tall flue pipe) pulls the flame away from the cone underneath the stove top and heats up both it and the oven. To light it, you simply put a little piece of paper on top of the cone, open the valve to wet the paper with diesel, and then apply a match. Some ships have huge stoves that work on this principle, with forced draft and adjustable flues, but I have only described one in its most basic form. These stoves, though dependable, are usually heavy and can take half an hour (or more) to heat up. Depending upon the ambient temperature, they also take a long time to cool down, which fact alone makes them hard to live with in the tropics.

We have all heard of accidents with stoves in boats. The worst I know of occurred when almost a whole family was burned to death, only a couple of miles from where we were anchored, through a wrongly installed alcohol stove. This was a long time ago, but the memory and the lesson are still there: Check your stove installation thoroughly, no matter what its reputation for safety; then use it intelligently.

It's over to you. The ship you purchase for the great chartering adventure may already have a reliable, adequate stove. Fine; stick with it. But if you decide to change, have a good look around and remember that you're aiming for safety and continuity. My preferences are butane and pressure kerosene, in that order.

45

THE CHARTER GAME

If you can gimbal your stove (arrange a pivot each side so that as the boat heels, the top stays level), then do so. Most cruising boats these days have gimballed stoves installed when they are built, but some, especially larger vessels such as *White Squall II,* have stoves that are fixed, and these should be fitted with "fiddles" or rails to prevent anything on top of the stove from sliding or being thrown off. The immediate area in which a stove sits, and the space around and above it, should be covered with noncombustible material such as asbestos board, and this should be sheathed with metal. Stainless steel looks well here and makes a practical as well as attractive "surround." An accessible "drip" tray below each burner is also a desirable feature.

It is always pleasant to sail into a bay at the end of a day's activity and know that barbecued steaks are on the menu for dinner. Pleasant, that is, for the charterers—and it can be for the skipper too, providing his barbecue setup is a good one. I have tried several methods of barbecuing, from a hibachi on a sidedeck to a "house type" barbecue on the bumpkin, and I wasn't really happy with any until a metalworker friend made one out of stainless steel that hooks over a stanchion on either side of the vessel aft. It is simply a stainless-steel box 24 inches by 15 inches by 5 inches made out of 18-gauge metal, and it has a grill on which the steaks, hot dogs, hamburgers, etc., cook. Under the grill (which can be adjusted for height) are the coals. With the whole contraption hanging on a stanchion outboard of the vessel, I can, with a good toddy grasped in one hand, barbecue happily, secure in the knowledge that there are no coals close to my precious deck, and that I also have a fair chance of keeping it clean as well.

REFRIGERATION

The difference between having refrigeration in a ship and not having it can be related to the difference between living and camping out. So a well-found charter boat must have a refrigerator or freezer—preferably both. Here again the size of the vessel and the space for a good-sized unit come into it; cost is also important. We chartered for eight years in the West Indies, taking up to six charter guests every cruise with a six-cubic-foot refrigerator in the galley and two insulated boxes on deck (which between them held a total of 300 pounds of ice), before we had a chance to install a freezer. When we first started in the game, we couldn't afford one; when we could afford one, we were too busy to build it in.

I have been shipmates with three types of refrigerator-freezers, all in their own way efficient, although very different from one another in operation. The first was a "demand" unit that I installed years ago aboard my 33-foot yawl *White Squall I* in San Francisco. It was a self-contained little 12-volt D.C. compressor-type outfit that would (the makers claimed) keep five cubic feet, including a little ice chamber, at the desired temperature. So I built a little 2½-cubic-foot box (half the capacity of the recommended one), heavily insulated it with poured polyurethane foam, and it was absolutely ideal when cruising in the tropics. Even in the sweltering port of Golfito, Costa Rica, with 100 percent humidity, the little unit faithfully came up with ice cubes "when the sun was over the yardarm." It was necessary, however, to run the engine for an hour or so every day to satisfy a craving for the amps, volts, and what have you, that the little plant devoured as it ran and switched itself on and off (in exactly the same manner as the average household unit).

The trouble with this type of refrigerating unit is that, in addition to the noise of the constant switching off and on, it needs a free flow of air (preferably cool) for the fan to blow onto the condenser. This is a drawback in (a) the tropics and (b) an engine room, which at times can be mighty hot. A water-cooled condenser would probably help a lot.

An absorption-type refrigerator is silent, economical (the tiny flame of a six-cubic-foot kerosene unit burns less than two gallons a week), and will always have a place aboard any ship I own. It must be installed level, and for best results, so the makers tell us, should have a good air space around it. However, I remember going aboard a 35-foot Swedish cutter in Tahiti, and out of a tiny kerosene fridge, which was built into the galley and appeared to have no air space at all around it, came a beer that was almost too cold. So, different ships, different longsplices!

When the vessel is heeled to a breeze, a refrigerator of this type can become temperamental and sometimes smoke, because the kerosene, which feeds the wick, surges in the fuel tank and the flame gets a little off-center in the boiler tube. In anticipation of this, it is a good trick before using the unit to cut open the top of the tank accompanying the refrigerator (these vary in size from one gallon to almost three, depending on the model) and stuff it full of brass or copper pot-cleaners. Then seal it up again. You won't be able to get as much fuel in as before, but the surge will be dampened down completely and your unit should work as well as ours does at sea.

Some absorption-type refrigerators have a butane flame for heating, while others have an electric element. My reasons for preferring kerosene over either of these is that its cost is negligible, it can be purchased anywhere, and we are legal wherever we go. Nor do we need to run a generator, which we would have to do if our fridge had an electric element.

I have a Belgian friend who, with the help of his wife, built their 40-foot twin-keel sloop *Magic Dragon* in Vancouver, sailed her to the Virgin Islands, and chartered very successfully. Shelley hung his absorption-type fridge on a steel peg off a bulkhead, fitted a furniture caster to both back bottom corners, and then used a hydraulic door closer on the top to dampen down the swing as she heeled. A very crafty bird!

The most popular type of refrigerators or freezers seen afloat today are on

ABOVE: *Gimbaled absorption-type refrigerator,* Magic Dragon. *(Photo by Shelley De Ridder)*
BELOW: *"Hold plate" freezer with refrigerator on top,* White Squall II. *(Photo by Ross Norgrove)*

the holding plate or brine tank principle. Briefly this consists of "plates" or "tanks" filled with a eutectic solution; pipes carrying refrigerant pass through these and the tanks are fitted inside an insulated box, which is the freezer. A compressor, driven electrically by a generator or belted off the main engine, handles the refrigerant, and the condenser (on the best installations) is water-cooled. The beauty of this principle is that everything can be done at one fell swoop—the batteries charged for the ship's lighting system and the freezer pumped down to zero (or below) once a day. We installed an 18-cubic-foot unit on this principle aboard *White Squall II* six years ago, and we run a generator one hour a day in the tropics to keep up to 500 pounds of meat frozen as hard as a board.

Before we leave the cool side of chartering, let us spare a little time for the humble ice box: it is necessary to carry ice to him, yes, but after you have, he'll never let you down. The inside measurements of the ones we have aboard are 32 inches long, 18 inches wide, and 15 inches deep; they have three inches of poured polyurethane foam insulation in the walls, 4½ inches in the bottom, and three inches in the lid. Located one each side of the wheel on deck with cushions covering their tops, they serve as seats while at the same time keeping ice up to eight days in the tropics.

It may seem strange that a ship with a freezer and kerosene refrigerator aboard still carries ice boxes on deck, but we always have. Some parties use a lot more ice than others, and although we can make the ice in the freezer, I

Plenty of ice cubes . . . .

. . . . for tall, cool drinks aboard Shangri-la. *(Photos by Dave Ferneding)*

have always found it an advantage to have the boxes on deck and keep ice, sodas, beer, etc., in them, so that people can help themselves whenever they want to quench their thirst, without going below to the galley. The ice must be carried aboard certainly, but on the bonus side is the fact that we don't have to put up with the sound of the generator making it. Indeed, some of the smaller charter boats rely solely on ice for refrigeration—and very successfully, too.

ELECTRICITY

Make sure you have plenty of juice. Gimballed oil lights hanging on bulkheads or coamings may be romantic and salty, but show me the woman who prefers to make up her face by the light of one of them and you've shown me the exception. Have them by all means if you will—they can be a good standby, and their glow produces just the right atmosphere at times—but the convenience of electric light, drawn from as large a bank of batteries as you can install or afford, is a must. They can be kept charged by an alternator or a generator driven off your engine; on larger boats, sometimes a separate generating plant is used or, alternatively, both.

Be a sport and give your auxiliary engine its very own battery, and after you have, don't go hooking up *any* other electrical contrivance to it— searchlight, radio, hi-fi, or the like. Make sure that the battery (or batteries, if you have both the room and money to spring for a bank) is there for one reason only—to start the engine. There is probably no charter boat afloat that hasn't run her lighting batteries down at one time or another; this does not matter too much as long as the auxiliary engine has its own separate fully charged bank that can be relied upon to start it immediately.

There has been much controversy about the merit of an alternator as opposed to a generator for charging batteries; the fact that the former gives more amps at fewer revs appears to be its main advantage. But since I have never owned an alternator (with the exception of our generating plant off which we draw only A.C. power), I cannot give firsthand information on their comparative virtues.

However, I have seen many yacht skippers in out-of-the-way ports and bays vainly trying to have alternators repaired, and this is what has probably influenced me to keep a cautious distance from them. Possibly the real reason I am a generator "buff" is that the two that are driven by the main engine of *White Squall II* have given such long and trouble-free service. The 24-volt generator that charges the starting batteries has been there for 18 years, and the big 32-volt, 70-amp belt-driven genny for the lighting bank has given sterling service for 12 years. The only maintenance necessary for either of them has been checking the brushes and cleaning the commutator *every* three or four years. And even I can do that.

A practice I have followed for years before buying such items as generator, bilge pump, wash-down pump, pressure water installation, echo sounder, autopilot, radio, batteries, and the like, has been to wander down to the nearest commercial fishing basin and see just what the local fishermen recommend. The average fisherman is a "jack-of-all-trades" who maintains his own gear while using it remorselessly year after year, and a talk with him can sometimes be an eye-opener. Not all that is sold can stand up to the constant use imposed upon it by a workboat.

Make sure that you have lights well placed throughout your ship, without wasting electricity. The modern tourist, whether he goes to the South Pole or darkest Africa, expects his comfort, so let's give it to him. Reading lights at the head of bunks, a light over or alongside a mirror placed here and there, a

A reading light over every bunk is a must in the charter game.
(Photo by Ross Norgrove)

light in the toilet or toilets—these are necessities. And don't forget the cook: a well-lit galley makes all the difference to the person preparing dinner.

Your charter boat should have lights—on the underside of her spreaders or, in a large vessel, on her deckhouse or superstructure—capable of illuminating her whole deck. These are only for intermittent use, such as when guests from another ship are either boarding or leaving at night, or when someone needs light to climb in or out of the dinghy, or on any other occasion when it is desirable for a short time to have light on deck. Most cruising boats have lights on their spreaders that can be switched on at night when changing sail or reefing, and while these are ideal for the reasons outlined above, a charter boat seldom uses them for this purpose. Ninety-nine percent of our guests prefer to be comfortably bedded down in a quiet bay at night instead of out battling the elements. Come to think of it, so do I!

Our ship must have navigation (running) lights and an anchor light or lights, and these must comply with the International Collision Regulations.

The arc of visibility of these lights—225 degrees for the white "masthead" light or lights (Rule 21a); 112.5 degrees for the green and red "sidelights" (Rule 21b); 135 degrees for the white "stern" light (Rule 21c); and 360 degrees for the white anchor light or lights (Rule 30)—is usually attended to by the manufacturer of the equipment, but the correct positioning of the lights and their proper use aboard is the responsibility of the captain. He must ensure compliance with paragraph 13, Annex 1, of the Collision Regulations, which states, "The construction of lanterns and shapes and the installation of lanterns on board the vessel shall be to the satisfaction of the appropriate authority of the State where the vessel is registered."

The rules tell us that each light must be visible over an *unbroken* arc. Make sure someone hasn't hung a coil of line in front of your starboard light, or lowered your ensign over the stern light and lashed it there (this sounds ridiculous, but it has happened). A sail must never blanket or interfere with the arc of visibility of a sidelight.

While we are on the subject of visibility—and this applies to all the navigation lights—it must be realized that the range of visibility laid down in the rules is the minimum only. I am firmly convinced that some of the collisions between small boats and large vessels at night are occasioned by the master or lookout of a large ship deciding that the tiny light he can see is that of another large vessel a long way off.

Have bright running and anchor lights, the brighter the better. And don't forget that the moment you see the reflection of another guy's light on the water, you're close. Sometimes too close.

Use the electricity you have sensibly, however. Even the largest battery bank can be run down quickly if lights are left burning for no reason. And keep an eye on your batteries; keep them topped up with water, always making sure that the plates are covered. Don't forget that they contain acid—have them snugly stowed in lead-lined fiberglass or hard rubber containers that cannot move no matter what antics the ship gets into. Batteries also need air, so make certain they are so placed in the ship that gas generated during charging can quickly be dissipated by ventilation. It is recommended (and in some countries mandatory) that batteries have a cover fitted over the box that holds them, so that tools or other metal objects cannot fall onto the terminals and cause a spark. Pegboard is often used for this; or sometimes a strong plywood cover installed at such a distance above the batteries as to give a three- or four-inch air space all around.

A way of keeping battery posts and terminals clean and free of corrosion is to wash them with a solution of bicarbonate of soda and water once a year. If they are then rinsed off with clean water, dried, and smeared with grease or Nocorrode before being reassembled, they should function perfectly with no power loss for another year.

The D.C. voltages used by the small-boat fraternity nowadays are usually 12, 24, or 32 volts, with now and again a vessel having 120 volts. The most popular, however, and the one found aboard most charter boats, is 12 volts. Fluorescent lights draw a fraction of the power of incandescent bulbs, so use

Cozy corner and library in Heart of Edna. *Note fluorescent light above bookcase and "just-in-case" kerosene light on bulkhead. (Photo by John Nicholls)*

them wherever possible. They may be hard to find for 24- or 32-volt systems, but they are available in abundance for the ship wired for 12 or 120 volts. So if your ship's electrical system will allow their installation, put them in—you'll get more hours of lighting from the power stored in your batteries if you do.

White Squall II has a little voltmeter, marketed under the name of Chargicator, hooked up to her lighting batteries. It is manufactured by Morse, and when I first came aboard some 14 years ago, I viewed it with suspicion as just something else to go wrong. As the years passed, however, I changed my mind—it has given uncomplaining service. I leave it switched on all the time and can see at a glance just how much "juice" is in the batteries and, consequently, whether they need charging.

An auxiliary generator giving A.C. power (120 or 240 volts) is a handy addition to the electrical equipment of any charter boat. Tools such as sanders, drills, etc., can be driven off it; it can run a vacuum cleaner, charge your batteries (through a convertor), and even power a guest's electric razor. The load the generator can take depends, of course, on how many watts it puts out; plug a power tool or appliance that takes 500 watts into a little generator that only puts out 200, and it will stop as quickly as if somebody had grabbed it by the throat. Equipment should be used sensibly and not be overloaded.

Small portable gasoline generator—nice to be able to use power tools. (Photo by Ross Norgrove)

Auxiliary diesel generators, such as the one we have aboard *White Squall II* (6 K.V.A., 240 volts A.C.), are seldom found in vessels under 50 feet in length because of the room they take up, and weight can also be a consideration. The small, portable, gasoline generator is a feature that has become increasingly popular over the last 10 years or so aboard vessels that don't have the space for a heavy, permanently installed electric power plant. These are available in a variety of voltages and capacities. Many of them, besides producing A.C. for tools, etc., will charge a battery at the same time and have the additional advantage of being air-cooled and portable (see photo).

With the wide variety of electrical and electronic equipment available today, it is a great temptation for the charter-boat skipper or cruising yachtsman to load his boat down with gear—gear that can make great demands on his D.C. power supply. So when outfitting your charter boat, or any other vessel, for that matter, be sure that your batteries have enough capacity and that your wiring is of such a size that they can handle the maximum load with ease. Have your electrical circuits, breakers, fuses, ground connections, etc., checked every year by a qualified surveyor, and make sure your alternator or generator delivering power to your batteries is of a minimum 50-amp output, or, if not, at least is capable of keeping them charged.

Diesel generator, vise, workbench, switchboard. Chargicator is at top left of switchboard. (Photo by Ross Norgrove)

PRESSURE SYSTEM

At one time I would have regarded a pressure water system as an un-necessary gadget. However, after having one aboard for many years, during which time it has pumped thousands upon thousands of gallons without giving a moment of trouble, I cannot but recommend strongly that a good one is a worthwhile addition to the equipment of any charter boat. The type we have is a P.A.R. (the heaviest-duty model the company makes), a little diaphragm and valve job. I bought an extra electric motor and sundry other spare parts when originally installing it aboard, but the only maintenance that has ever been necessary has been the replacement of the two neoprene valves and diaphragm every couple of years—a half-hour job.

FAUCETS, SHOWER, AND WATER

We have spring-loaded faucets over washbasins, galley sink, etc., and these again I recommend unreservedly. You have to hold the faucet on to get water, which means that some charter guest cannot lock himself (or herself) in the head, turn on a faucet, and merrily let it run as if Niagara Falls (rather than the capacity of the ship's tanks) were behind the water supply. Our shower also is spring-loaded, so it works only when a little chain is pulled down and held down. This releases the built-up pressure between the shower head and a micro switch on the pump unit in the engine room and—hey, presto—the little installation throbs away and water squirts out of the shower head.

The shower head should have very fine holes to enable a shower to be taken with a minimum of water. Incidentally, the drain that one of these little units places on a battery bank is infinitesimal. *White Squall II* carries a little over 300 gallons of water, and this is ample for a one-week charter cruise with eight aboard, just as long as all hands use water sensibly.

The material used for a vessel's water tanks is, I feel, worthy of mention here. Some ships have stainless-steel tanks, which, if made correctly of first-rate material, are very good. Tinned copper (with the tinning on the inside) is also excellent. Galvanized tanks can give good service, and I have known them to last for 12 years. When new, they should be well washed out, because sometimes for a short while the water can "taste" and be cloudy. This soon disappears, however, and these tanks can keep water in perfect condition.

Steel tanks, which are very popular in some parts of the world, should be cement-washed inside to prevent discoloration of the water and to keep it "sweet." For this, an inspection door in the top of the tank is necessary if a good job is to be done, and the "wash," which is a mixture of cement and water, is brushed over the inside of the tank and door, which is then bolted in place. The whole thing is filled with water after 24 hours. If the cement is left longer or if it is allowed to set before the tank is filled, it can become brittle and fall off. Steel tanks need "rewashing" from time to time.

Fiberglass water tanks are often molded into a ship when she is built; just as frequently they are custom-made to fit the space allocated in a vessel. They can be excellent, and if built strongly, can last for many years. But they often have one drawback: When you take a drink of water, you taste fiberglass. To guard against this, it is a wise precaution to steam the insides of the tanks thoroughly before they are used. If a vessel has integral tanks, or tanks built in so that they cannot be removed, they must first be emptied before steaming. Then steam (from a hose pushed down the filler pipe, or, better still, into the inlet fitting on the tank itself) must be allowed to flow into the tank (or tanks) for at least two hours.

Since the average yachtsman does not usually have a steam pipe at his beck and call, the sudden need to use one may seem to present a problem, but if he can find a gallon can and a Primus—or any other small stove plus a piece of rubber hose (preferably a tight fit in the top of the can and a loose fit into the tank)—he can do the job easily enough by: (a) filling the gallon can half full of water; (b) placing it on top of the Primus, which should be as close as possible to the tank; (c) connecting both can and tank by rubber hose; and (d) lighting the stove and allowing the water to boil, so that steam is forced along the hose into the tank for at least two hours.

If the fiberglass water tanks are removable, take them out to do the job and suspend them upside down over the can. The whole idea of introducing steam into a fiberglass tank is to "cure" the resin, and it is a way to ensure that the water will not have an odd taste. An easier way of steaming a removable or new tank than the can-and-Primus method is to take it to your favorite laundry; talk to them nicely and they'll probably let you use a steam hose for a few hours.

Wooden tanks built of marine-grade plywood are as good as any; if painted inside with paraffin wax, they will last a good 15 years. I built wooden tanks for our schooner 10 years ago and painted them inside with Gluvit, an epoxy, while I was assembling them. I used wooden fillets along the joins, which were epoxy-glued and fastened with bronze Holdfast nails. Delrin through-hull fittings were utilized for inlets, outlets, and vents. These tanks keep water perfectly and don't seem to have aged at all. They should continue to give good service for years to come.

To remove the chlorine taste, we use an Aqua-clear activated charcoal filter between our pressure pump and the main line off which all faucets draw water. The chlorine is either in the water when we fill our tanks or put there by us if we have any doubt at all about the "potability" of the supply. I prefer to be heavy-handed with the chlorine (instructions for how much to use are on any bottle of bleach, e.g., Clorox). Let the water sit for an hour or so in the tanks so that the additive can do its stuff before pumping it through the filter as you need it. In this way you avoid any risk of "turista"—or whatever the favorite name for it is—among the people aboard.

In most cases when chartering, the ship's water comes from a reliable source, such as the main supply of a busy port, but now and again we pick up guests in obscure, out-of-the-way places, which usually means that we top off our tanks there also. And this always calls for the chlorine treatment.

Carry your own hose aboard. We have two plastic hoses. Each has a male fitting on one end and a female on the other, so that in addition to the convenience of being able to join them together quickly, after using the water and draining it all out, we can screw the ends together for the sake of cleanliness before stowing the hose away. Each hose is 100 feet long.

The amount of water carried aboard varies from ship to ship, and some have enormous tankage. The amount of water needed depends on the size of the vessel (which goes hand-in-glove with the room she has for tanks), how many people she has aboard, and how long she will be away on a cruise.

I know of charter boats getting along fine with 200 gallons or less, but these are smaller vessels that carry fewer people and usually use salt water for washing dishes. (Dishwashing uses more water than anything else.) Often a little hand or foot pump drawing water from a through-hull below the water-line is installed in the galley for this express purpose.

Water from a shower can drain into a holding tank in the bilge, which in turn is pumped out, or, as in the case of *White Squall II*, is pumped directly from the shower stall over the side by a little Jabsco pump.

THE TOILET

The toilet, or "head" as it is usually called, must be as trouble-free as possible for both the charter guests' convenience and your own peace of mind, because if for some reason it gets clogged up, then you know who will have to fix it. This—and if necessary I can speak emotionally on the subject—is to be avoided at all costs.

The easiest "head" to use is the one that flushes in the same manner as a regular household job, sending the waste swiftly into the sea in installations where the toilet is above the waterline. Alternatively, the waste is collected in a sump tank, usually in the ship's bilge. The cistern that feeds the toilet is then automatically pumped up (often by a little Jabsco), and the whole unit is ready for use again. The bilge tank is pumped out at your convenience at sea by a "macerator" pump, which you pray will never fail. Macerator—marvelous word! This method, or its equivalent, is mandatory in certain parts of the world, and some marinas have the facilities to pump out a ship's sump tanks and so save the vessel a trip to sea.

I feel it is incumbent upon me to say something about sump tanks, though I recoil at the thought of having one aboard. Just think of sailing around with the sump tank full and not being able to empty it! Upon reflection, though, it is not so much having the tank aboard that makes me break out in goose bumps; it's the knowledge of whose job it would be to fix that pump if it got gummed up or refused to go on duty. That prospect alone is enough to make a man sail to the other side of the world and set up shop there—anywhere he doesn't need a sump tank!

Something else that can give the prospective owner of a sump tank pause for thought is the location of the vent. Every tank, whether it is intended for water, fuel, or waste, must have a vent pipe, and it is usual to continue this above decks and fasten it to a coaming or deckhouse. Here it lives snugly out of the way, its top bent over and down in a half-circle to prevent sea or rain water from running back down it and into the tank. Be as crafty as possible about the positioning of this vent, for it can make all the difference to the success or failure of your floating fun. One almighty roll of the ship with the sump tank half full of waste can send enough gas out of that vent pipe to make all hands on deck look incredulously at each other.

A friend informed me recently that he had finally "whipped" the vent pipe problem by running it 18 feet up his mainmast. He used clear, nontoxic hose, and after fastening it every foot with a U-shaped clamp, he inserted a half-circle of copper pipe in the top, in the same manner as a deck or coaming vent. He tells me that it is highly successful and has made all the difference to life aboard. He still has his macerator pump down below, but his troubles on deck have gone with the wind, so to speak.

Clear, nontoxic hose led up Masada's mainmast from toilet sump tank in the bilge. All ventilation troubles "gone with the wind!" (Photo by Ross Norgrove)

To operate within the law, for the charter skipper who is required to collect all waste aboard in a sump tank, I will advise this: Have your tank (or tanks) made of strong, durable material, such as stainless steel or mild steel. In the top, have a good-sized plate, at least 12 inches in diameter, that can be unbolted for inspection and cleaning. Install a manual "no-clog" pump (diaphragm Edson type is ideal) as an alternative to your electric macerator in case it breaks down; and hope for the best.

We have always used the largest hand-operated toilets manufactured by Wilcox-Crittenden, and they have given excellent service, needing only routine maintenance from time to time. It is possible to fit a chlorinator (a little gadget that it is claimed "purifies" waste) to most hand or electrically operated toilets, and several models are available commercially in an attempt to satisfy local regulations. It depends on what part of the world you intend to charter in, and no single rule applies here.

Have a washbasin, mirror, racks for towels and hand towels, holders for toothbrushes, etc., in every toilet area. And while we are still in this important place in the ship, I might point out that there are a number of earthy little plaques available that can be displayed in the head to inform the user that a marine toilet can be temperamental at times. The one stating that, "Nothing, but nothing, is to be flushed down this toilet unless it has been eaten first (toilet paper excepted)," is as good as any to get the message across.

The one responsibility that guests have aboard a charter boat takes place in the head: they must be held responsible for how they operate it and what they put down it. The strategic location of any notice (or notices) informing them of the correct procedure should be planned carefully. We have placed instructions on the inside of the hinged toilet lid, and I have always considered this a good place. A friend, however, has gone one step further on his boat. In addition to installing a notice on the inside of the lid, he has cunningly placed one on the back of the toilet door, so that a user meets the instructions eyeball to eyeball, so to speak.

I had never thought that the mere pumping of a toilet could instill in anyone a feeling of prestige, but I actually had a charter guest announce one time, "You know, Ross, when I've got that handle in my hand, I feel as if I'm running the ship."

STOWAGE

Try to arrange as much stowage as possible for your guests' clothes. Again, this varies with the size of the vessel and the number of passengers she has to accommodate. If each person can have a good-sized drawer or locker, it is ideal; this, along with one large or two medium-sized closets for suits and coats to hang in, will suffice. If your ship has private cabins with ample drawers and locker space, then this does not, of course, apply; it is intended to be regarded only as a minimum.

The amount of luggage people arrive with varies with the individual and in most cases depends upon his (or her) experience as a traveler. But, by and large, people who charter are not overburdened with baggage. They still will have at least one suitcase apiece, though, and it can be a problem to figure out where to stow these bags when you pick up in one port and drop off in another. So give this a certain amount of thought when planning or buying your ship. I stow suitcases in the forepeak, the engine room, and at times in the lazarette. Some charter guests prefer to keep a small suitcase with toilet articles, etc., in their cabins, or at the foot of their bunks. Now and again your people will be experienced yachtsmen who arrive with all their gear in canvas duffel bags—a charter skipper's dream!

If you are working out of a port to which you will be returning at the end of the charter, there is no need to take the suitcases along at all. Have a good locker ashore, and, after your guests have unpacked aboard, stow their empty luggage in it. Then it's well out of the way for the entire trip.

Aboard vessels short on locker space, it is common to see the little fishnet hammocks (sold by marine stores) slung against the hull or lining alongside the guests' bunks for them to stow various items of equipment. These hammocks vary from about four to six feet in length and can hold a surprising amount of gear, such as swimsuits, informal clothing, cameras, beach towels, lotions, etc.

When building lockers or drawers into a vessel being fitted out for the express purpose of chartering, the wise architect, shipwright, or do-it-yourselfer will provide as many as he can reasonably fit in—as opposed to the bare minimum he thinks he might need. It seems that no matter how much stowage we have on a ship, we always wish we had more, so the sensible utilization of the room at our disposal is of prime importance. The range, size, and design of vessels used in the charter trade are so varied that to particularize, and suggest that hanging lockers should be of one size while drawers should be of another, is impossible. Obviously, a 35-footer cannot have the same amount of stowage space as the average 60-footer, so the problem of where to fit lockers and what size they should be varies from ship to ship.

In a cruising boat being adapted to chartering, it is often possible to divide a large existing locker into two or sometimes three compartments. I have known smaller boats that overcome the problem of daytime stowage of sheets, pillows, etc., by providing a zippered bag of colored material or toweling (to match the decor of their cabin) for each bunk. The bedding is packed inside the bag in the morning and spends the day there, with the bag becoming a not-unattractive cushion.

In addition to the allocation of lockers and/or drawers for the guests' clothes, stowage room must be organized for ship's stores such as towels, sheets, food (canned and fresh), beverages, tools, spares, rope, lifejackets, medical kit, and other incidentals. In larger vessels, the location of stores and provisions is not usually important—not to the ship, that is. In a smaller boat, it can matter a great deal. Make sure the location of heavy stores, such as cans of ham, fruit, and vegetables, sends her down evenly on her marks. For instance, a quarter or half a ton of provisions packed into the bow may put her down by the head, which neither you nor the ship would be happy about in a following sea. Conversely, stow those provisions aft and her performance may suffer to windward. In general, heavy stores should be placed at or near the center of the vessel, and as low down as her available locker space will permit.

The order in which all stores or provisions are stowed on board is largely common sense. A successful charter boat (and there is no reason why any properly run and outfitted vessel cannot qualify as such) uses a lot of food. Make sure you know where everything is after it's stowed away; few things are more infuriating than needing something you know is on board and not being able to find it. Get into the habit of putting the same things in the same place. When we first started in the game, we made a drawing of the ship showing the position of every food locker, numbered them on the drawing (Port 1, 2, 3; Starboard 1, 2, etc.), and made a note of what each locker held. After a while, and with a few modifications, our blueprint was not necessary and hasn't been for years. But it's still there if we need it, and the same lockers are still used for the same stores.

VENTILATION

Adequate ventilation, especially in the tropics, is necessary for the comfort of all aboard. It can be achieved with windscoops over hatches, large skylights, the careful positioning of ventilators, and portholes. Ventilation in a warm climate is usually a compromise on an oceangoing yacht, because deck openings, through which we might expect a liberal passage of air, are generally kept down to a minimum when a ship is built. The reasons for this relate to both structural strength and the safety of the vessel, such as the possibility of being caught in a gale at sea.

As a result, an ocean cruiser can be uncomfortably warm below when anchored in a tropic bay unless ingenuity is used to coax a free flow of air through the ship. This can be accomplished in various ways. The use of "windsails" over hatches and skylights is probably the most popular method of directing the wind below decks, where it can make all the difference to living conditions.

Dorcas *has ventilators—all Dorade-type, too! (Photo by Ross Norgrove)*

Windsails or scoops can be anything from an old piece of canvas, "jury-rigged" and spread by a broomstick over the lee side of a hatch (so that the wind hits it and obediently heads on down below), to tailor-made master-pieces that hoist on a halyard or lift and have wide mouths held open by nylon ties and bottoms that clip or button in a variety of positions on the coaming of the hatch or skylight down which the air is being directed. A simple "scoop" over a hatch can be made by hoisting a three-foot-wide by six-foot-long piece of canvas or sailcloth (with a wooden spreader at its top) on a halyard, and making the two bottom corners fast to small screw eyes situated on the outside of the coaming. A piece of light nylon line leading from each outboard end of the spreader can be led forward (or to windward) and made fast to lifeline, stanchion, or whatever is convenient. These ties should be well tightened so that the top of the windscoop leans over the perpendicular and gives the wind no option but to go below. This rig is successful at anchor even when it is raining, for the hatch can be closed partially, so the rain runs off the canvas onto the deck. Thus, especially if the hatch is fitted with wedge-shaped boards at the sides, only air comes below.

Some vessels have air conditioning, but this necessitates having a generator hammering away all the time, week in and week out, with its attendant maintenance, which is something I couldn't live with. Air conditioning really is a matter of individual preference. If you want it, then install it, but its presence aboard is not necessary for your ship to succeed in the charter game. I can testify to that.

In addition to the canvas windsails we rig for the comfort of charter guests, and our regular ship's ventilators, which we adjust to suit the wind direction, there are six stainless-steel wind scoops, which we poke out three portholes on each side when at anchor in a bay. The airflow from these scoops into the cabins can be increased or reduced simply by twisting the scoops around.

AWNINGS

A lot of living is done on the deck of a charter boat, and if it is to be enjoyed in any comfort at all, a good awning is essential. In the tropics, an awning is such an accepted part of a ship's equipment that its absence is unthinkable. For a charter boat to be without one would not only detract from the measure of enjoyment our guests (to say nothing of ourselves) derive from its shelter, but without it, the fairest of them would be fried to a crisp!

A charter boat's awning should be strong, waterproof, and easy to put up or down. Never use light synthetic material, as I did when making the awning for my little yawl years ago; it would not lie quiet, and it crackled, popped, and flapped in the lightest of airs. It leaked, too, and, being white, generously

Windscoops pushed out through portholes when at anchor make a big difference in temperature below decks. (Photo by Ross Norgrove)

Moorea, Tahiti. Note windscoops, port side forward—also the mate's garden aft of the gallows frame. (Photo by Carl Moesly)

allowed the sun to glare right through—in short, it was more nuisance than it was worth. The grey, green, or blue Vivatex used by many Caribbean charter yachts is ideal. Vivatex is a treated canvas that is waterproof, rot-resistant, and can be sewn easily by the amateur wanting to make his own awning.

It is a popular misconception that an awning is needed only as a sunshade; that is its prime function, yes, but many is the night I've stretched out on a mattress atop our deckhouse and, with a tropical shower thrumming down on the canvas a few feet above my head, gone to sleep secure in the knowledge that since the cover didn't leak, I would stay dry.

Don't design a complicated awning for your ship. Sometimes when on charter it will be up and down twice a day, and if there is anything you don't need, it's an awning that takes all hands and the cook to set it up or stow it away. Our awning on *White Squall II* has a half-inch-diameter Dacron line running fore and aft along the center or "ridge"—this makes fast at its forward end to the mainmast, and aft to the permanent backstay, onto which is hung a two-inch by three-inch by eight-foot spreader of painted fir. The

ABOVE: Eight-foot wooden spreader. BELOW: Awning rolled out, hooked on to a shackle in the port rigging, main halyard shackled on to lifting points. Note roping all around and along center. (Photos by Ross Norgrove)

ABOVE: Awning hooked on both sides forward. It is now ready to be made fast to the mast and the spreader. BELOW: Awning hoisted. Main halyard holds it up, ties to the main rigging and stanchion tops keep it from flapping. (Photos by Ross Norgrove)

ABOVE: Awning rolls forward and ties when not needed to cover cockpit area completely.
BELOW: A Bimini-type awning sheltering the cockpit area. (Photos by Dave Ferneding)

sides of the awning, which also have half-inch Dacron line sewn in, hook onto rings that are permanently seized to the two forward mainmast shrouds and at their aft end are set up tight by the line's being hove through holes at the outboard ends of the spreader.

The center of the awning is hooked onto the main halyard and is lifted, which tightens the whole thing. The flaps, which drop 14 inches from the fore and aft side lines, have light pieces of Dacron (four each side) to tie them down—these make fast to the tops of stanchions. The awning is 28 feet long by 14 feet wide, and the two of us can have it up in 10 minutes—and with help, in half that time.

The Bimini-type awning (see photo) that can stay in position all the time or be quickly disassembled is ideal for smaller (up to 50 feet) boats. These awnings can stand a surprising amount of wind and also—especially when equipped with side curtains when at anchor—give adequate protection from a tropic sun.

BUNKS, MATTRESSES, AND COVERS

Gone are the days of the "donkey's breakfast"—the straw palliasse onto which the sailor lowered his salty frame to cork off a few undisturbed hours (he hoped) in his watch below. It has long disappeared over the horizon, in company with colza oil sidelights, single Spanish burtons, and salt horse from a keg at the foot of the mainmast. The donkey's breakfast was no sleep inducer! The departure of this lumpy, black-and-white-ticked companion of the old sailing scene is unlamented, for if it were still with us, the chances of coaxing a steady trickle of charter guests and their fair companions away on a cruise would be mighty slim.

The modern-day charterer, at the end of the day's activities, which have probably included enough sun, salt, and spray to make him feel an affinity with his "gung ho" brother of square-rig days, expects a comfortable sack. Fortunately, we can give him one. There are many types of mattresses to choose from—kapok, sponge rubber, innerspring, and polyfoam are but a few. Once again it is a matter of personal preference, and it also depends on the use intended for the cushion. I prefer polyfoam not less than four inches thick for bunks that, during the day, are expected to serve as seats or settees (such as in a dinette, which becomes a double bed at night with the table lowered) and for mattresses that have to be shaped to the hull, as is usually necessary for forward bunks or quarter berths. For fixed berths, I cannot get past regular innerspring mattresses. We have three kinds aboard *White Squall II*—foam rubber, polyfoam, and innerspring; in my book, the innerspring, for comfort, leaves the other two for dead. Innerspring mattresses are heavier, however, and consequently more awkward to move around, so I have only placed them in bunks whose stowage space underneath is accessible by way of drawers or locker doors. In cases where stowage under bunks can be reached only by removing or folding back the mattress, polyfoam is hard to beat, however.

A word about polyfoam: It is light and therefore easy to move around, which is convenient when the occasion arises for diving under a bunk for dry stores, fruit juice, or necessities such as rum or gin. In fact, these cushions are so light that it may seem expedient (especially when stowing stores for a cruise) to put them on deck out of the way so as to have more room down below. But herein lies a trap: the first puff of wind may whisk them away over the side. An hour or so later, the perspiring mate and skipper come on deck to find that their mattresses have put to sea without them. . . .

So have a care when using foam for deck cushions, or when bringing mattresses on deck from below for any reason. It's convenient and inexpensive to have buttons, clips, or eyelets in permanent deck cushions to keep them in place, and it is a whole lot easier to pass a light line around a mattress temporarily on deck than to have to up anchor and go in search of it.

A bunk covering must be capable of protecting the mattress underneath from moisture caused by a spilled drink or someone sitting down to lunch in a damp bathing suit, so bear this in mind when shopping for material. There are a number of vinyl or other coverings that "breathe" and at the same time fulfill this requirement.

For a floor covering, I like carpet throughout the ship. It can be "indoor-outdoor" or just the regular household variety; we have tried both, and since we change it every three or four years, the lasting quality of one as opposed to the other is of no great consequence to us. We make it a house rule that anyone who has been swimming should dry off before coming below, and this is always acceptable to guests.

THE TABLE

People who go away on a cruise together like to sit in a group when they eat and discuss the day's activities—the great sail they've just had, the fish that Jimmy caught, the coral on the reef they snorkeled over, and so on . . . all the things that go into the making of a memorable vacation. So be sure your table is big enough for all hands to sit around at one time. I built our gimballed table aboard *White Squall II* before we ever started in the game, and it is five feet long and two feet, eight inches wide, with a pivot at its fore and aft ends and 200 pounds of lead underneath in a box, which is an integral

LEFT: Dinette-type table aboard Heart of Edna— *room for guests and crew to eat together. (Photo by John Nicholls) BELOW: A table big enough for all hands to sit around,* White Squall II. *(Photo by Ross Norgrove)*

part of the whole thing. When the ship heels, the lead compensates for it and the table top stays level—nothing slides off onto the floor. It will seat eight.

Although we try to anchor whenever possible in a calm bay for the night, there have inevitably been times when we experienced a rolly anchorage, and Basseterre, St. Kitts, is one of them. On one occasion a group from Connecticut boarded us at Guadeloupe for a two-week charter up through the Leeward Islands ending in the Virgins, and St. Kitts was one of the stops on our itinerary. Never—except perhaps at the atoll of Wailangilala in the Fiji group (where it was like being anchored in the middle of the ocean)—have we rolled so much, but our gimballed table spilled not a drop.

The dinette type of table is often seen aboard charter boats. Since it is frequently situated close to the galley, it is popular with ship's cooks, who in general agree that the shorter the distance between their domain and the "eatery," the better!

THE DINGHY

A good dinghy complete with outboard occupies a position of high priority on a charter boat's list of equipment. Carry one as large as possible and do not worry about looks; your dinghy is going to be a little workhorse, so if she looks the part, so what? She will be used for swimming, diving, and picnicking excursions; she will carry groceries, ice, booze, fish, turtle, coral souvenirs, shells, spearfishing equipment, lobsters, and lots of people. Ideally, she should have a fairly flat floor to give her stability. If a 160-pound person can stand on the gunwale of a dinghy without bringing it any closer to the water than six inches, then she will pass.

And you must be able to row her. I do not mean to paddle her with little oars until someone comes to your rescue and tows you in. Where you're going, you're on your own a lot of the time, and in any case (if I may digress for a moment), I firmly believe that if a man is prepared to venture "outside the breakwater" in any vessel, then he'd better be prepared to get back under his own steam. Help the other guy whenever possible, but never ask for it yourself unless you're certain you need it.

But, back to the dinghy: Make sure she *can* be rowed; have good strong oars and rowlocks, and then you have a good auxiliary rig for the odd occasion when your outboard quits. This does not happen often, but it can; you can shear a pin and not have a spare; you can even run out of gas!

Below are the main points I consider desirable when choosing a dinghy, skiff, dory, tender (call it what you will) for a charter boat:

(a) As large as possible. *White Squall II's* dinghy is 12 feet, 6 inches long and will carry eight in a calm, four in a moderate breeze. It is fiberglass.

(b) Light enough to be dragged or carried up a beach by two or three people.

(c) Stable enough for a man to stand on the gunwale.

(d) Capable of being rowed easily and towed astern with safety.

(e) Rugged enough to stand some hard knocks against jetties, concrete landings, occasional rocky beaches, etc.

(f) Flotation built into it.

(g) A smooth fender around it and, in particular, no leads, cleats, or protrusions on the bow that can damage the stern of the ship. (I have never owned a dinghy yet that hasn't attempted to ram me now and again during the night!)

The dinghy should have a good anchor with a fathom or two of light chain and eight or ten fathoms of line attached to it; a tool kit carrying *new* spare outboard plugs, shear pins, and sundry basic tools; a bailer and a large sponge. In some parts of the world local regulations require that a lifejacket or its equivalent (buoyant cushion, etc.) be carried for each person in the dinghy.

I built a wooden box for our dinghy a short time back; it houses the outboard tank and tool kit while doubling as a seat. I wish I had thought of it years ago. The box has a wooden cleat screwed to its after end, and this slides under the center thwart. The forward end has a bronze pad eye screwed to it, and this lashes down to an eye bolt in the keelson. All this means that it cannot move when underway or float around when the dinghy

ABOVE: Dinghy box, holding tank, gas funnel, and tool kit.
BELOW: With the lid on, it becomes a seat or a picnic table.
(Photos by Ross Norgrove)

collects water from rain or other causes. The fuel line to the outboard passes through a small hole high on the after end of the box; it is protected from water leakage by the angle of the hole, the dinghy seat, and the lip of the lid, which also shelters it.

Rubber dinghies have a large following in certain parts of the world and are often used by charter boats as tenders. I consider that their suitability depends on the area a charter vessel is working. In some predominantly sandy areas they could be fine, but for taking gunkholing or shelling parties around coral reefs, where the dinghy frequently gets bumped against ledges or outcrops, they could have a short life. Also, they are difficult to row in anything more than a small harbor chop.

The lightness of rubber dinghies can also make them vulnerable. On one occasion, we stopped at Lord Howe Island on a passage back to New Zealand from Australia in my little yawl. We were using a rubber dinghy as a tender that particular trip, and one day after a walk ashore, we returned to where we had hauled it up the beach, only to find it was no longer there. We discovered it finally—deflated and beyond our ability to repair. One of the fierce puffs of wind that hurtle down from the mountains around the lagoon had picked it up and dumped it on a barbed wire fence about 300 feet away. We found it only after much searching, with several rips in it—lying in a field on the other side of the fence, being thoroughly inspected by a couple of cows.

One of the most important features for a rubber dinghy that is expected to carry charter guests is compartmented construction—that is, the ability to still float and support people even if it is holed.

THE OUTBOARD

Outboards of between three and ten horsepower, depending on the size of your dinghy, are satisfactory unless you are catering to waterskiers. As far as model or make is concerned, it is largely a matter of personal preference. I have always used Johnsons or Evinrudes, and found them both satisfactory. Some of my friends swear by Seagulls, some by Mercurys; in Tahiti, Chryslers were popular. Another friend of mine is happy with his eight-horsepower Yamaha. My advice is to ask around among the pros, have a look at what is giving good service year in and year out, and then make up your mind. Remember that it is almost never possible to run a charter boat's outboard in fresh water to flush it out, so be sure the model you buy doesn't need this sort of attention.

We have always carried two outboards and have made a practice of running them each a month at a time on the dinghy. The reason is that the biggest favor you can do an outboard is to run it; and if, in the middle of a cruise, the one currently in use gets "something in its throat," it can be replaced immediately with the spare, which you know will function with no time lost. The one that has given trouble can be repaired in your spare time, or by an outboard shop when you arrive back in port.

SNORKELING EQUIPMENT

Having your cake and eating it too is an experience that all too few people in this world enjoy; and if there is one facet of the chartering game that brings full awareness of this happy state of affairs, it is snorkeling. To be able to introduce people to the underwater world and to hear their oohs and ahs is compensation enough, but to be paid for it as well is like sprinkling an already iced cake with gold dust.

If your ship accommodates up to six charter guests, buy eight or ten sets of snorkeling gear. A set consists of mask, swimfins, and snorkel. Don't be chintzy. Buy good-quality equipment; it is easier for beginners to use and will last twice as long as second-grade stuff. (Charters involving scuba equipment are covered in Chapter 5.) Stock up on various sizes of masks and flippers; a child or an adult with a small or narrow face needs a different mask from someone with a face like a full moon. Carry small flippers for small feet, and vice versa; some guys (I'm one of them) have feet like a geography map.

If the snorkels you buy don't have some red or orange Dayglo tape on top of them, apply it yourself. It makes all the difference in checking the whereabouts of your snorkelers once they are in the water.

We always carry a "lookbucket" aboard for the person who wishes to "snorkel without getting wet." This is really an inverted bucket that is often

Every charter boat working in the tropics should carry snorkeling equipment. (Photo by Dave Ferneding)

75

made of black plastic with Lucite glued in the wide end. To use it, it is only necessary to put it over the side of the dinghy (it will float on top of the water) and look down through it. Many elderly people, and others who, for a variety of reasons, prefer not to go into the water, have enjoyed the view of coral reefs, fishes, and old wrecks through our lookbucket.

A lookbucket can also be used from the dinghy for spotting something dropped over the side in a bay; for checking on the ship's anchor cable or ground tackle, which may now and again get snarled around or hooked up on a coral head; for searching for a reef to dive on; for identifying lobster holes; or for looking for shells in knee-deep water. Whether chartering or just cruising in the tropics, I would not be without one.

THE BOARDING LADDER

One of the advantages associated with equipping a vessel for the convenience of charter people, and in trying to leave no stone unturned for their comfort, is that the crew of the ship lives and operates aboard a craft that is efficient to the nth degree—a not-unpleasant circumstance.

The boarding ladder, another link in the chain of important accessories for

Boarding ladder, White Squall II—rubber feet rest against the hull; a bronze pipe step underwater is for swimmers. (Photo by Ross Norgrove)

the well-found charter boat, is often given only cursory attention during the fitting out of vessels used only on weekends or for an occasional cruise. Often it is a light, temporary affair, spending most of its life stowed in the lazarette or "somewhere" in the ship. In our case, however, we need a solid, dependable boarding ladder that a child, an 80-year-old, or a 300-pounder can use with confidence.

The length of the ladder from water level to deck varies, of course, with the size of ship and the height of her topsides. *White Squall II's* ladder, which is put over the side as soon as we anchor in a bay, is 48 inches long by 21 inches wide. The sides and steps are 1" x 6" painted fir; bronze, 1⅛-inch-diameter pipes, which continue on down 16 inches below water on both sides, are joined together at the bottom by a length of the same pipe to form a rung for the convenience of swimmers. This bottom underwater step was originally wood (a continuation of the ladder), but it made the whole thing so buoyant that when anchored in any sort of a roll or slop, the ladder would try to float free. This was impossible because of the way it is fastened to the ship, but the bottom would float out, so in the end I cut it off a few inches above water, bolted the pipe step on down below, and so cured any desire it ever had to cause us trouble.

Both sides of the ladder have half-round brass the length of their outboard edges to save them from the chafe frequently occasioned by boats or

A Mediterranean-type boarding companion. (Photo by Ross Norgrove)

dinghies unloading passengers; a handhold is cut between each step, which has a covering of nonskid tape. A bronze eye bolt in each side near the top matches up with two in the bulwarks, and a ⅝-inch-by-24-inch stainless-steel rod slides through all four to keep the ladder firmly in place. Twelve inches above the bottom are two sponge rubber pads, to save paintwork where the ladder rests against the hull.

There are, of course, many types of boarding ladders and just as many ways of attaching them to your vessel. I have only described the one that, evolving through experimentation, trial and error, has proved adequate aboard our ship and has a solid, dependable "feel" when in use. Charter guests feel confident as they clamber up and down.

Many ladders are too narrow or are not fastened securely enough to the ship; either of these conditions can bestow a sense of insecurity upon the user at times. This is to be avoided like the plague by anyone hoping to succeed in the charter game. Make sure your ladder is steady, secure, and reliable; just to have it hooked over the top of the caprail or bulwarks is not sufficient. For instance, on a number of occasions when cruising the Tonga Islands with a party aboard, we've had native canoes alongside, bumping and banging the ladder, which, because of its ruggedness, suffered not at all. A ladder less sturdily built or secured would have had a tough time of it. It's sometimes hard to make natives understand that they're beating up your ladder—unless you can speak their language.

The Mediterranean ladder or "companion," with its little grating top and bottom, its stair treads neatly leading down at right angles to the side of the vessel, is shippy and suits larger cruising yachts very well. In fact, I have nearly weakened and fitted one several times, but on occasion, in a harbor chop, I've picked up or dropped off people at a ship so equipped and found it awkward. The dinghy can sometimes drop on a small sea and come up hard underneath the lower grating, which can be tough on fingers if they happen to be in the way.

FISHING TACKLE

It is seldom that conscientious fishermen charter a sailing craft for their vacation. A real dyed-in-the wool fisherman, to whom heaven is the feel of a rod or line in his hand every spare waking hour, does not in general care two hoots whether he's standing on an old pier waiting for the ebb, rolling around in a leaky dinghy in the middle of the night, or sitting in the fighting chair of a $200-a-day sportfisherman. It's the fact of his line being over the side that counts, not where he is. But while not catering exclusively to fishermen, the average sailing charter boat usually carries equipment aboard for the use of guests who might enjoy hauling in a fish now and again. It can all add to the fun of vacation.

A light rod with a spinning reel for use when at anchor in a bay, or for fishing from a dinghy, can be a lot of fun for people of all ages, and it is a much-used and appreciated piece of equipment aboard any charter boat. In addition, we have always carried a sturdy rod and reel to be used for trolling when underway. The reel has a good 50 fathoms of 60-pound-test line on it, the best swivel we can buy, and our favorite lure.

This choice of lure depends on what our latest kick is. Sometimes it's a feather jig, sometimes a silver spoon or a wooden plug—it depends on where we are. Sixty-pound test may seem heavy to the points-conscious I.G.F.A. man, but when you're doing a good nine knots with wind abeam enjoying your sail, and old Charley hooks a big one, then he'd better be able to horse him in without any of the fishing tackle carrying away. You can't kick a sailing vessel astern, and it is unthinkable to luff or drop the genoa to slow her down.

If you're fishing for fish and not sport, have 30 fathoms of 400-pound-test line (I prefer braided nylon) out astern, a good swivel, one fathom of wire leader (preferably flexible), and your favorite lure. On the inboard end, in a one-fathom bight of the line, buy or make a rubber shock absorber out of automobile innertube. This will make all the difference between catching or losing the big fellow who's heading for Australia at 20 miles an hour when he takes your hook.

And that's it. Baited handlines on a charter boat are "out," in my book. There's too much chance of someone piling up a tangle on deck and putting his foot in it at the precise moment Mr. Big down below decides to leave for some other territory with the bait in his mouth. Not much chance of that? O.K., but to be on the safe side, if you *will* have handlines aboard, make sure that none of them is above 20-pound test or, in any case, is always of a weight that will break before it pulls someone over the side. The easiest and safest approach to this problem is not to carry any.

RADIOTELEPHONE

A charter boat is expected to have a ship-to-shore radio aboard, and while its prime function is its use in case of distress or emergency, in some parts of the world it can play an important role in the overall success of the ship as a business venture. I have been able to confirm dozens of charters over our radio that otherwise would have had to wait until we got into port; instead of possibly losing business, we were able to confirm it.

Most charter guests, once aboard, divorce themselves completely from the cares of home and office and settle down to enjoy their cruise—away from the shackles of civilization, secure in the knowledge that for a precious week or two, no secretary, boss, or family can make demands upon their time. Now and again, however, we get someone in a party who has important business—a deal that he feels he must check up on—and in such cases our radio plays an important role. In some countries or localities, it is possible to be "patched" into the regular telephone system and so talk to anyone in the world. From the Mamanutha group (Fiji Islands), we talked regularly to Miami, Florida, through the Lautoka operator who performed this service. In the Virgin Islands it is possible to call anywhere by contacting the marine operator in St. Thomas, who will "patch" you through. I remember one beautiful day sailing on a broad reach down Sir Francis Drake Channel in the Virgin Islands and one of the girls in the party we had aboard was busy describing over our R/T to her sister in Detroit (where it was snowing) just what it was like to be aboard. . . .

In some remote areas, such as the San Blas Islands or the Galápagos, a very powerful set is needed to "get out," but with the single-sideband (S.S.B.) radios available today (and mandatory in many countries), this is becoming increasingly possible.

"Ham" radios are worth mentioning here also, even though their use for business is taboo. However, their range is so spectacular that many cruising and charter boats have them nowadays. The knowledge of someone, somewhere, being able to hear the emergency or distress signal (which we all hope never to have cause to transmit) can be reason enough for a long-ranging boat to have a ham radio aboard.

One piece of equipment that should never be underestimated is the VHF (Very High Frequency) radio. It is line of sight, yes, but if you're disabled, in danger, and are trying every possible means at your disposal to summon assistance, an aircraft can pick up a VHF signal where any other means of getting her attention would fail. With this possibility in mind, some vessels even carry aircraft radios.

Distress signals by emergency position-indicating radio beacons (EPIRBs) are now included in the Collision Regulations (section "n" Annex iv). The small, self-contained sets available today can, some makers claim, send a distress call over more than 30,000 miles of ocean for eight days. Aircraft or ships "home in" on the signal.

When choosing an R/T for a ship, there are several factors to be considered, not the least of which is cost. However, even when cost is not a major factor, the maximum power demand of a set must not be more than the vessel's electrical system can easily supply. So before buying an R/T, consult all literature available on the set and make sure your batteries can handle it. The size of the R/T you install can sometimes be influenced by local regulations; some countries have very stringent laws, while others could not care less. The responsibility for ensuring that his radio equipment is adequate rests squarely in every case on the charter captain.

While an R/T aboard a charter boat is handy for transmitting messages and picking up local gossip, the main reason for its being aboard is its use in case of distress. The correct international distress frequencies are 2182 kHz or 156.8 MHz, and every charter-boat operator (whether he is required to be licensed or not) should familiarize himself thoroughly with the correct procedure. Although this chapter is intended to cover only the ship and her equipment, it would not be complete without the inclusion of distress and urgency procedure. Just to have a radiotelephone aboard is not enough; every operator of R/T equipment must know how to use it in an emergency.

DISTRESS AND URGENCY PROCEDURE

Distress

If in imminent danger and immediate aid is required, use the spoken word "MAYDAY," preceded by the alarm signal if possible.
(1) Switch to 2182 kHz or 156.8 MHz (Channel 16), international distress frequencies. (Any other frequency may be used if it is known that the nearest station or ship is keeping watch on that frequency.)
(2) Say "MAYDAY" three times.
(3) Say this is (ship's name and call sign), repeated three times.
(4) Say "MAYDAY" (identification of the craft).
(5) Give your position—Latitude, Longitude, or bearing and distance from a known geographical position.
(6) State nature of distress and type of assistance that is required.
(7) Give any other information that may assist rescue, such as color, length, type of boat, etc.; also number of people aboard.
(8) Listen on the same frequency for acknowledgment.
(9) If any other ship interrupts, say "SEELONCE MAYDAY."

Urgency

If "MAYDAY" is not warranted, but urgency is required for the safety of ship or person, use "PAN" "PAN."
(1) Switch to 2182 kHz or 156.8 MHz (Channel 16), international distress frequencies. (Any other frequency may be used if it is known that the nearest station or ship is keeping watch on that frequency.)
(2) Say "PAN" "PAN" (3 times).

(3) Give the name of the station required (3 times).

(4) Say this is (name of ship . . .) 3 times.

(5) Give urgency message.

(6) Listen on the same frequency for acknowledgment.

Cancellation of Distress or Urgency Calls and Messages

DISTRESS and URGENCY calls and messages must be cancelled if it is subsequently found that assistance is not required.
Example—
Say "MAYDAY" (once) ALL STATIONS (3 times), this is: (ship's name and call sign), 3 times. Cancel my earlier MAYDAY, help no longer required."
The operator may say the words "SEELONCE FEENEE" to indicate the end of radio silence and give all stations permission to resume normal operations.

If You Hear a Distress Message

(1) Listen carefully; do not transmit. If possible, write down the message and the time.

(2) Listen for acknowledgment from a coast station or any other vessel. Try to determine whether you are the ship in the best position to render assistance, or whether some other vessel is better located or equipped.

(3) If no acknowledgment is heard, or if yours is the logical boat to take action, reply to the "MAYDAY" call as follows: "(name of craft in distress), this is (name of your own ship and call sign). Received "MAYDAY" (position, course, and speed toward distress scene and estimated time of arrival)."

(4) If you are not the logical ship to render assistance, continue to listen in and maintain radio silence.

(5) If other radio traffic interrupts, say: "SEELONCE DISTRESS, this is (ship's name and call sign)."

When retransmitting a distress message, a station must say "MAYDAY RELAY" (three times), then give her identification.

Securité

If you hear the word "SECURITE" (pronounced "SAY-CURE-E-TAY"), this will indicate that a navigational or meteorological warning is to follow.

Radiotelephone Alarm Signal

The alarm signal generating device (ASGD) is used in conjunction with a radiotelephone transmitter to transmit a distinctive alerting signal on 2182 kHz. The signal is heard as a high-pitched tone followed by a lower-pitched tone at quarter-second intervals. This sequence is repeated continuously for 30 to 60 seconds. The purpose of this signal is to attract the attention of persons on watch, and, at some stations, to actuate automatic devices giving an alarm. The alarm signal must be used only to precede a distress call or manoverboard emergency.

Some radios have provision for this alarm built into the set; separate units are available for use with other sets.

Misuse of Radio Distress Signal

There have been incidents when the distress call "MAYDAY" has been sent out by vessels that were not at the time in immediate danger, and here the attention of boat owners, yachtsmen, and fishermen is drawn to the use of the urgency signal "PAN," which indicates that the call is urgent and concerns safety but does not necessarily imply that the vessel is in imminent danger or requires immediate assistance.

It is advisable to paste alongside your radio a copy of the procedures described above. If you ever find yourself in an emergency situation, it is far more convenient to have the correct steps in front of you in black and white, than suddenly to have to hunt for or remember them. Keep the batteries from which your radio draws its power fully charged; it is recommended that the batteries be situated high enough in a vessel so that in the case of the ship's making water in an emergency, they are not quickly flooded and put out of action.

Be conversant with R/T use and protocol. Your set is a valuable piece of equipment—look after it. It may be needed when you least expect it. For instance, in early 1972 we were anchored at the island of Ogea—approximately 200 miles east of Suva, Fiji—and were informed that a native girl in the village was ill. We went ashore, were taken to a native hut, and found her lying on a pile of coconut matting, with a foot and leg swollen out of all recognition. She had a puncture wound on the sole of her foot, out of which her father had dug a fishbone several days before, and this seemed to be the cause of the trouble. I bathed the wound, applied a sterile dressing, elevated her foot slightly, and made her comfortable, but I was not at all happy with her condition. It was dark when we arrived back aboard the ship, and I don't think I've ever been so worried in my life. That girl was in agony and, as I saw it, there was blood poisoning, so I called Suva Radio on 2182 kHz to inform them of the fact. I received no reply, so changed the call and transmitted the "PAN" (urgency) signal on the same wave band, describing it as a "medical emergency" and addressing "any station."

After four hours, a voice replied, saying, "This is the United States Coast Guard icebreaker *Staten Island* answering the vessel with the medical emergency, over."

Never before or since have I been so pleased to hear a voice. The *Staten Island* was on her way from the Antarctic to the United States and was 320 miles north of us when some wide-awake radio operator aboard picked up my signal. I spoke to a doctor aboard the Coast Guard ship, who asked me all the pertinent details regarding the girl's age, condition, etc., and told me that I could do no more. But she had to have medical attention as soon as possible.

The icebreaker then tried to raise Suva on 2182 but without success; then Honolulu came in, then Auckland, New Zealand, then Sydney, Australia—stations thousands of miles apart. Finally Sydney called Suva on the phone, and they came on the air. The *Staten Island* took over the transmission, medical assistance was arranged for the next morning, and everybody was happy—and through radio, a very sick girl received aid she desperately needed.

Distress Signals

Rule 38 Annex IV of the Collision Regulations, tells us that:
(1) The following signals, used or exhibited either together or separately, indicate distress and need of assistance:
    (a) A gun or other explosive signal fired at intervals of about a minute.
    (b) A continuous sounding with any fog signaling apparatus.
    (c) Rockets or shells throwing red stars fired one at a time at short intervals.
    (d) A signal made by radiotelegraphy or by any other signaling method consisting of the group ... --- ... in the Morse Code.
    (e) A signal sent by radiotelephone consisting of the spoken word "MAYDAY."
    (f) The International Code Signal of distress (N.C.).
    (g) A signal consisting of a square flag having above or below it a ball or anything resembling a ball.
    (h) Flames on the vessel (as from a burning tar barrel, oil barrel, etc.).
    (i) A rocket parachute flare or hand flare showing a red light.
    (j) A smoke signal giving off a volume of orange-colored smoke.
    (k) Slowly and repeatedly raising and lowering arms outstretched to each side.
    (l) The radiotelegraph alarm signal.
    (m) The radiotelephone alarm signal.
    (n) Signals transmitted by emergency position-indicating radio beacons.
(2) The use or exhibition of any of the foregoing signals, except for the purpose of indicating distress and need of assistance, and the use of other signals which may be confused with any of the above signals is prohibited.

(3) Attention is drawn to the relevant sections of the International Code of Signals, the Merchant Ship Search and Rescue Manual, and the following signals.

    (a) A piece of orange-colored canvas with either a black square and circle or other appropriate symbol (for identification from the air).

    (b) A dye marker.

The decision to indicate distress and call for assistance is one that should not be taken lightly. But, once made, it has far more chance of succeeding if it is done correctly.

Any signal, in addition to the ones above—I'm personally not too fond of (h)—can be used to indicate distress. For instance, we always carry a small signaling mirror (with a hole in the center) in the dinghy, "just in case."

Parachute signal flares fired into the air by a gun and giving off a red light are possibly the most popular of night signals. They can be seen for miles and should be regarded as a necessity by the conscientious charter-boat skipper when outfitting his vessel. A "Very" pistol is handy also. Hand-held flares are worthy of inclusion in a distress kit, but be sure you are familiar with their proper use. There are some double-ended ones that will produce dense smoke from one end for daylight use or a flame at the other if required at night. I prefer the individual flares that have a wooden grip at one end and are clearly marked "smoke" or "flame" at the other.

Distress equipment (flares, cartridges, rockets, etc.) is perishable and has an expiration date stamped on it, after which it must be renewed.

Have your distress equipment all together in a waterproof bag or container that can be reached easily from on deck, or, if not, immediately available in a locker below. Most seamen live out their lives without ever needing to use distress gear, but if the need arises, we must know the drill and have the proper equipment at hand without having to search for it.

FIRE EXTINGUISHERS

Portable fire extinguishers should be displayed prominently throughout a charter boat and should be inspected annually by a qualified surveyor or technician. If the port or country you are working out of has regulations that compel the ship and her equipment to be inspected every year, then the number, type, size, and location aboard of extinguishers will be stipulated.

In many cases, however, the responsibility for fire-fighting apparatus rests with the charter-boat captain himself, and he must ensure that the number of extinguishers is sufficient, that they are of suitable size to deal with an emergency, and that they are distributed intelligently throughout the vessel. Every living space should have its own fire extinguisher, and each should be readily accessible. An engine room should have its own extinguisher, and large engine rooms should carry two. Gasoline engines, in addition to having a backfire flame control or "flame arrestor" fitted to the carburetor, should have a fixed CO_2 fire-extinguishing system in the engine room that is actuated automatically; there should also be some provision for it to be operated from on deck. I like to see a large extinguisher (10 pounds or more) near a forward hatch and another aft, in such a position that either one can be reached quickly from on deck if necessary.

The types of portable fire extinguishers carried aboard these days are usually dry chemical or carbon dioxide (CO_2). Foam-type extinguishers, while efficient, are rarely seen on boats nowadays because of the fearsome mess they make. Once started, most models keep going until they are empty, and the residue they leave sticks like fury to anything it touches. Dry chemical extinguishers are inexpensive and have the advantage over other types in that they are able to be recharged aboard. We have several "kits" on *White Squall II* that we purchased from the suppliers for this express purpose. Dry chemical extinguishers should be equipped with a gauge or indicator to show that normal pressure exists within the cylinder. CO_2 extinguishers are clean and leave no mess; they can put out a fire almost as quickly as switching off a light, and can be used again and again before recharging.

It should be noted that while it is easy enough to have fire extinguishers

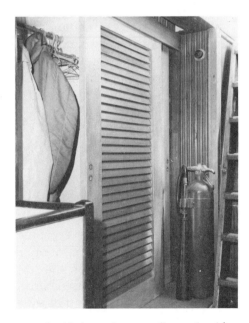

Every cabin . . . .

. . . . should have its own fire extinguisher.
(Photos by Ross Norgrove)

aboard a ship (all we have to do is go out and buy them), they can be considered efficient only if they are installed within easy reach, and if *everyone* aboard knows how to use them.

LIFERAFTS AND LIFEJACKETS

In some parts of the world, local rules insist that vessels "carrying passengers for hire" be equipped with a liferaft (or rafts) capable of supporting passengers and crew in an emergency. A charter boat working in such an area will have to be equipped in accordance with these regulations, which will state clearly just what the requirements are. Often, however, a charter vessel sailing among tropic islands comes under no rules whatever. In fact, many a charter captain has been lured into the game by his desire to shake free of signs, lights, and little pieces of paper that are forever telling him what to do. This desire to be independent is understandable, and one of my reasons for writing this book is to show that it can be achieved (I've done my own thing for years). But while we may be masters of our own skins and do what we like with them, we can't with other people's; as soon as we accept somebody's money to take him away on a cruise, we also accept full responsibility for his safety.

The inflatable liferafts available today usually come fully equipped with emergency rations, signaling apparatus, medical kit, etc. In my opinion, no charter boat should be without one of adequate size—whether it is required by law or not. When buying an inflatable, it is advisable to arrange for the sale to be subject to the raft's passing all tests at a liferaft testing station, being repacked, and issued with a current certificate. I insisted upon this precaution on one occasion when we were buying a new inflatable raft (a name brand, too!), and it didn't pass the test; it had three holes in it.

Once your liferaft is on deck in its cradle, don't forget to tie the line (when pulled, it will cause the valve on the air bottle to open and inflate) to something on the ship—mast, handrail, eye bolt, etc. This may seem pretty obvious, but there have been cases where ships have foundered and liferafts—uninflated and in their fiberglass containers—have floated away while people drowned. Such a tragedy occurred in the Pacific a few years ago, when an interisland ship sank in a cyclone with great loss of life. A few days later, one of her rafts (still in its container) was discovered on the shore of an island miles away from the disaster. The children who found it rolled it along to a village, someone pulled the string (which had never been made fast aboard the ship), and before the villagers' astounded eyes, a rubber "house" appeared in front of them. The last I heard of the raft was that a native family had moved in and taken up permanent residence. . . .

87

Carry an approved "adult"-size lifejacket aboard for every adult, plus several small ones for children. Every crew member or passenger should know where his lifejacket is. I prefer to have them in a locker clearly marked "lifejackets," or neatly placed in a rack below the deckhead at the foot of each individual bunk. They should all be of a "preserver"-type design; once fastened to a person, it will keep him in an upright, head-back position in the water, even if unconscious. The jackets should be examined annually, and if outdated or damaged, promptly renewed.

MEDICAL KIT

We carry our first-aid kit in a plastic box of the type used to hold fishing tackle. It has three shelf compartments that telescope back toward the lid when it is opened. This means that we can see quickly, without rummaging around, where individual items are. It has the additional advantage of being portable. A medical kit carried by a charter boat should include:

Kaopectate—2 large bottles; also a small bottle of paregoric.
Laxatives—Fruit Lax and/or Milk of Magnesia.
Eyedrops—Murine or equivalent.
Sleeping pills; also painkillers such as aspirin and codeine.
Seasick tablets—Marazine, Bonine, etc.
Antiseptic burn cream.
Antiseptic liquid, such as Dettol, to be used in water for bathing small wounds.
Merthiolate or Mercurochrome; also tincture of iodine.
Vaseline gauze, such as Optulle, for burns and abrasions.
White petroleum jelly for small burns.
Sunburn cream.
Calamine lotion or equivalent for itching.
Bandages—1", 1½", 2", and 4" (several of each), plus medicated, individually wrapped gauze squares.
Elastic Ace-type bandage.
Triangular bandages (2 large).
Adhesive tape—1" and 2".
BandAids and "butterfly" closures.
Cotton-tipped swabs such as Q-tips for applying antiseptic creams and removing small foreign bodies.
Absorbent cotton—large roll.
Scissors—medical, with blunt end.
Tweezers—two sizes.
Thermometer.
Plastic resuscitation device, such as "Venti-breather." This comes in a box with instructions for use included.

The above is the minimum that should be carried aboard. It must be realized that first aid is exactly that, and no more ambitious step should be taken by an unqualified person. It is one thing to swab out a small cut and quite another to set a broken limb or diagnose a stomach pain. Professional medical advice and help is usually available at the other end of your radio, and the prudent charter captain will always know how to reach help in an emergency.

A good first-aid book (there are many available) should be carried and stowed alongside the kit. Whether the captain has attended a course of first-aid lectures or not (and this is strongly recommended), he should study the book and understand its contents. The use of the resuscitation device for mouth-to-mouth artificial respiration is something he must be completely conversant with.

MISCELLANEOUS

Carry three or four sets of safety harnesses for children. They're handy items of equipment to have aboard and it can make all the difference to your peace of mind (to say nothing of the parents') if the kids are wearing them when sailing.

At least one ring or horseshoe-shaped lifebuoy should be carried on each side in a quick-release cradle. Each lifebuoy should be attached to the ship by a strong line, minimum length eight fathoms, fastened to the buoy by a clip that can be released if the buoy is to be used free.

A powerful hand-held searchlight is commonly given high priority, so its inclusion in a ship's list of equipment is worthy of mention. I personally don't find much use for one, and our light has been in action only half a dozen times in twice that number of years. However, it is aboard and ready for use if needed.

A good hand-bearing compass, in addition to the steering compass, is one piece of equipment I wouldn't be without. Ours is a Sestral and lives in its rubber bracket (supplied by the company) above the chart table. A similar bracket is situated at one side of the aft hatch, and when taking bearings, running fixes, bearings in transit, etc., it is in use constantly. After any navigational exercise is over, our hand-bearing compass is returned to its bracket away from the "main stream of the flood"—out of the way of any human traffic that might bump or damage it.

A manually operated bilge pump should be considered essential by the owner of any vessel, whether he is chartering or not. A charter boat, without question, should have one of large capacity. It should preferably be "choke-free." An Edson type or Whale diaphragm is ideal.

A hand-held, battery-powered electric lantern (or two) has a place aboard any charter boat. It is handy for the inevitable shore parties at night (either coming or going) and can be used aboard in the event of a power failure. Flashlights (we have three in bulkhead clips throughout the ship) should be carried, plus spare batteries. And let's not forget the humble kerosene hurricane lamp and a packet of candles!

We usually have two fenders suspended over the side, just aft of the ladder, for the dinghy to rest against when we are anchored in a bay. These, along with two more that are stowed on deck with our docking lines, can also be used when tying alongside a dock.

The list of miscellaneous equipment could go on and on—shackles, paint, brushes, etc., for bosun's stores; engine, outboard, and electrical spares; D/F, radar, autopilot, strobe light—you name it. More stuff is available all the time, and while Sir Francis Drake didn't have a zinth of what we have today when he sailed his *Golden Hind* around the world nearly 400 years ago (with the instincts of a good charter skipper, he made a profit too!), there is no reason why we shouldn't take advantage of modern-day technology and make our navigation and life at sea simpler and safer.

In this chapter I have dealt with the equipment I consider that a vessel in the charter trade should carry to be well found, but since no field of endeavor caters more to individual tastes than the charter game—and no fraternity is more fickle than the floating one—it is inevitable that some skippers will consider my tastes either more spartan or more opulent than theirs. To which I say, "Fine; load what you like aboard, boys—just as long as it is in addition to what we have suggested here." As Henry Ford said, "Paint it any color you like, as long as it's black!"

Chapter Four

Logistical Problems and Solutions

THE FOOD

If any single factor contributes more than another to a vessel's success in the charter game, it is the food that guests are served when away on a cruise.

Once your party is aboard, the whole success or failure of the business revolves around the galley. The food must be "first cabin" all the way.

It makes no difference whether your ship is glittering, whether the beaches and bays you visit are enough to send the most morose charter party into transports of delight—if the grub's no good, or if there's not enough of it, you'll never get them back. And you will have canceled out all chance of ever getting their friends.

It is a funny thing, but it seems that no matter how exotic a part of the world we work in, or how conscientiously we strive to give our guests a memorable time, the first question they are asked by friends and family on returning home is, "How was the food?"

If the answer is, "Good!"—or, better still, "Excellent!"—you've got them hooked and you'll get 'em again, along with old Charley and Alice next door, and some of the guys at the office.

If the answer is, "Well . . . so, so," or, "Could have been better," then no matter how glowingly you, your boat, or the area in which you've voyaged is described, it will bring you no business. You'll never get back the gang you've just catered to—and you've got more chance of being struck by lightning than you have of ever getting their friends.

The answer, of course, is *never* scrimp on food. Buy the best, and buy plenty of it. And try to serve them the type of food they prefer.

Once a charter is confirmed with a deposit (*see* Chapter 5), contact your charterers, asking what their food dislikes or allergies are, along with their liquor or beverage preferences. It is most important to serve no food that people may dislike or that they may be allergic to. Avoid the food they can't, don't, or prefer not to eat. For example, some have an aversion for brussels sprouts, some cannot eat fish, some don't like rice or veal. Sometimes the guests' religion may prevent them from eating certain meals. We are continually loading stores aboard in the charter game, and it is just as easy to buy what people want as to stock up with any old thing and hope for the best.

Individual preferences at mealtimes are rarely acknowledged aboard a charter yacht. It is hardly possible to cook steak for three members of a group, spaghetti and meatballs for two, and fish for one after flogging a 48-footer to windward for most of the day. So, it is very important that the menus you have chosen and stocked for are palatable to all hands.

It is a pretty safe bet that if the food you serve a guest is much the same as he gets at home—only better—you'll go over big.

Serve the Frenchman his duck *à l'orange*, after aperitifs and suitable hors d'oeuvres; give him the correct wines; finish off with flaming crepes suzette—and he'll be happy. I've yet to meet the American who would turn his nose up at a rare, juicy steak, with vegetables, baked potato, and fresh salad.

Have Bols aboard for your Dutch charterer, and if you can hash up a good rijstafel, you'll probably win a place in his heart. Give an Englishman kidneys and bacon for breakfast with, maybe, mushrooms on toast, and it will earn you an appreciative look. If you can make good veal scallopini, your Italian charterer will probably tell his buddies. And so on.

It is difficult to generalize, but usually when people are away from home, they will, it seems, try a "native" meal for a kick or on the side, as long as the food they are used to is there to fall back on. But if you dish them up *only* food that is endemic to the region and with which they are totally unfamiliar, most of them will not be happy.

Again, of course, there are exceptions. Some people (I'm one of them) eat like a vacuum cleaner and will polish off any kind of food anywhere they can get it. However, they do not make up the majority of the charter guests. In any event, we just don't have to worry about those who will eat anything.

The fact that certain ethnic groups prefer their own food was demonstrated one day on the wharf at Suva, in the Fiji Islands. The huge S.S. *France*, with the best *cordon bleu* in creation aboard, had dropped anchor in the bay during the course of a voyage around the world, touted as the "most expensive ever." The first boat full of passengers tied up at the dock, the tourists surged ashore, and one of them was heard to say to an Indian taxi driver, "Take me to a hamburger joint, buddy—I just gotta have a goddamn hamburger!"

Aboard *White Squall II,* the meals served during a typical one-week charter in the tropics are as follows:

First Day

Breakfast
Chilled fruit juice, and/or vegetable juice. Dry cereal if desired. Eggs (any way), bacon, hot cornbread with butter, preserves, coffee, tea.
Lunch
Chicken salad, lettuce, tomatoes, cheese, pickles, plain and rye bread. Fresh fruit salad, iced tea, coffee.
Hors d'oeuvres (before dinner)
Smoked oysters and crackers, dip, assorted nuts.
Dinner
Broiled barbecued steak (best possible quality), baked potatoes with butter or sour cream, green beans, carrots, tossed salad, hot rolls. Chilled peaches and ice cream, coffee, tea.

Second Day

Breakfast
Fresh chilled grapefruit, link sausages, scrambled eggs, raisin bread toast, butter, preserves, coffee, tea.
Lunch
Pizza with avocado salad. Cold sliced pineapple with raw sugar, iced tea, coffee.
Hors d'oeuvres
Caviar, crackers, celery pieces stuffed with dip, nuts.
Dinner
Roast lamb with mint sauce, roast potatoes or rice, green peas, carrots, hot rolls, apple pie and cream, Irish coffee, tea.

Third Day

Breakfast
Chilled fruit juice and/or vegetable juice. Dry cereal if preferred. French toast with maple syrup or jelly. Canadian bacon, coffee, tea.
Lunch
Ground sirloin hamburgers on toasted buns. Coleslaw, tomatoes, pickles, potato chips, fresh fruit, coffee, iced tea.

Hors d'oeuvres
Small squares of bread topped with cheese and ham, then toasted. Coconut chips (*see recipes*), black olives, nuts.
Dinner
Prime rib roast of beef, mashed potatoes, broccoli, carrots, tossed salad, hot rolls, cheesecake, cream, coffee, tea.

Fourth Day

Breakfast
Chilled papaya slices with freshly squeezed native limes. Eggs à la Minine (*see recipes*), blueberry muffins with butter or jelly, coffee, tea.
Lunch
Cold cuts (if roast beef of previous night was a big one, possibly slices of this served cold in addition to other cuts—ham, salami, etc.), cheese, pickles, two kinds of bread, butter, mayonnaise, cookies, iced tea, coffee.
Hors d'oeuvres
Shrimps in sour cream sprinkled with paprika, crackers, stuffed olives, nuts, potato sticks.
Dinner
One-half broiled lobster per person, lemon and butter sauce, carrots, beans, potatoes. Tossed salad in cavity of lobster, hot rolls. Lemon pudding with whipped cream, Irish coffee, mints.

Fifth Day

Breakfast
Fresh chilled grapefruit, bacon, banana and rum pancakes with maple syrup. Coffee, tea.
Lunch
Toasted club sandwiches, sweet pickles, tomatoes and cottage cheese, potato sticks, fresh fruit salad, iced tea, coffee.
Hors d'oeuvres
Caviar and crackers, dip, whelks (West Indian top shell, *see recipes*) with hot garlic butter sauce, assorted nuts.
Dinner
Barbecued spareribs, steamed vegetables (potatoes, green beans, carrots), hot rolls, tossed salad, bread pudding, (*see recipes*), coffee, tea.

Sixth Day

Breakfast
Chilled fruit juice, and/or vegetable juice. Link sausages, eggs (any way), hot cornbread with butter and preserves, coffee, tea.

Lunch
Hot dog and baked bean casserole, rolls, pickles, beets, cookies, iced tea, coffee.
Hors d'oeuvres
Camembert cheese and crackers, black olives, banana chips (*see recipes*), nuts.
Dinner
Stuffed double pork chops (*see recipes*), baked sweet potatoes, broccoli, salad, hot rolls. Chocolate layer cake, Irish coffee, tea, mints.

Seventh Day

Breakfast
Chilled fruit juice and/or vegetable juice. Dry cereal if desired. Eggs Benedict (*see recipes*), coffee, tea.
Lunch
One-half avocado per person—stuffed with lobster, crabmeat, or shrimp salad. Rolls, fruit cake, iced tea, coffee.
Hors d'oeuvres
Anchovies on crackers, coconut chips, stuffed olives, nuts.
Dinner
Barbecued chicken, corn on the cob, coleslaw, hot rolls, butter or margarine, orange pineapple pie, coffee, tea.

Recipes

Below are some of the less-familiar recipes used in the preceding menus:
Eggs à la Minine—Chopped meat (ham, cooked bacon, chicken, or beef), can of celery or mushroom soup, toast, eggs. Stir chopped meat into soup. Heat. Pour mixture over toast. Place poached egg on top. Sprinkle with parsley.
Eggs Benedict—English muffins, sliced ham, eggs, hollandaise sauce. Split and toast English muffins. Cut ham same size as muffin. Place ham on muffin. Slide poached egg onto ham. Cover with hot hollandaise sauce.
Stuffed Double Pork Chops—Place one chop on top of another, or cut deep pocket in double-thick pork chop. Put seasoned stuffing between, and hold together with wooden toothpicks. Place in baking dish and bake at 350 degrees F. until half done (approx. 30 minutes). Place a thick slice of cored apple on each double chop. Sprinkle with brown sugar. Continue cooking until tender.
Bread Pudding—Toast and butter bread on both sides. Place in baking dish. Sprinkle with raisins and cinnamon. Beat two eggs. Add ½ cup sugar, ¼ teaspoon salt, two cups milk to eggs. Mix well and pour over toast. Let stand 10 minutes. Press down to ensure mixture is soaked up by toast. Sprinkle again with cinnamon. Bake in slow oven (325 degrees F.) about one hour.

Banana Chips—Peel green bananas. Slice very thin. Fry in oil until brown. Drain on paper. Sprinkle with salt.

Coconut Chips—Crack mature coconut and remove meat. Peel off dark skin. Slice white meat very thin. Place on tray and bake in oven (350 degrees) until golden brown. Sprinkle with salt. These can be eaten immediately or stored in an airtight jar, in the same manner as nuts.

Whelks, or West Indian Top Shell—These are sea snails and can be gathered around the tideline. They should be cooked under pressure for 35 minutes. Serve hot in their shells with steaming garlic butter. Remove animal from shell with toothpick. Discard entrails, dip in sauce . . . ahh!

The Pacific trochus are bigger and sometimes harder to get (you usually have to dive for them), but they can be cooked in the same manner and have a similarly delicate taste.

Meals, of course, can vary with the locality in which a charter vessel is working, the availability of certain ingredients, and, not infrequently, the nationality of the guests. Also, the cooks' personal preferences and specialties come into it. The preceding menus are intended as a guide only; they are ones that we have found to be acceptable to charter guests and also reasonably easy to produce by someone who has other duties aboard in addition to cooking.

Often we have been unable to purchase all that is required for certain meals. Lobsters, for instance, may be unobtainable, in which case we would serve fish wherever possible. Some guests who have a marked preference for steak may, in correspondence beforehand, express a desire for it twice in a week. For a change, we may serve corned beef and cabbage one night or roast leg of pork, spaghetti and meatballs, meatloaf, chicken and dumplings, turkey with West Indian seasoning, or 12-boy curry and rice. The kinds of meals served depend on what is available and on how well stocked the stores are in the area a charter boat is working. This can also have a direct bearing on how much can be charged for a charter cruise.

WINES, LIQUOR, AND BEVERAGES

We have always served wine with dinner, and at noon, too, if guests desire it. Carry some good red, rosé, and white wines aboard, plus champagne, together with liqueurs and a good after-dinner brandy. Wherever possible, discover your guests' liquor preferences before they get aboard. Even if you carry a wide variety, you could run out if they all drink the same thing.

Carry several kinds of beer—in cans wherever possible. Bottles of beer take longer to cool and can break. The same with sodas—ginger ale, lemon-

Bar, removable glass rack, liqueur glasses, barograph, clock, thermometer, TV, tape deck, cassette player, and radio—aboard White Squall II. *(Photo by Ross Norgrove)*

ade, orange, coke—get them in cans. Many guests in their correspondence specifically request diet colas. They seldom drink them once on board, it seems—in fact, most guests lose their diet somewhere between home and the ship—but buy some just in case.

We make all drinks available at any time to charterers and let them help themselves. This may sound like an encouragement for guests to get on the sauce and stay on it from the beginning of the cruise until the end, but except for one party (whose incredible capacity for liquor gave us conversation for months afterwards), it has never happened.

Price yourself high enough, and you won't get drunks. People usually go to a lot of trouble, and travel a long way, to get aboard. In almost every case, they are too smart to waste the investment, especially if the charter price is a hefty one: to get their money's worth and to see everything, they just have to be sober.

Usually charter guests have a few beers, gin and tonics, sodas, etc., during the day, and a pre-dinner cocktail session (in which I participate wholeheartedly). The successful business executive or professional man— the type of person most likely able to afford a vacation on a well-found charter yacht—is seldom a lush.

My advice is to make the booze available. Don't stinge on it any more than you would on the food.

PAPER PLATES

There is much to be said for the use of paper plates at breakfast and lunch: it expedites cleaning up at a time when everyone is anxious to get underway. It also saves on water. We have never had even the most discerning guest complain of their use at these meals.

It is possible to purchase wicker "plates" that hold the paper plates and so make them stiff and "usable." Shop around for these; they make all the difference in the use of paper plates.

ACTIVITIES

Typical activities for a charter cruise among a group of islands in the tropics might be as follows:

Crew arises seven A.M. Some guests have a swim while breakfast is being prepared. A big pot of coffee is brought up on deck under the awning, along with cups, cream, sugar. Eight A.M. (or thereabouts), breakfast.

Wicker holders for paper plates (breakfast and lunch) and a table big enough for all hands, White Squall II. *(Photo by Gray Somers)*

Nine-fifteen, all cleaned up, awning down, sails up and underway. Guests take the wheel if they feel like it (some take turns the whole trip). Beers, sodas available—guests help themselves.

Anchor for lunch and guests swim off the ship. Keep an eye on them. Make sure they can handle themselves in the water. Tell them to swim toward the bow—the boat usually lies head to wind, and small waves, current, or a combination of both, can carry them astern.

Guests frequently have beer, bloody Mary, gin and tonic, etc., before lunch.

One-thirty P.M. Lunch over, sails up and underway. Sail to, and anchor off a submerged reef, close to overnight anchorage, for snorkeling and skindiving. From there proceed under power to anchorage selected for the night.

Cocktails (at any time). Dinner, seven or seven-thirty P.M.

If the ship has anchored in a suitable area, sometimes the guests go ashore for a stroll after dinner. Other times, over after-dinner liqueurs and drinks, they may talk, play cards, have a singsong, or listen to the hi-fi. Some turn in early or visit friends cruising in another boat sharing the anchorage.

Another day the charter boat might not stop for lunch but keeps sailing until the next overnight anchorage is reached. Here all hands go ashore to a restaurant, with native entertainment and, perhaps, a dance.

The next morning, after breakfast aboard, it is quite common for the charter crew to take on ice and some fresh provisions while the guests explore the native market, or go on an island tour to take photographs, or view some natural or historic point of interest.

Either before lunch or afterwards, the ship, with the full party and crew aboard, is sailing toward her next overnight stop. Often another charter boat will be leaving at the same time for a similar destination, so we make a race of it.

After a swim in clear, tepid water, hors d'oeuvres and a leisurely cocktail "hour," all hands are ready for dinner—a hard life!

The reason for dining around seven or seven-thirty P.M. is to enable the crew (especially on a two-handed boat) to get the dishes washed and all the cleaning done early enough to obtain a good night's rest. Even with dinner at seven-thirty, it is seldom that the table is cleared, all dishes washed, and the galley cleaned before nine-thirty P.M. To have dinner any later can make it a long day.

In parts of the world where guests insist on eating later, the charter boat either has a larger crew to deal with this contingency (such as a full-time cook and steward) or if shorthanded—which is more usually the case—does not get underway as early the next day.

Breakfast and lunch aboard a charter boat working a warm, equable region are often served on deck. In fact, it is a common thing for all hands and the cook (let's hear it for the cook!) to picnic ashore on a beach. This can be very popular with parties. It is usual on such an occasion to take all the "fixings" for lunch—plus drinks, ice bucket, and a big canvas or plastic table cloth—in the dinghy and set up the picnic spot ashore a short distance from the water's edge.

An important item of equipment that should always accompany the paraphernalia brought from the ship for a picnic or cookout is a large garbage can. If the chosen spot already has receptacles for this purpose, then you don't need to bring your own can ashore, but in any case, the disposal of ship's garbage is the charter captain's responsibility. He must make certain that any place selected for a picnic is left exactly as it was before he, his crew, or his guests used it. In many places, the indiscriminate disposing of refuse is illegal.

Make sure that none of the guests litter. It is usual either to put garbage in cans ashore or dump when well out at sea. Quite apart from the health point of view, or the fact that we might be breaking the law, is the aesthetic aspect. Few things can be more offending to the eye than a littered beach. Or to be snorkeling over a beautiful coral reef and to see a rusty can or broken bottle down there among the anemones and sea ferns.

Dinner aboard at the end of the day, with all the trimmings, can be an occasion to remember—best china, everyone wearing a shirt at the table (usually shorts and bare feet underneath), an appropriate tape of background music, a good meal, a fine wine. . . . And that's the whole idea; that's what it's all about in having your cake and eating it, too! If they're enjoying it, you're enjoying it. It's not hard to do—buy the best (we've covered that) and keep your ship clean, really clean.

I prefer to make each guest responsible for his or her own bunk. Some keep it spick and span, some don't. One person may keep a bunk area as neat as a new pin for the entire cruise while his counterpart may have it (and keep it) looking as if a cyclone passed through within five minutes of being aboard. To which I say, "O.K." If a guy wants to live like a slob, let him. Just as long as *you* don't. The galley, the toilets, the floor, the decks, the dinghy (don't forget that the dinghy serves the same function as an automobile—it gets a lot of use)—they all must be clean.

SNORKELING

As was mentioned in the previous chapter, snorkeling can be very popular with charter parties, especially those taking cruises in boats working a tropical region where warm, clear water encourages anybody wanting to try.

Some guests are completely familiar with the equipment used in this fascinating pastime, and whenever an excursion (usually by dinghy) is made to a coral reef or sunken wreck, they will expertly don mask, snorkel, and flippers and take to the water. Many charterers, however, are totally unschooled in the use of snorkeling gear and regard the sport as a most mysterious one—something they couldn't possibly do. All of which, of course, is bunk. Almost anyone can be taught to snorkel, and even the most skeptical can be indoctrinated in the art if the technique used to teach them is slow and easy. Age does not seem to be a drawback, either. We have had people in their seventies, who had hardly put a big toe in the sea for 40 years, become lyrical over the new world suddenly opened to them.

In most cases, it seems to be a person's introduction to snorkeling that determines whether or not he (or she) becomes a convert. Place someone timid (having his first try at it) among a bunch of gung-ho skindivers bound for a spearfishing expedition on the ocean side of a barrier reef, and you could scare the wits out of the guy. Teach him the game in easy stages, and one day he might lead the way.

Our business in the charter game is to give people a safe, enjoyable time, a glimpse of our way of life, of the environment we live and work in—one that, usually, is completely alien to their own. Snorkeling for someone who has never done it, or who has been too shy or nervous to try, can add a new dimension to his or her charter cruise. Introduce them to it carefully.

The first essential is a mask that fits comfortably and does not leak. The whole success or failure of a person's initiation into snorkeling often can be traced back to this. To test a mask, to see if it suits, a would-be snorkeler should leave the headstrap hanging free, hold the mask lightly against his or her face, and draw in a sharp breath through the nose. A well-fitting mask will suck tightly in around the edges if given this treatment, and will not let in any air. An ill-fitting one (or wrong size) will allow air to leak in between the edge and the wearer's face. If this happens, try another mask. Keep on trying them until one is found that is a good fit and until suction can be created. A mask must be able to pass this test before the headstrap is adjusted and used to hold it in place; otherwise, it will leak water when actually in use.

Once newcomers to snorkeling have been fitted with masks, have them sit around on deck wearing this piece of equipment, familiarizing themselves with breathing through the mouth only, before proceeding any further. They should be instructed not to expel any air at all through the nose, as this can fog up the face plate.

Swim fins or flippers—either term fits—can be tried on before or after the mask-fitting exercise. A flipper should fit comfortably on the foot and not be too tight. A flipper that has been dipped in a bucket of water beforehand is easier to get on than a dry one.

Breathing in and out through a snorkel is the next step, and it should be practiced while still wearing the face mask and sitting comfortably on deck. The snorkel can be either attached to the mask strap by a rubber or plastic loop or pushed up between the strap and the wearer's head. The mouthpiece of a snorkel should fit snugly in the mouth of the user, and the whole thing should be flexible enough for him to turn his head without discomfort.

The next move is to introduce them to the game, and for this—especially with an older group—it is an advantage to be able to take them to a quiet beach. Repeat the mask and breathing drill, then lead them one at a time into waist-deep water. Many people find it easier, once they reach the water's edge, to turn around and walk in backwards with flippers on. Once our aspiring snorkeler is standing in the water, have him (or her) bend over until his face plate is about an inch below the surface. Make sure the top of the snorkel is well above water, and that no water can get down it as they breathe in. After making certain he can competently use the equipment thus far—and that his mask doesn't leak—go back into shallower water. Here, he can stretch out full length and, with his hands on the bottom, practice using flippers, mask, and snorkel at the same time.

Some do not progress very far beyond this stage and are content to fin slowly around, their mask just barely in the water, enjoying the sight of small fish, coral, sea ferns, or whatever else the area has to offer. Others, however, develop into competent snorkelers and skindivers very quickly.

Often a charterer will have taken a diving course and have passed an examination. Possibly his experience will be limited only to a pool. He probably is good—he may be very good—but it will depend upon the standard of the instruction he has received and also his own temperament as to how he conducts himself when finally using snorkeling equipment on a charter cruise. A safe rule of thumb, no matter what qualifications a guy has (or says he has), is to conduct his first snorkeling or diving excursion in a quiet, sheltered area.

Although we have seldom taken parties who wanted to dive to the exclusion of everything else, many experienced divers have been aboard. With such groups, we have done a lot of spearfishing.

Spearfishing as a sport—diving free, with only a mighty gulp of air, as deep as you can go for 30, 50, or (if you're one of the "royals") 100 feet or more—has many adherents. When you've swum into a cave on the track of a grouper, and you have no tank but only as much air as your lungs will hold, and when you eventually nail him, you're starting to feel that little gulp of tightness way down in your throat that tells you you're overdue. By the time you tear him out, fighting like a tiger on your spear (he's got a life to lose too), and you head for the surface, you know if you make it that this is one helluva sport!

Spearfishing with a tank on is not a sport; it is slaughter, and it is rightly becoming illegal in many parts of the world.

Keep your snorkeling gear in good condition. Inspect the edges of masks where they fit against the face. Any mask with a deteriorated or split edge should be replaced, because it will let in water. Face plates can be kept clear by cleaning with toothpaste and fresh water; keep an old toothbrush handy for this job. Zippers on diving equipment or bags can be kept in good working condition with silicone spray.

Introducing people to snorkeling can add tremendously to their enjoyment of a charter cruise, and it is often one of the factors influencing their return a year or two later. It can be a great satisfaction when they do come back and confidently don the equipment to know that you were the one who taught them in the first place.

LINEN AND LAUNDRY

It is usual for a charter boat to have three changes of linen—sheets, pillow-cases, towels, hand towels, beach towels, washcloths, and dish towels for the galley. A busy vessel usually has one change ashore at the laundry and two full changes aboard. On boarding the ship, guests are given two sheets, one pillowcase, one washcloth, one towel, one hand towel, and one large beach towel. Sheets and pillowcases are expected to last one week, which is the length of an average charter.

Sometimes extra towels are needed during a cruise. Keep a good stock. Make sure your beach towels are good long ones. It is quite usual for a charter guest, smeared from top to toe with sunburn cream or lotion, to take a towel on deck and stretch out on it to work on a tan. If the beach towel is a short one, the surrounding cushions or deck can become oily and, possibly, stained. All this is part of the game, but to help keep your own blood pressure down to an acceptable level when a slippery customer heads for your natural teak deck with her beach towel under her arm, make sure you've supplied her with a big one.

TIME BETWEEN CHARTERS

After a charter party has disembarked at the end of a cruise, the most important item on the ship's agenda is how long it will be before she next puts to sea.

Many factors contribute to the length of time a vessel spends in port between charters. If she is new to the game, she will in all probability not be as heavily booked ahead as other boats working the same area. Some of them may have been there for years. Or if the region she is chartering in is not easy for people to reach, she may be in port for a week or more—even much more—before sailing again. In this case her crew will probably have time for a breathing spell and be able to attend to ship's business and chores at an easy pace. However, if she is heavily booked, fitting the maximum number of trips possible into a "season" (and here I am referring specifically to a crewed charter boat), she is going to be mighty busy.

I do not believe a "turnaround"—the length of time between arriving in port after a charter cruise (typical length, one week) and sailing again on another—should be less than 24 hours. In the time between disembarking guests and sailing again with a different party aboard, a charter-boat crew must attend to every detail necessary to ensure that their vessel is a completely restocked, efficient, self-contained unit.

The following is a typical list of what must be done:

(1) The ship cleaned from stem to stern. Hull, decks, deckhouses, ice boxes, cockpit should be cleaned, along with the interior. Toilets, showers, galley, refrigerators, floor, bunks, mirrors—they must be spotless.

(2) Wash ship's laundry (sheets, towels, etc.) ashore, load clean laundry aboard—make certain you have enough.

(3) Meat order. Wherever possible—and especially in the case of a quick turnaround—place the order with your favorite supplier a week beforehand, so that it is deep-frozen and ready when you want it. We have often confirmed or ordered our meat over the radio.

(4) Groceries, vegetables, and fruit. This is usually the biggest order. Make your list well in advance. Inspect whatever correspondence you have received from the incoming charter party regarding food dislikes or allergies. This can often influence what you purchase.

(5) Beverages—liquor, beer, wines, sodas, liqueurs. Check your correspondence and stocks and order accordingly.

(6) Main engine fuel (diesel or gasoline), outboard gas, lube and outboard oil, stove fuel (butane, kerosene, alcohol, etc.).

(7) Water.

(8) Ice.

(9) Attend to whatever job needs doing aboard. There is usually something, no matter how we plan it otherwise. It may be that we have to change the fuel filter cartridges or water filters, or a pump washer in a toilet, or a stove burner. It may be necessary to attend to the case of asthma the outboard contracted a couple of days ago, or discover why the starboard spreader light didn't work last night. I've never done a trip that there wasn't something.

In some ports it is possible to place the entire stores order with one supplier, such as a ship's "provider," and have it all delivered. I have never had this luck. Often when we have been busily going from one store to another in a little island port in an endeavor to buy everything needed for a coming charter, I have thought how nice it would be just to sit aboard and twiddle my thumbs—to sit under the awning with a cold beer, while everything was delivered to the ship's side. But we can't have everything. To be operating a sailing ship in the tradewinds, to be able to sit on deck in just the minimum amount of clothing day or night is a privilege in itself. To have all the restocking of the ship attended to by someone else would be almost too much. (Must say I'd like to try it, though!)

Unless you belong to the small band of fortunates working out of ports where shore facilities are so organized that a few phone calls will bring everything (and I mean *everything*), you can figure on doing a lot of running around yourself. For this you need wheels, either your own or hired. In St. Thomas, I shared a VW van with Bob and Fergie, two other charter skippers. This was an ideal setup, and our rule of "the boat stocking for a charter gets the wagon" always worked. We did this for years, and when now and again two of us would be buying stores on the same day, we took turns. Most of the time, however, our old heap sat rusting away under the coconut trees while we sailed around the islands. In all other ports I have used taxis.

Once your stores are aboard, stow them carefully, making sure you will know exactly where every item is during the cruise to come.

Leave your ice until last, unless you have no freezer or refrigerator and it is needed for preserving frozen stores. In our first year of chartering, the only refrigeration we had was ice boxes, and we found that frozen meat placed in them at the beginning of a one-week charter was thawed, but in good condition and edible, at the end.

For those who need or prefer to carry ice, make or have made some ice bags. An ice bag should be constructed of heavy canvas or sailcloth and be capable of holding a 50-pound block of ice. A bag 24 inches long and 15 inches high will do this with ease. The handles can be made of webbing and should be stitched securely to the bag, passing in one piece completely underneath so the handle on one side is connected to its counterpart on the other side.

Bags constructed in this fashion will last for years and will make all the difference to the labor of an ice-loading exercise, especially if you are faced with ferrying the stuff out to the ship in a rolly anchorage. They can also help to influence a taxi driver suddenly faced with the request to carry ice in the trunk of his precious cab. If you have good ice bags, plus an ingenuous manner (an asset to any charter skipper, either ashore or afloat), then you're a winner!

Some ice houses provide only shaved ice, and while this may not last as long as good, clear ice in a block, the fact that it can be poured in and out of a bag is a convenience.

THE CHARTER GAME

To arrive in port at the end of a charter and, over a period of 24 hours, attend to all the jobs necessary to get going again with a fresh group aboard, is an accepted part of the charter scene. For a crew working their ship (and themselves) as hard and as conscientiously as possible to take advantage of a "season," this is a necessary program in many parts of the world.

Once you're in the swing of the game, 24-hour turnarounds are not too bad unless something unforeseen happens. On one occasion, right in the middle of the season, we arrived back in the bay at the end of a trip with a major leak in a water tank. It had occurred suddenly the night before, and we'd just managed, by utilizing water in a spare tank on deck, to make it through the remaining 12 or 14 hours of the charter without any inconvenience to our party. It was patently obvious, however, that the leak was serious; this was not a one- or two-hour job to be put off until next morning. We were scheduled to sail in 24 hours with a group we'd had the year before.

First things first! We bought our stores, loaded them aboard, stowed them away, and by eleven o'clock that night I was able to begin the project. It took all night. After I had removed the lead (200 pounds) from our swinging table, unbolted it, pulled up the carpet and then the floor, I was able to get to the tinned copper water tank. I uncoupled it, eventually got it up in a position to work on, and discovered the trouble. Two rivets holding a baffle inside the tank had been torn loose by the surging of water. It was the rivet holes that were allowing the precious liquid to pour out into the bilge.

A permanent repair was impossible under the circumstances; I did not have the equipment for it. So I sanded down to bare, shiny copper around each hole, warmed the metal slightly with a propane torch, cleaned it with acetone, and applied fiberglass and Caulktex (synthetic rubber) patches.

By seven o'clock the next morning, everything was back in place; the tanks were filled with water and it was time to rush off and get 300 pounds of ice. Then scrub the decks . . . clean the hull . . . then the dinghy . . . buy a couple of new fishing lures . . . digest the news from my wife (who had been feverishly cleaning up all evidence of last night's emergency) that the water tank was holding O.K. . . . and a shout from along the dock, "Hi, Ross; hi, buddy!" . . . our party had arrived and the show was back on the road.

It is possible, of course, to get going in less than 24 hours, and while most of us have done this at one time or another, it can be tough duty. The speed of a ship's turnaround, as well as the pace at which her crew is forced to work (at such a time), is often influenced by the area she works. If the locale is a remote one, there may not be frequent air service. Sometimes there is no option but to get going again with a new party almost as soon as you arrive back in the bay. Such was the case with the *Golden Cachalot*, a big three-master working the Galápagos Islands. She had the toughest schedule we'd ever seen.

One plane a week flew from Ecuador to the little island of Baltra and picked up the party that had just completed a cruise. It also brought a new group, plus the stores. The *Golden Cachalot* had a big crew, and she needed them. The hive of activity aboard as people packed and left, as the crew cleaned ship, bunkered, watered up, stowed provisions, and as the new party arrived, convinced us that even our toughest 24-hour turnaround had been a breeze compared to this.

But if quick turnarounds become necessary to take advantage of a season at its peak, they do not go on forever. As a busy period tapers off, a vessel usually has much longer spells between charters. Three or four days, weeks, or even months can pass before she goes out on another cruise. This commonly depends on what area of the world a ship works; often an impending winter or hurricane season is responsible for lack of business.

Some operators do 12 or 14 weeks and then take it easy for the rest of the year, and here it gets down to how well the individual is fixed financially. This usually has a direct bearing on how hard he wants to work.

We did 30 weeks, year after year, and I consider it was too much. If you want to have your cake and eat it too, be satisfied with 25 weeks. In addition to allowing you time to have fun, this much business still allows you to make money if your charter fee is high enough (*see* Chapter 5).

A vessel doing 25 weeks will do a number of 24-hour turnarounds; she will have slack periods of a week or two at times between charters, and possibly a longer spell of a couple of months. A typical breakdown of her activities, with time off for her crew, is as follows.

Number of charter weeks	25 weeks
Average 3 days between charters	11 weeks
Time estimated for haulout	2 weeks
Time estimated for maintenance	6 weeks
Vacation for crew	4 weeks
Taking it easy—fun—"prospecting"	4 weeks
	52 weeks

As can be seen, the 25 weeks outlined above are not consecutive, and they do not leave the crew free to "goof off" for the remaining 27.

The average of three days between cruises, totaling approximately 11 weeks, represents a period where the crew works as hard as they ever do when actually out on charter. Running around after provisions, stocking up, tidying and cleaning in preparation for a trip can be a whole lot more demanding on the operators of a charter boat than when they are eventually sailing and earning their bread and butter.

The two weeks allowed for a haulout is, of course, only approximate (the skipper's responsibility here is discussed in the next section), and it represents the total length of time between arriving in port after a charter, hauling, restocking, and sailing again. It could be shorter if haulage facilities exist close to the charter boat's base of operations, or longer if she must travel to a port to be hauled or lifted clear of the water.

In the Caribbean, we always hauled twice a year and allowed one week on each occasion. In the Pacific we averaged a haulout every nine months.

It was Lord Nelson, I believe, who said, "Nothing spoils ships and men more than ports!" Be that as it may—and although I suspect that the Admiral's famous statement was inspired by the sight of some of his Jack Tars (who had probably been pressganged in the first place) disappearing over the nearest hill whenever he made port—it is often as nice to arrive in port as it was to leave it.

After cramming as much business as possible into a "season," it can be very satisfying to sail back into the bay knowing that the pace set for the next few days, weeks, or months will be one of our own choosing. The company of other crews is usually something that can also be anticipated with pleasure, for few other occupations breed empathy of the type existing between operators of ships employed in the charter trade. Each vessel is a little world unto itself, a self-contained unit dependent entirely upon the ability of the people running it to keep it that way. And "keeping it that way" is what

After a series of charters, it's nice to be a family again. The Riddells aboard Gay Vandra *at Athens. (Photo by Emily Riddell)*

contributes more than anything else to the feeling of brotherhood. We are all in the same boat here; we all have our problems and our moments. It is not easy to preserve this little floating world we live in in its entirety and to be successful at the same time. Nothing worthwhile ever is.

Of the compensations available to those who are efficient charter-boat skippers, however, not the least is the knowledge that they are members of a unique, almost way-out band. We operate independently, each in his own way. We pass at sea with a wave, meet briefly in little island ports while on charter, and often only really get together when a season is over and the guests have gone home. While customers are with us, we are at our best; we have to be, in both ability and manner. When they are not aboard, our responsibility is directed toward the maintaining of our world by preparing both the ship and ourselves for the next influx of passengers. It's also nice to have time to shoot the breeze with each other. . . .

The six weeks allowed for maintenance, the four weeks for vacation (usually a complete change of scene away from the chartering area), and four weeks for "prospecting" (sailing around looking for new territory) and having fun are not just figures plucked out of thin air. I believe they contribute as much to continuing success in the game as do the 25 weeks of charter.

MAINTENANCE

The more competent a charter skipper is at maintaining his ship and her equipment, the more money he will save. A charter-boat captain should be a Mr. Fixit. The more jobs you can do with your own two hands aboard your vessel, the less chance there will be of a holdup due to an equipment breakdown while away on charter—or anywhere else, for that matter.

If you've just bought a boat with the intention of giving the charter game a whirl, make every effort to familiarize yourself with her equipment. Keep an equipment file and fill it with all available information on *every* piece of gear— mechanical, electrical, or manual—that is installed aboard your ship. Read the engine, generator, and refrigeration manuals (instead of novels) until you know all her gear inside out.

Some people are better at this than others, and I do not for a moment wish to give any impression that I am a member of this upper echelon of Mr. Fixits. I'm not. After more than 30 years full time in the floating game, I can service most things aboard my ship, but not as well or as quickly as a lot of people I know.

It is an interesting challenge to accumulate the know-how to deal with various problems that arise on a vessel working for a living. However, whether you have a natural ability or not, it is possible. Through asking questions, studying manuals, watching the moves of every "pro" you come across, you can assimilate a lot of information. Store it away in your head. Write it down wherever possible. If I can do this, anybody can!

If you can't trace an electrical fault in the wiring or in a generator, ask someone who can to show you how. A charter guest who happened to be an electrical contractor showed me how to trouble-shoot with a voltmeter during a 10-day charter years ago. I am still not a pro, but even knowing just a little has saved me a lot of grief (and money) over the years.

Pick up information on how to deal with various problems whenever you can. A drowned outboard for instance. . . . I have a charter skipper friend who can deal almost in jig time with an outboard that has taken an involuntary swim. Fergie boils several gallons of fresh water in every pot, pan, or kettle he can find. While the water is heating, he removes the spark plugs from the outboard. The next move is to pour the water (it must be piping hot) into a large, clean, plastic garbage can (every charter boat has a couple of them or their equivalent) and lower the outboard upside down into it until the entire crankcase, cylinder head, and electrical components are submerged. Hold it thus while someone else cranks it over for five or ten minutes. The hot, fresh water will get into everything, washing all the salt out and heating up the metal. Pull it out of the water and keep cranking. When all water is pushed out of the cylinders through the plug holes, squirt in a tiny amount of 30-weight oil. Crank her over a few more times and install new plugs. Then put the outboard back on the dinghy and give her a good, hard run.

Carry every spare you can think of—light bulbs, fuses, wiring, solder, injectors, valve springs, pump impellers, cotter pins, gasket material, copper fuel pipe, fuel filters, plumbing fittings—all that you can sensibly store aboard.

A lot of charter skippers are pack rats. I'm one of the worst or best, depending on which way you look at it. All sorts of gear, without any conscious effort on my part, finds its way onto my ship. On one memorable occasion at Yacht Haven, St. Thomas, I realized that I was not the only skipper afflicted with this almost uncontrollable passion.

Most of us 50 or so charter-boat operators rented or shared large lockers ashore in a building that was owned by the hotel. I held one in partnership with Bob, owner-skipper of the *Bounty*, a 55-foot bugeye ketch. Great changes were being planned by the hotel, and part of the program was the redesigning and building of bigger and better lockers. We were all notified of this project and informed that if we had any "junk"—broken engine parts, old wire, dead batteries, pensioned-off outboards, pieces of pipe, outdated fittings, etc.—to pile it up outside in a big heap and they would take it away to the dump for free. This was hailed as a tremendous idea. Various members of the floating fraternity ransacked their lockers, throwing unwanted "junk" onto a pile that, over a period of only a day, grew and grew.

Early the next morning, long before the dump truck arrived to cart it all away, I wandered ashore to inspect the heap. Bob, surprisingly, was already there, as were about two dozen other charter skippers. I thought I'd be the only one. I moved along one side of the pile, and the first thing I spied was a piece of bronze pipe about two feet long. It was a good two inches in diameter and threaded at each end. What a find! Then I picked out a piece of rubber hose—suction hose. Across from me, I saw Bob, eyes alight, drag a length of half-round brass from under a coil of wire. Around us, others were doing the same thing.

The whole heap—except for a pile that would hardly have filled a wheelbarrow—disappeared back inside the lockers.

While the tendency to accumulate and hoard all manner of "treasures" is not only confined to operators of charter boats (I know a few cruising characters who, as pack rats, could teach us all a thing or two), it must be remembered that a boat carrying cargo—in our case, passengers—does not usually have room for an unlimited assortment of spares as well.

Therefore, while it is recommended that the well-found charter boat should have a good supply of the parts most likely needed in case of equipment failure, every nut, bolt, washer, impeller, etc., must have a reason for being aboard. And, just as important as having the stuff in case of breakdowns, you must know where you have stowed it on the ship. But know when to stop. It is possible for a charter skipper with a large boat to go to extremes and load his vessel down with so many spares that it is almost as easy to sail a couple of hundred miles to the nearest ship chandler for a part than to start hunting for it aboard. Just thought I'd mention this. . . .

In *White Squall II*, we carry enough bottom paint for a least one haulout, plus enough regular paint for one complete fitting out and touch-up maintenance between charters. This, of course, does not apply if you're confined to an area that is "down by the head" with ship chandlers; then it is just a matter of taking a few steps up the street to buy whatever you need whenever you need it. However, not all of us have this convenience, and some of those little dots on the chart that represent the island groups we work in can often be frustratingly short of the bosun's stores we need. If this is the case, and to fulfill his maintenance schedule, the wise charter captain will always think six months ahead by ordering paint, varnish, thinners, brushes, and sandpaper by mail, or fully stocking up when he is in a port where all these supplies are obtainable.

If a charter skipper is determined that by this time next year his boat will be in better shape than she is this time this year, he will keep up with his maintenance. It is obvious that a maintenance schedule should be planned well in advance. The haulout, usually the main event in the program, should be booked far enough ahead so that it does not clash with dates already offered to, or taken by, future charter parties. Long before it is time to haul, or be lifted clear of the water for antifouling and checking of underwater fittings, a charter captain should determine as closely as possible just what he intends to do once his ship is up on the hard. He should prepare for it by purchasing whatever materials he considers necessary for any of the various jobs.

Most vessels, and especially those carrying considerable electrical equipment, will need underwater sacrificial zincs replaced at least once a year. Several systems (Capac is one) are available as an alternative to zincs and will, the makers claim, completely take their place. If your ship is thus equipped, and you are happy with the setup (your propeller hasn't fallen off lately), then zincs will not be on your shopping list. However, if your ship does need them, have them aboard, all drilled and ready to install.

Once hauled or lifted clear of the water, give your underwater fittings the eye. Is the propeller pitted at the ends of the blades? If so, possibly cavitation is the cause. It has been my experience that the installation of zincs on the hull, above and below the propeller aperture, will completely nullify this trouble.

Disassemble a seacock. Any discoloration of metal? Can the parts be tapped with a lead hammer without being affected at all? If electrolysis is present, they may disintegrate, or sharp edges will crumble. If this happens, examine them all, together with your through-hulls. If your ship has a bowsprit, inspect the bolt or shackle pin where the bobstay makes fast to the hull fitting at or near the waterline. The same applies to the bumpkin stay.

Is the transducer painted with antifouling, the same as the rest of the ship below water? Mine is, and despite instructions from the manufacturer stating that this will impair its sensitivity, it is accurate enough for me. The point here—and one I cannot get past—is that if the face of the transducer is not painted, it soon gets so foul with barnacles and other underwater growth that it will not record anything anyhow!

Clean inside every through-hull fitting with a stick. Any obstructions? If you have been lying in harbor where there is a predominance of weed—such as Morro Bay on the California coast—it may be necessary to clear engine intakes and raw water filters. Do all this now, while you're on the ways. Don't risk wishing you had done it once you're back in the water.

Give your rudder gudgeons, pintles, and bottom bearing a thorough inspection. Are they worn?

How about the stern bearing? When steaming at low revs, was there any vibration aft in the ship? If there was, the stern bearing probably needs replacing. Maybe your shaft will need drawing and inspecting for wear and scoring.

Is too much water coming in through the stuffing box? It may need repacking. I prefer to let a generous drip come in while we are steaming, so that the stern gland remains cool. This water is pumped out by a small

A "bit of growth" resulting from an unpainted transducer face.
(Photo by Carl Moesly)

submersible electric pump located in the bilge aft. A grease nipple in the engine room, from which a copper pipe leads to the stuffing box aft of the gland, is given a few pumps with a grease gun after the engine has been in use. This puts a skin of grease around the shaft and prevents water from coming through the gland and into the ship while under sail or at anchor.

Is your radio ground O.K.?

It is not necessary to be a licensed marine surveyor to look for all these things and to make decisions on them. There is nothing I have outlined that is anything more than common sense.

Just to haul your ship up on the ways and walk away whistling while the yard scrubs off and slaps on a coat of paint is not good enough. Many yards will not allow the crew of a vessel to do any work below the waterline when she is hauled or lifted clear of the water. O.K., so be it, but the master of every ship, large or small, is the one who is ultimately responsible for the condition of his vessel when she goes back in the water. So make sure, after she's scrubbed off and before any paint can cover things up, that you go around her underneath with the foreman or person in charge. Make a list of what needs doing and be certain it has all been attended to before you go back into the water.

If you are hauling out on one of the little slipways that exist in some island groups—where often rafferty (Rube Goldberg) rules are the only ones existing—have a good look at the ways before trusting your precious ship to them. We broke an axle in Tahiti on a cradle that we had been assured was *très forte!"* Our 60-ton bulk dropped four inches. And that South American port where we were hauled out sideways . . . Santa Maria!

THE CHARTER GAME

Unpainted sumlog. Note the relatively clean ship's bottom after 11 months in the water. (Photo by Carl Moesly)

If your boat has a long keel, have a look at the length of the cradle she will be expected to fit in. Is it long enough? Will it accommodate her beam? If she has a short keel, measure the distance between the cradle bearers. Are they too far apart for the keel to bear on at least two? If so, and you have no alternative but to use the slipway, insist that heavy planks (preferably hardwood, minimum four-inch thickness) be spiked fore and aft to the bearers for the keel to sit on.

Carry either a set of plans or photos showing the dimensions and shape of your boat underwater. I have always used photos, for the simple reason that I don't expect to get them back. I take along three. One shows the ship, side on, sitting in a cradle and showing her full profile. Another is a shot from about a hundred feet forward, showing her underwater sections. The third shows her stern sections, rudder and propeller, taken from aft. On the back of the photos, I write her dimensions and weight.

If, however, your ship has a short keel, or an underwater shape that makes her tricky to haul, photos are not good enough. You must have a set of plans for the yard to inspect before they do a job such as this.

Regarding bottom paint, and the frequency with which a vessel should be antifouled, no single rule applies for every part of the world. In many temperate regions, if a good-quality bottom paint is used, it is possible that a ship will have only a light scum on the bottom after a full year in the water. I have had this experience in New Zealand, and after antifouling with the same paint before sailing for the tropics (Tonga Islands), I was forced less than seven months later to sail 450 miles to Fiji to haul, as we were becoming foul.

I have yet to find the bottom paint that will give the same service regardless of what region the ship is working.

114

Gay Vandra *hauled out for a haircut and a shave at Aegina, Greece, before a charter season.* *(Photo by Emily Riddell)*

If you intend to stay in an area, have a talk with the skippers of other trading and charter boats based there. Ask them what bottom paint gives the best service. Wander through local shipyards, and you'll usually get the straight, unvarnished truth from the guys who scrub ship's bottoms and put the paint on. If you get close to them, they can give firsthand information on what paint does, or does not, collect growth over a given length of time. Don't ask the yard owner or boss. Normal business practice forces the guy to plug the brand he stocks, and it may be no good.

In a country where charter boats come under government inspection, it will probably be mandatory to haul twice a year—once for a full survey and six months later for a "haircut and shave." In each case, the vessel will be coated below the waterline with antifouling, so the necessity for a paint that will last a year, and may cost twice as much as one only good for six months, does not arise.

Never stop criticizing and inspecting your own equipment. The more sound and safe you can make it, the more confident you'll be of its ability to stand up to the wear and tear of the charter game and not let you down. Keep a running survey going. Check your standing rigging, turnbuckles, shackles, toggles, running rigging, and anchoring gear.

Maintenance takes place aboard every vessel working for a living. A refrigerator or an engine can break down just as easily in a "maintenance-free" glass hull as it can in a wooden, steel, or ferro one.

115

THE CHARTER GAME

Make a master list of the maintenance you consider will be necessary aboard your ship for a year ahead. Break the list down into parts. Make one for little jobs—such as sail inspection for chafe (usually the most damaging thing to any sail)—engine oil changes, disassembling and oiling of mast and sheet winches, overhauling anchor windlass, wheel steering (wires, pulleys, sheaves, pins, quadrant and (if hydraulic) pump, oil leakage and joins), bilge ventilation and stove (don't just assume that your stove will perform trouble-free forever without any maintenance). If you have a "sniffer" aboard, test it regularly so that you are certain it will work. Test the one between your eyes at the same time.

The list will vary, of course, from boat to boat. But write down every job you can think of, and attend to them in order of importance.

Bigger jobs, such as main engine overhaul, rigging replacement, installation of new water tanks, building more storage lockers in the galley, etc. (this always goes over big with the cook), are usually left for the off-season. They warrant a separate list. A busy charter boat, with only a few weeks between seasons and a big job to attend to, must make certain that all materials and labor necessary for the project are arranged well in advance.

Have little or no varnish on deck. Even though our rail, hatches, and skylights are all teak, they are painted; only the wheel and binnacle are varnished. The reason is that paint lasts a year and varnish usually only four months when exposed to tropic sun and salt spray. Since a charter boat is first and foremost a workboat, there is no time for revarnishing when we are busy and, while nothing looks better than gleaming brightwork on a ship topside, nothing looks worse if it is neglected.

It is usually possible to recruit labor in various ports or islands to assist with maintenance. The ability of help so employed, we have found, varies greatly; often language is also a consideration. In St. Thomas, we had Alvin, a native boy from Antigua. Alvin was no Rembrandt with a paintbrush, and his Calypso had me baffled for years, but as a worker he was without peer. In Tahiti, we had Gaston, who spoke pure Tahitian and about four words of French. I speak English (I think) and three words of French—marvelous conversations!

If it seems I have devoted a lot of space to maintenance and placed too much emphasis on these tasks, it is only because it is an inescapable fact of the floating life. We cannot live in our boats and work them without maintaining them also. We can't just sit in a boat as we sit in a house. Boats float (or they're supposed to); they also take us places; and if we play our cards right, they'll provide us with a living as well.

Conscientious attention to maintenance is part of the overall picture of success. And success in the charter game, as in any other enterprise, can seldom be regarded as luck.

TOOLS

A good tool kit is essential to attend to the servicing of equipment that is necessary to keep a charter vessel a going concern.

Start off with the basics: claw hammer, engineer's hammer, set of punches, cold chisels (several sizes), hacksaw (plus spare blades), adjustable wrenches, pipe wrenches, water-pump pliers, screwdrivers (many sizes), plus a good vise (and the means of mounting it). Work up from there.

Some equipment, such as autopilot, sheet winches, and macerator pump (glory be), may need special tools. Make sure you have them aboard.

A good tool kit is something in which we can all take pride, and it will pay for itself a hundred times over. Socket sets, wrenches (combination, box, and open-end), Allen wrenches, drill bits, pliers, files, flaring kit, tap and die set, soldering kit, sidecutters, tin snips, Visegrips, electric drill motor, sanders, jigsaw—if you can't afford all this to start with, confine yourself to the essentials and keep adding extra items (after a while they all look like jewels) to your kit. And don't forget carpenter's tools—fine-tooth panel saw, large and small planes, wood chisels, hand drill, square, and measuring tape.

Some people couldn't care less about tools; they treat their acquisitions as just another thing to buy and their presence as an inevitable part of the ship's equipment. I cannot subscribe to this attitude. In addition to being a life member of the pack rats club, I am also a compulsive tool collector. Hardware stores are my jewelry stores. My wife can leave me in the tool section of any store and go off shopping for hours at a time, secure in the knowledge that I'll hardly have budged an inch from the spot where she left me except, perhaps, to have made a few purchases to add to my precious collection. Once I have them aboard, I feel as if I have achieved a victory if one of them (especially a recent purchase) is suddenly needed for a job.

Sometimes there are several of one kind of tool in a cruising or charter boat's kit. There can be (and usually is) a reason for this.

In 1951 we entered the 1,300-mile Tasman race from Auckland, New Zealand, to Sydney, Australia, in my 33-foot yawl, *White Squall*. On the way across (we were about four days out), the compass light suddenly went out. It was midnight, raining, and the good old Tasman Sea was treating us to some of her famous weather. We tried another bulb—no luck. One of the little wires leading into the socket had carried away. We searched the ship from end to end for a small screwdriver and found we didn't have one aboard. So we filed a big one down, and several frustrating hours later, we were able to attend to a job that should have taken only a few minutes. Since then, I've carried several tiny screwdrivers. There is one in among the ship's cutlery; there are two or three among my tools; there is one in the locker where I keep spare electrical gear. I am particularly confident about the position of this last one, because it speared me not long ago when I was fishing around in there for a fuse. I have never needed any of them for an emergency—not yet. But I will one day, and I'm all primed for a celebration when I do.

BOSUN'S LOCKER

A bosun's locker can usually be regarded as an addition to the ship's tool kit. Timely use of the contents of both is sometimes necessary to keep her operating.

It should include a large and small sailmaker's palm, several sizes of sail needles (these can be kept in a small jar full of oil, or covered with grease in a flat, hinged tin), beeswax and/or already-waxed Dacron thread, wooden splicing fid, marlin spike, marlin (waxed and plain), several paint scrapers (I prefer the three-cornered type), scraper files, putty knives, and several sizes of shackles. All of these items should be kept in a portable ditty bag.

In the paint locker section of the bosun's store, there should be paint-brushes (various sizes), paint, thinners, varnish, sandpaper, epoxy glue, instant "super" glue, penetrating oil, silicone (in paste form for track slides and in a spray can for zippers), tapered "softwood" plugs (each one marked to fit a through-hull), hand cleaner, and a bundle of rags.

This list represents the minimum. The range of gear usually depends upon the amount of locker stowage space aboard and how long the ship will be working away from a port where supplies are obtainable. The construction of the ship, her superstructure and her interior, can also have a bearing on the contents of the paint locker. Carry all you have space for, or think you may need. Be ruthless with old cans containing only a little paint. A can with a tiny amount of paint in it is seldom worth keeping for any length of time: the can takes up valuable space and the paint in it will usually have thickened underneath a tough skin. Give such contents of your locker the deep six when you're well out at sea, or dump them ashore.

Paint often spoils in a can because the lid is not replaced correctly. If the groove in which the lid sits becomes filled with paint and some is allowed to remain there while the pot is open and in use, it may be difficult to bed the lid firmly back in place. If you punch four holes in the groove as soon as you open the can, this problem is largely circumvented. The paint that inevitably runs into the groove after a paintbrush has been dipped in, or paint is poured from the can into another container, trickles through these holes and back into the can. Replace the lid firmly, tap it down with a hammer, and your paint has *every* chance of keeping for much longer than if the lid were put back on any old way.

Look after your equipment. Spray or wipe tools with a fine oil to keep them from rusting. Wash out paintbrushes in diesel fuel before stowing away; this ensures that the bristles will stay soft. Before using them again, wash them in thinners.

Make certain your spare shackles are really spares, and can be used in a hurry when necessary, by greasing the threads on the pins and leaving them finger-tight.

It is an exceptionally well-equipped vessel that has the tools (and knowledge) aboard to deal with all maintenance and any emergency. However, we can do our best and, in doing just that, derive an enormous amount of satisfaction from the result. Many jobs are attended to by charter skippers aboard their ships by using the tools, materials, and know-how carefully accumulated beforehand.

CARE OF DINGHY AND OUTBOARD

Your dinghy and outboard are a combination that mean a lot to you. Look after them. Never forget that even though the dinghy may be equipped as completely as you can arrange or afford (with outboard, tank, oars, anchor, tools, lifejackets, etc.), and though you may, and should, look on it with pride, it is defenseless against neglect. The dinghy has much in common with the ship herself; both are completely dependent upon us.

A charter boat's dinghy is as much a workboat as the ship herself. It gets hard use. We expect it to perform without fault after being overloaded, dumped on beaches, hauled over gravel, and towed in all sorts of weather. It can, and will, do all of this if hard use is tempered with a little care and attention.

I like to see an outboard well shackled to an eye bolt in the transom of a dinghy: an outboard so attached cannot be stolen easily (the robber needs tools) and it will stay fastened to the dinghy and not be lost over the side in the event that its clamps are tightened insufficiently.

Outboard manuals often advise the use of a padlock and chain. While this may be ideal for some individuals, those words were not written for me—nor, I suspect, for a lot of people like me. I always lose the key or discover, when I want to take the outboard up onto the ship, that the key is ashore, going the rounds of the stores in the bottom of my wife's handbag. So I end up unscrewing a shackle after all.

Having shackled your outboard securely to the dinghy, continue to give it a little more attention. Tilt it up when not in use, so that the gearcase and propeller are clear of the water. If you don't, these parts will soon have a growth on them. Inspect it regularly, making sure it pivots easily and that the throttle is free and does not stick. Grease it as per the handbook. Install a filter in the line between the gas tank and the motor so that water, from condensation in the tank or from any other source, cannot reach the carburetor. At the intervals recommended by the manufacturer, take the motor off the dinghy to change the oil in the gearcase.

The eye bolt in the bow of a dinghy, to which a painter is made fast, is often not strong enough to take the continual use imposed upon it by the charter game. Sometimes a dinghy is towed astern for the whole cruise; often the eye bolt is utilized as a lifting point when bringing the dinghy aboard; year in and year out, the towing eye is subjected to strain. A lot of them just can't take it. If you have any doubts about the strength of the eye bolt on your dinghy, replace it with a bigger one. I replaced the ⅜-inch-diameter bronze eye bolt (installed by the makers) with a ½-inch-diameter stainless-steel one about eight years ago. The latter almost fell apart when it was taken out last year for inspection. We have another bronze one in there now that looks strong enough to hold down a gun carriage on a ship of the line. It is ⅝ inch in diameter—and woe betide anything it comes in contact with! Incongruous though it may look, it should be able to do its job without giving trouble, such as carrying away when the dinghy is being towed in a bit of a slop.

Even the most hard-nosed charter captain needs only one experience of turning in his tracks in even moderate weather to pick up his dinghy—adrift after the eye bolt has parted—to become a believer. It can be a hell of a job, because usually there is no other point forward on the dinghy to fasten to and still be able to keep on towing it. So, some way, somehow, after a "volunteer" has jumped down into it, or has swum to it with a line, the dinghy must be lifted aboard.

I have not had this problem for some years now, and I never want it again. But I have two friends who, only a few weeks ago, found themselves in a similar predicament to the one I have just described.

Barry and Faith left the Great Barrier Island for a 40-mile run in *Masada*, their husky 55-foot cutter. The weather was calm; southeast winds of 12 to 15 knots were forecast. They decided to tow their 13-foot fiberglass dinghy rather than lift it aboard and, before leaving the bay, Barry (he must be clairvoyant) decided to tie a short auxiliary line from the dinghy end of the painter around the center thwart. When they were about 15 miles out, the ⅜-inch-diameter bronze eye bolt in the bow of the dinghy parted. The dinghy swung around on an angle to their course and started to take water over the gunwale as it was pulled along sideways. There ensued a busy 20 minutes or so as they luffed up, hove to, and, at the expense of much bumping and scraping on the ship, the dinghy, and themselves, they got it aboard. This dinghy now sports a great galvanized steel eye bolt in the bow. . . .

After having satisfied ourselves that the eye bolt on the dinghy will do anything expected of it without complaint, the next step is the choice of a suitable painter and the means of fastening it to the eye. I prefer nylon line with a minimum diameter of ½ inch for this job. Not only is a painter of this size strong enough to deal with the jerk of a dinghy being snapped back onto its course when being towed under sail in a following sea, it is also of a comfortable size to handle and, being nylon, has a desirable amount of stretch.

A dinghy painter may be fastened to the eye bolt with a fisherman's bend or a bowline, it may be spliced around a thimble and then shackled to the eye, or, after spreading the thimble until there is enough of a gap for the eye to pass inside (after which the thimble is closed again), the painter is passed through the eye, around the thimble, and spliced.

The first of these methods is temporary at best and not good practice over the long haul. The second is often seen and is usually dependable as long as the shackle pin is moused and then well riveted over. The third method is by far the best, in my opinion. It does my heart good to see my painter passing completely through the eye in the bow of the dinghy, around a stainless-steel thimble, before being spliced back into itself with five good tucks, which are then tapered off. But then I'm a member of the club—I'm one of the guys who has had to pick up his dinghy at sea!

If all this sounds like any charter-boat captain who tows his dinghy is nuts, and that he should always lift it aboard, no matter what, consider that: (a) a lot of our runs are short and in relatively sheltered waters; (b) our dinghies ("shoreboats" would be a more realistic term) are usually big ones that entail time and effort to get aboard; (c) most charter boats run as shorthanded as possible. Our days are full of work, and to secure a dinghy aboard or in davits, only to put it down into the water again in a few hours or less, is something we avoid wherever possible. I have known smaller charter boats (35 to 40 feet) that work exclusively in sheltered waters and use dinghies of a size that would be almost impossible to bring aboard, so they have no alternative but to tow.

For an open-sea passage between islands, however, the dinghy should always come aboard.

The length of a dinghy's painter is also something to be considered. Ours is 20 feet, and once made fast aft, on board the ship, it does not fall in enough of a bight to get underneath and around the propeller when we are maneuvering under power. This is the sole reason for its length. The end is spliced back in a nine-inch "soft" eye that can be conveniently dropped over a winch, cleat, or bollard.

Some boat owners use a floating line to take care of the possibility that a painter might sink down and be wound around a propeller when the ship goes astern. Another school favors small foam or plastic floats positioned about three feet apart all the way along the painter. My choice is nylon line (because of its strength and ability to stretch) of a predetermined length that makes it impossible to form a deep enough bight to reach the propeller under any conditions.

In cases where a dinghy tends to yaw when being towed in a following sea, bend a strong line onto the painter and slack away until the dinghy is 50 or 60 feet astern and riding on the "upward" face of a sea—that is, on the windward side of the crest. Make fast to the towline a five- or six-pound weight on about a fathom of line after 30 feet or so of towline has been payed out (or at a point that will be roughly halfway along the line when the dinghy is a satisfactory distance astern); this will help take the snap out of the towline as strain comes and goes, due to the surging and often uneven speed of both craft.

When a charter boat is anchored in a bay, her dinghy, dory, punt, or skiff (it goes by all of these names and gets called a few more at times) is expected to be available for instant use. Whether the charter captain is in the habit of tailing the dinghy off the stern when at anchor or laying it alongside, it is an advantage to have a couple of fenders close to the boarding ladder for it to rest against when people are using it.

I have a system I have adhered to for years. Weather permitting, day and night, the dinghy lies against two fenders just aft of the boarding ladder on the starboard side. If the anchorage is tidal, causing the ship to swing with the current while the dinghy moves in another direction with the wind, I pass up a stern line and make it fast well aft on the ship. Every night before retiring, if the weather allows for the dinghy to lie alongside, and whether the locale is tidal or not, the painter is led forward of the boarding ladder and firmly secured aboard the ship. The dinghy stern line is made fast aft. If I consider that there is enough of a wind blowing for the dinghy to behave itself and not creep up under the stern and deal the ship a foul blow during the night, I tail it off from aft in the towing position by its painter.

Dinghies and outboards are often damaged through the landing facilities (or lack of them) in some ports. A dinghy that has been tied up nonchalantly and left without a thought for its welfare can easily be injured. Wash from passing craft can cause it to pound on rocks, a breakwater, or a concrete wharf; a rising tide can trap it underneath a bridge or jetty; a falling tide can leave it hanging on a painter that was tied too short and cause all its contents to empty into the bay; other boats using the landing can bang into it. The trick in avoiding all this strife is to have someone aboard land the shore party and then take the dinghy back to the ship. We have often done so. My wife gives me a call when it is time to pick her up by using a little walkie-talkie she carries in her purse. During her absence I am usually engaged in some routine maintenance job aboard, and I keep a large set going on her wave band. We have used this arrangement for over 10 years in both the Caribbean and the Pacific, often to the enormous entertainment of natives in out-of-the-way places. And for those who spurn the use of electronic aids to summon the dinghy, a powerful set of lungs can be very effective.

On occasions when all hands are going ashore, and even the skipper has been talked into leaving his vessel, it will be necessary, once at the landing, to tie up the dinghy and leave it. In this case, drop your dinghy anchor (ours is a 15-pound CQR—*see* Chapter 3) over the stern when about 30 feet from the steps, jetty, or landing. Land your party and then, while someone you can trust holds the end of the painter, haul the dinghy stern-first for six or eight feet away from the landing. Inside the transom, the dinghy should have a cleat to which the anchor line is then made fast. The person on the landing hauls on the painter to dig the anchor in and also to bring the bow of the dinghy back to enable you to step ashore. It is impossible to generalize, for hardly any two dinghy landings are the same, but, having done all this, it is usually possible to take the painter 10 feet or so to one side or the other and make it fast. Ideally, the dinghy should now be positioned clear enough of the landing so as not to be in the way of other boats using it, and free of any obstruction that might damage it.

When tying up a dinghy among a cluster of other small craft inside a

Stern anchor out, outboard tilted up, painter made fast to the "off" side of the dock. This charter boat's dinghy is out of the way of any other small craft using the landing and is clear of any obstruction that might damage it. (Photo by Ross Norgrove)

sheltered yacht basin or marina, it is generally not necessary to go through the drill of using a stern anchor. In this situation it is usually possible to make the painter fast to a post or cleat and walk away secure in the knowledge that your shoreboat will come to no harm. However, one or two of the things you do, or don't do, will help demonstrate whether you are a reasonably knowledgeable seaman and courteous—or a bad one who couldn't care less.

Never tie your dinghy painter over the top of the other guy's. Often, in a sheltered boat harbor, when 10 or 15 dinghies tie up to the same pontoon or landing, several of them will have no option but to make fast to the same post or cleat. When this happens, and there is no alternative but to tie to a point already in use, pass your line around underneath all the others and make fast with a bowline, or make a second turn and finish off with two half hitches around the standing part of the painter. The advantage of using one or the other of these knots is that either can be tied or untied without disturbing any painter already there.

The other "no-no" is: Don't tie your dinghy up too short. Give the other guy a fair go. A small landing or float can accommodate a large number of dinghies if they are made fast with painters that allow them to float 12 or 15 feet clear. Even two or three dinghies tied up short to a small landing stage can make it difficult to use.

Have your ship's name painted on the transom of the dinghy, preferably on both outside and inside. This is popular, and often mandatory, with insurance companies. And while on the subject of insurance, I should mention that it is possible that some aspiring charter skippers will regard my concern for the welfare of the dinghy as being unnecessarily noble and decide, "What the hell, mine's insured . . . why should I care if it gets knocked about or lost?" This attitude can be disastrous. It can be responsible for the loss of a dinghy, which may, because of the region the charter boat is working, take months to replace. A fully equipped dinghy, lost a few days before an impending series of charters—charters calculated to bring in $20,000 to $30,000—will be sorely missed, and the fact that it is insured will be small consolation if it can't be replaced immediately.

Something that can damage a dinghy and its contents, no matter how efficiently we tie it up, is the attention of vandals. We experienced this on an occasion when we picked up a charter party at the island of St. Maarten in the West Indies. We dropped anchor in the bay the day before the charter and that night, by prearrangement, made our way ashore to a hotel to meet and have dinner with our party. We moored our dinghy (under the attentive eyes of a small band of youngsters) with an anchor over the stern and the painter fast to a little pier. On our return, we found the starting cord had been ripped out of our brand-new outboard, handfuls of stones had been thrown into the dinghy, and one of the oars was missing.

Since then, we have always picked out the biggest kid among any group watching us tie up the dinghy. We give him 25 or 50 cents and tell him he'll get the same again if, on our return, the dinghy and outboard have not been interfered with. So far, this system has never failed. . . .

RESPONSIBILITY

Webster's tells us that responsibility is a "state or quality of being responsible." From that eminent source, then, we can deduce that as soon as customers trickle down the gangplank, or board our craft by any means, we, as masters of the vessels they ship away in, are placed in that state. We are accountable for their safety and their welfare. As soon as the skipper of any vessel accepts a fee to take anyone anywhere, he must accept full responsibility for their safety while aboard. This usually means that he also has the job of debarking them at a designated place and, in most cases, at a stipulated time. Even if it is only a one-day sail—out of the bay and back—the degree of responsibility is the same.

My intention in stating this is not to discourage the intended charter-boat captain. It is only to point out a fact that is inescapable, and one he must be fully cognizant of. It is a fact accepted by hundreds of charter-boat operators every day all over the world.

This state into which responsibility, by its definition, places us need not be one of jangled nerves or a heightened pulse rate; it need not leave us vowing that the next job we take will be on a farm. Far from it. A well-fitted-out charter boat can offer as safe and unique a vacation as it is possible for people to have. The ultimate ingredient, however, and the one that makes it possible for a charter boat to operate safely year after year with a minimum of fuss, is the master's acceptance of the responsibility vested in him when he takes command. It is this acceptance that will drive him to keep up his maintenance, continually check lifelines, lifesaving gear, stove, fire extinguishers—each and every one of the things covered in this book, plus anything else particular to his ship or the region he is working. All this is not hard; it is, as much as anything, a state of awareness that a charter captain must develop and retain in order to make a success of his job.

Besides the responsibility involving life and limb, there is the moral one. These people—our customers—pay good money to come away in our ships. If we don't pull out all stops to show them a good time, then we are just not doing our job.

Unless we are on a "ferryboat" run where the calls we make this week are to the same places as last week, we should do everything possible to suit the charter cruise to the party aboard. This may involve shelling expeditions for one group, raildown sailing for another, snorkeling and beachcombing another, a little sailing interspersed with walks ashore another . . . and so on.

It can be very satisfying at the end of a cruise when guests are leaving to know that in addition to having coped successfully with their safety while aboard, we have also been responsible for making and keeping them happy.

SEAMANSHIP

Seamanship, both basic and advanced, is adequately dealt with in any number of manuals devoted wholly to the matter, so a step-by-step discussion of it is not the province of this book. It is assumed that the intended charter captain has his favorite publication on the subject; it is also hoped that he studies it.

My sole reason for including a passage on seamanship is to point out to the aspiring charter skipper the fact that in the handling of his vessel, he will be expected by his guests to act in a professional, assured, competent manner and to show that with a little forethought, it can be done successfully. It is not necessary for half a hundred sailors to be leaping and bounding around the decks of a ship to the accompaniment of whistles, loudspeakers, yells, and shouts to get a vessel alongside. Witness a merchant freighter. She arrives in the middle of the night and docks with hardly a sound. Quickly, too—all hands want to get back into their bunks! There has been no noise and no running; no merchant seaman in his right mind would run when he could walk anyway. There she is in the morning, all 10,000 tons of her, tied up only a cable away from where we are anchored, and we didn't hear a thing. It is exactly this type of competence, this standard of seamanship that we must strive to emulate.

For the crew—often only a man and woman—the running of their 50-, 60-, or 70-footer to the standard expected of them takes a certain amount of planning and practice. For example, let's start with docking.

We have been away for a week's charter cruise with a compatible group aboard. Everyone has had a fine old time. They have swum, snorkeled, taken turns at the wheel, sunbathed, walked on golden beaches; they have hauled a few fish in over the stern as we've sailed along; they have been well wined and dined. As we sail into the bay where they will debark, all hands are suntanned and happy. We round up into the wind, drop the sails, and several of the guests help us "skin" them up into a harbor stow. Everybody is commenting on what a wonderful time they've had. All we have to do now is to lay the old girl alongside the dock and the voyage is over.

Now is no time to make a mess of things—like carving a 10-foot splinter off the dock on account of having misjudged our speed and distance. Or sticking our bronze stemhead fitting (anchor and all) through the varnished transom of that big power-cruiser berthed up ahead because we didn't test the reverse gear before we made our approach. Now is the time to dock our ship in a workmanlike, if unspectacular, manner. For this, we need lines to secure her with, fenders, and the knowledge of how our vessel can be expected to perform in various circumstances.

We will assume that our craft is a typical auxiliary sailboat of 55 feet. Her engine gives her adequate power to maneuver and it drives a right-handed propeller. This last is usual for a single-screw vessel, but it is important to know, for occasionally a boat will have a left-handed wheel. A right-handed propeller is one that, when viewed from astern, turns in a clockwise direction, or to explain it another way, the top moves to the right. The opposite, of course, applies to a left-handed propeller.

The rotation of the propeller has a great influence on how a ship maneuvers, especially when all, or most, of the way is off her and she is reversing.

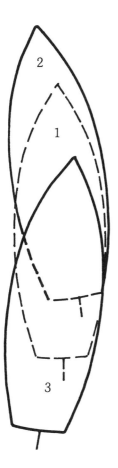

Effect of a right-handed propeller on a single-screw vessel. (The opposite applies to a ship with a left-handed propeller.) (1) Vessel stationary, rudder amidships. (2) Engine in gear ahead, rudder amidships. Stern swings to starboard, bow to port. (3) Engine astern, rudder any position. Stern "cants" sharply to port, bow to starboard.

127

A right-handed propeller will drive a vessel's stern to starboard (bow to port) when going ahead with rudder amidships, and her stern (usually no matter what her rudder angle) sharply to port when going astern. It follows, then, that a single-screw vessel with a right-handed propeller is easier to dock port side to, and a single-screw vessel with a left-handed propeller is easier to dock starboard side to.

Back to our charter party! We are moving in toward the dock with this contented gang aboard our 55-foot ketch. Our intention is to lay alongside with neither fuss nor bother. Let's not botch up the job! Our ship has a right-handed propeller, and we are docking port side to. Over the port side we hang three rubber fenders spaced so that the ship will lay against them when alongside; we also prepare our lines. There are four of these—a bow line, a stern line, and two springs. Each line is one-inch-diameter nylon and has an eye spliced on one end big enough to drop comfortably over a large bollard or pile.

The most important line in the whole docking procedure is the after spring. In this case we will take it off the port shoulder, a little more than one-third of the length of the ship, back from the bow. Once that's ashore, she'll do everything but talk to us!

The object is to berth at a speed slow enough to give steerageway. So a cable (approximately 200 yards) from the dock sees us well slowed down. It is here that we give her a little nudge astern to make sure our reverse gear is working.

Out of gear, and at a speed not greater than dead slow, we approach, at an angle of about 15 degrees, the spot where we will tie up. As it passes over the position our stern will occupy, the bow is three to six feet out from the wharf (this depends on how quickly the stern will cut in when we reverse, and varies from ship to ship). The other half of the crew who is standing at the port shoulder—our mate, wife, or girlfriend—passes or swings the after spring ashore.

As soon as that spring is over a piling or bollard, we give her a kick astern—then out of gear again. Just moving now, our port side about two feet away and parallel to the dock and with our mate slacking the spring around a strong cleat, belaying pin, or bitts aboard, we approach the desired position.

We've nearly reached it—a tiny kick astern, then out of gear again. Our mate has her eyes upon us. A nod. She turns up on the cleat, making the spring fast, and as soon as her hands are clear, we engage the engine in gear, dead slow ahead.

The ship is alongside now, held by her after shoulder spring, which is fast ashore at a point roughly level with her stern—and kept there by the force the engine is exerting on it by ticking over in gear ahead. We now adjust the wheel to a position that will keep the ship's centerline parallel to the side of the dock and leisurely tie her up. The bow line will go out ahead; the stern line goes aft along the dock, and our forespring will lead from the port quarter forward to a point on the dock roughly level with our port shoulder. With all lines fast aboard, we can now bring the engine out of gear ahead and shut it down. If we've done a good job, with a total lack of yells, barked commands (I'm not game to bark at my wife anyhow, are you?), and frantic running around the deck, nobody will even comment upon the performance. If we've done a *very* good job, we have a chance of collecting the highest praise it is ever possible to get. A charter guest who has been busily packing a suitcase below just might come on deck after the engine is stopped, gaze around, and say, "When did we dock? I thought we were still at sea!"

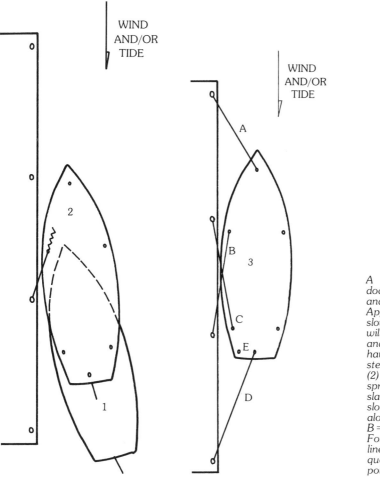

A normal docking, or docking with wind and/or tide ahead. (1) Approaching dock dead slow; a short kick astern will take way off the ship and in the case of a right-handed propeller, cant stern in toward the dock. (2) Port after shoulder spring ashore and being slacked as vessel moves slowly ahead. (3) Fast alongside. A = Bow line. B = After spring. C = Forespring. D = Stern line. E = Stern line frequently comes from this point.

129

To get her away from the dock, we start the engine, move the after spring line from the port shoulder, and lead it either through a bow chock or to the farthest point available forward, where, in either case, we make it fast. If there is no one handy on the dock to stand by this line and tend it as we leave, now is the time to double it up. The eye is taken off the dock aft and dropped over the samson post or other point well forward on the ship; the bight of the line is taken *underneath* the eye of the forespring and around the dock bollard athwart the bow. This is then made fast aboard to the same point (samson post, cleat, or bitt) occupied by the eye. With bow line, stern line, and forespring let go and aboard, a couple of good fenders hung over between the port shoulder and the bow, and our wheel hard over to port, we give her a gentle kick ahead, then out of gear again.

Three things will have happened: (1) Our stern, helped by the fact that we have a right-handed propeller, and also because of the hard left rudder, has moved out to starboard; (2) The ship has moved slightly ahead, tightening the after spring; (3) This spring now is holding our bow, with fenders in between, against the dock. Another kick ahead—we leave the engine in gear

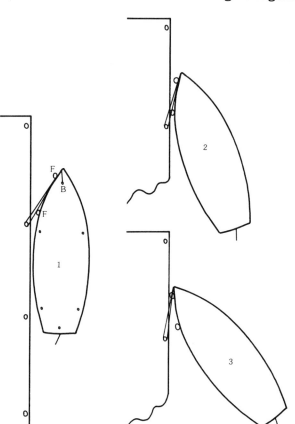

Kicking the stern out with a doubled-up spring off the bow. (1) Short kick ahead with hard left rudder—then out of gear. F = Fenders.   B = Doubled-up spring. (2) Slow ahead as first fender bears against the dock. (3) Second fender doing its job now—nearly ready to put engine out of gear, haul spring aboard, and kick astern. (4) and (5) Ship going astern, all lines and fenders aboard. (6) Short kick ahead with hard left rudder. (7) Astern—rudder in same position. (8) Out of gear, rudder amidships; ready to come ahead or to starboard.

and her stern walks out to starboard. Our mate, standing by forward with a spare fender "just in case," looks aft and with a nod signals that we can't go any farther without the chance of marking up the paintwork.

We wait with engine out of gear while she gets the spring aboard, and then, leaving the helm hard a-port, we give the ship a good kick astern. With the bow 15 or 20 feet clear of the dock, and our stern canted sharply to port by the action of the right-handed propeller going astern, we slow down, come into neutral, put her in gear ahead, and give her a short burst with about half throttle. This straightens her out for another kick astern; then out of gear, wheel amidships, engine in gear ahead, and we are clear to go off in any direction. If we're lucky, our mate will by now have all fenders aboard and be busily engaged in coiling down the docking lines. If today is not our day, she'll be standing by to take the wheel, and we do it ourselves!

All docking procedures are not the same as the ones outlined above. For instance, if we wish to dock starboard side to with our right-handed propeller, the fact that the ship's stern will cut to port when going astern (tending to throw it away from the dock) must be considered. A large single-screw ship deals with this situation by dropping her port anchor a couple of ship's lengths from the berth. With her engine stopped, a few shackles or

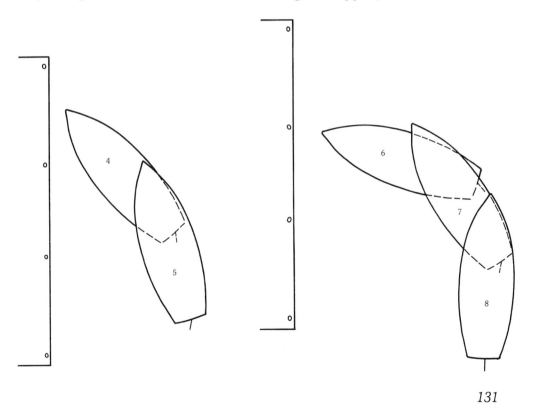

"shots" out (each is 15 fathoms), dragging her anchor along the sea bed, the ship approaches her allocated docking site, her head tending to be pulled to port and her stern subsequently canted to starboard, or toward the dock.

When a short distance—sometimes only 20 or 30 feet—from her desired position, a smart kick astern will almost stop her, and at the same time bring her stern to port, away from the dock. If good judgment has been exercised in the dropping of the anchor, the angle and speed of approach, and the timing and power of the kick astern, she will now be parallel to, and 10 or 15 feet out from the dock.

Heaving lines go ashore; head lines, stern lines, springs, breasts are taken to wharf bollards; and the ship's capstans pull her gently alongside.

If all has gone well, with the very minimum of commands via ship's telegraph (from bridge to engine room), the captain might pick up some kudos when, in the bowels of his ship, one engineer mutters to another, "Couldn't-a done better myself!" That is high praise indeed. On the other hand, if much backing and filling has been necessary to work the vessel into her berth, a great number of engine movements will probably have been required. In this case, there will be no doubt in anybody's mind (among the "down-below" gang, that is) that the Old Man has once again made a mess of it.

(I've never been in a ship yet where the engine-room department wasn't certain that if *they* were in command, she'd dock without fuss or bother—just like parking a car! It works the other way, too, on a freighter. Among the "topside gang," everyone from the deckboy up knows that if only he could get into the engine room, he'd get another four or five knots out of the old girl—easy!)

The rigmarole of dropping an anchor to "cant" her stern in to starboard and "snig" her bow out to port is seldom necessary aboard a charter boat when berthing starboard side to with a right-handed propeller. A standard treatment of this situation is to approach the intended position as close to parallel as possible to the side of the dock. Approximately a ship's length away from the berth, a short kick ahead with hard left rudder will cant the ship's stern toward the dock. A touch astern will almost stop her; the after spring—from the starboard shoulder this time—is dropped over a bollard or piling, and the battle is won.

If the stay alongside is to be brief, such as picking up or dropping off someone, a vessel will often run no other line ashore but her after spring. Her engine, ticking over in gear ahead and exerting a constant strain on this line, keeps her alongside.

The technique I have described in running an after spring from either the port or starboard shoulder may not find favor in the ranks of those who do not have a cleat or bitt there to make fast to. To which I say, put one there.

132

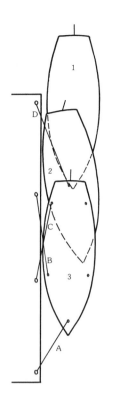

LEFT: Docking starboard side to with right-handed propeller. (Same tactics apply to vessel with left-handed propeller berthing port side to.) (1) Approach parallel to the side of the dock, dead slow. (2) Short kick ahead with hard left rudder cants stern toward dock. (3) Smart burst astern pulls stern away from dock and almost stops her. After spring is taken from starboard shoulder, made fast aboard and, with engine in gear slow ahead, tie-up proceeds in usual manner. A = Bow line. B = After spring. C = Forespring. D = Stern line. BELOW: Docking with wind and/or tide astern. (1) Parallel approach—after spring ashore from port quarter. (2) Engine out of gear—after spring being slacked from port quarter until vessel reaches desired position. (3) Ship positioned by after spring slacked from the port quarter. A = Bow line. B = After spring. C = Forespring. D = Stern line. E = Stern line frequently comes from this point.

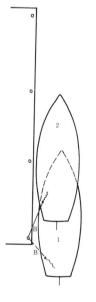

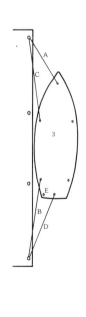

WIND AND/OR TIDE

WIND AND/OR TIDE

Alternatively, install a lead in your bulwarks or rail at this point and pass the spring through it. Whichever way you do it, it will pay. I am certain that without the convenience of being able to take our after spring lines from this point aboard *White Squall II,* Minine and I could never dock her two-handed under some conditions.

In my book, there is only one other place on either side of the ship from which an after spring can run, and that is the quarter. If you're coming up to dock with a strong tide under you or a brisk wind astern (or both), and you're obligated to berth stern to the elements, run your after spring from the quarter of whichever side you're making fast to the dock, and she'll lie alongside without cracking an egg.

Don't run your after spring from the bow when docking. Besides placing an unfair strain on the rigging (as the spring, leading aft to the dock, comes hard against it), it can chafe on deckhouses and be more nuisance than it's worth. I can speak of this from a recent experience.

A few months ago, we were returning to our own ship after a short cruise with friends (another couple) on their 58-foot, 35-ton ketch. Before proceeding farther up-harbor to their mooring, it was decided that we would top up water tanks at a convenient finger pier. The only points aboard the ship that could be used for making lines fast were the windlass forward and a cleat each side aft. This left us no option, as we nudged up to the dock, but to run an after spring from the bow—in this case, the windlass. We were approaching the pier upstream and managed to get a line onto the first of the pilings we came to. This we used as an after spring off the windlass. We never did get alongside. With a three-knot ebb sweeping out through the pilings at the end of the pier, the strain on the fore rigging became intolerable as, with the hefty diesel thumping away below, the spring line came hard against the sidestays as we drew closer to parallel to the dock. With our pivoting point so far forward, and the strong tide on our starboard bow, the closer we came to the pier, the less in control we seemed to be.

We could have made a big deal out of it, such as using a lengthy head, or breast line, taken from the windlass along the pier toward the shore. But our only reason for being there was to top up tanks, so we dropped back and hung off a short bow line to accomplish the job. However, it was an interesting exercise, and one that left us all permanently thumbs down on the efficacy of an after spring led from the bow in anything but textbook conditions.

As can be seen, other factors besides the rotation of a propeller can influence the docking of a ship. The charter-boat skipper, in his desire to act like a pro, is well advised to study the various docks and the conditions generally prevailing around them in the area he works. He will probably be berthing his vessel at all of them in time, and prior knowledge of the height of

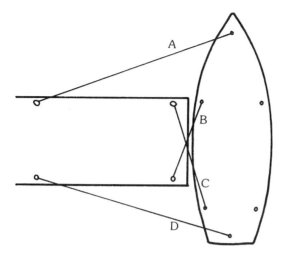

Typical tie-up across the end of a narrow dock. (It is usually possible to nudge up slowly and get an after spring ashore off the shoulder. The vessel goes ahead on this until all the other lines are run ashore and made fast aboard.) A = Bow line— in this case sometimes known as "breast" or "head line." B = After spring. C = Forespring. D = Stern line—in this case sometimes known as "stern breast line."

a dock, the position of pilings or bollards to drop a line over, the depth at low water, direction of ebb and flood and prevailing wind can all contribute to the decision of just how he will lay his ship alongside.

Watch the other guy. Study his tactics. Should that schooner berthed on the other side of the estuary have turned and docked head to wind, instead of tying alongside with wind astern? What would you have done? And the guy who, with the breeze blowing onto the face of the dock, dropped his anchor a good 150 feet upwind, and after digging it in, kept giving her scope until his stern was a few feet away from the pilings where he passed up a line. Good move? You're damn right it was! He bunkered, filled his water tanks, then loaded stores and people off the dock, straight over his transom. All he had to do to get going again was to let his aft line go and steam slowly toward his anchor, hoisting sails as he went. He hove his pick aboard and was away and laughing, boiling out of the bay on a close reach before any of us could say "Jack Robinson." If he'd berthed alongside, the wind would have pinned him there like a fly and he'd have had one hell of a time getting clear.

File all this away in your mind. Try never to make the same mistake or miscalculation twice. My ears are burning as I write this, for we all make mistakes. The fellow who maintains he hasn't has either never handled a vessel or is lying in his beer. The big thing is to try to learn by them—both your own mistakes and those of the other guy.

It is seldom that two vessels handle the same. Even sister-ships can have their own idiosyncrasies. Years ago I took the controls of the sister to my little 33-foot yawl, to move her from the windward side of the dock to a more sheltered berth at a leeward marina, and I was astounded at the difference. The two ships were the same in design, they both had right-handed propellers, but whereas my boat, after gathering sternway to port, eventually could be made to respond to the rudder and actually steered astern in any direction, my friend's vessel would not. I pondered the reason for a long time, until I examined her one day on the ways and found that she had a bigger propeller aperture. Apparently that made the difference.

I categorically stated earlier in this section that a right-handed propeller will cause a ship's stern to cut sharply to port when going astern, and to starboard when in gear ahead (with a left-handed propeller, of course, doing the exact opposite), I have made no mention of why it is so.

The forces that influence a vessel's performance under power are generally discussed under three headings: wake current, transverse thrust, and screw race or current.

Of these, the easiest to understand is wake current, which is caused by the vessel's passage through the water. This current is strongest at the surface and gradually diminishes to zero strength at the keel. Transverse thrust is present when a propeller is turning. Here, the angle (pitch) of the propeller blades sets up a current, which may be resolved into both a transverse component and a fore and aft component. Of these two, the transverse force is small in comparison to the fore and aft force, which drives the ship ahead or astern.

Screw race or current is both suction and discharge. It is caused by the turning of the propeller, and, through its action on the surrounding water, is responsible for a ship's forward or aft motion. The discharge race—that is, the body of water pushed by the propeller (whether going ahead or astern)—is stronger than the suction.

With transverse thrust, the athwartship component of the obliquity or pitch of the propeller blades does not account for the slewing of the stern. In theory, the thrust to one side should be equal to the thrust to the other, because the upper and lower blades pass across equally each way in the course of a revolution. However, the propeller churns and breaks up water near the surface to a greater extent than deeper down, with the result that the lower blades cut through more solid water than the upper ones and thus must overcome greater resistance. The difference between these transverse pressures slews the stern to starboard when going ahead, but more sharply to port when going astern—as the forward flow of water from the propeller washes up against the hull and retards the sternway of the ship. This reduces the fore and aft component relatively to the transverse component.

Unequal blade thrust is another factor responsible for the cutting of a ship's stern (one with right-handed propeller) to starboard when going ahead with rudder amidships, and to port when going astern. It is caused by the angle between the propeller shaft and the horizontal. The greater this inclination, the more water is in contact with a descending propeller blade as a ship moves through the water—which has the effect of increasing its pitch. In a vessel with a right-handed propeller, this has the effect of exerting thrust on her starboard side, and with rudder amidships, cants the stern to starboard and the bow to port when going ahead. The same vessel, when going astern, has her stern canted to port, by both the action of transverse thrust and the amount of extra force induced on the starboard side aft by the discharge current from the propeller washing against it.

It is seldom that an auxiliary sailboat has twin engines, but since many types of vessels are used in the charter game, a brief mention of the maneuverability of ships so equipped is in order. Twin-screw vessels are usually a joy to handle; with one engine in gear ahead and the other going astern, the average twin-screw ship can turn in her own length. It is usual for the propellers of such craft to revolve in opposite directions. Both, when viewed from aft, turn outboard; that is, the starboard propeller is right-handed and the port propeller left-handed.

Twin rudders, each one situated behind a propeller, are more efficient than one central rudder, as the wash (screw race) acts on each rudder independently, whether in ahead (discharge current) or astern (suction current). Either ahead or astern, the screw assists the action of the rudder immediately aft of it, resulting in more overall efficiency in both the steering and maneuvering of the vessel than with a single rudder centrally located. When both engines are going ahead at the same revolutions, with rudder, or rudders, amidships, the transverse effect of one propeller is nullified by that of the other, which is turning in the opposite direction. All things being equal, the ship then steers a straight course.

When maneuvering a twin-screw vessel, using one engine ahead and another astern, it will be seen that both propellers in this case turn the same way. Transverse thrust with some vessels under these conditions is very obvious. Over a period of several years, when I was handling a twin-screw tug equipped with four-bladed propellers, each exceeding 11 feet in diameter, I never ceased to marvel at the effect of this thrust. The tug's stern could be made to walk to one side or the other, as if a couple of giant hands down below were responsible.

Suffice it to say that if a man is reasonably efficient in the running of a single-screw ship, he'll win at a walk if he ever gets two throttles and two propellers to play around with.

In cases where a twin-screw vessel is being docked under only one engine, a different set of circumstances arises, and these can vary greatly from boat to boat. Deep draft, shallow draft, windage of hull, deckhouses and/or spars, distance from keel to propeller shaft, a central rudder or twin rudders—all come into it, and here it is up to the skipper to know his vessel. How will she respond when berthing if an engine decides to quit or you're only running on one to conserve fuel? Which side should you dock?

Any time I have done this, and with not a small vessel (900 tons), I have berthed the same side to as the working engine and used the tying-up procedure that applies to a single-screw ship.

THE 'DO'S'

Get to know your ship. They all have their different little habits under sail or power. If you're new aboard, find out how much room she takes in stays. . . . Will she handle under mainsail alone in the final stages of anchoring under sail? Is she easy and safe to gybe? Hard-mouthed under some sail combinations and easy under others? Discover everything you can about your boat before you ever take a party on a cruise. They'll expect you to *know*.

The words "under weigh" define a vessel in the act of weighing (hauling aboard) her anchors. The term "underway" applies to a vessel "not at anchor or made fast to the shore or aground," which means that once you've got the hook aboard, let go the dock lines, or cast off the mooring pennant, you fall into this category. Be ready for it!

Before committing ourselves to being "underway," there are a number of things we should do: Helm should be put hard a-starboard to hard a-port, then back amidships. Fuel and water tanks sounded. Oil sump of engine (or engines) dipped. Boarding ladder and fenders aboard. Running lights and horn checked. All loose gear stowed on deck and below. If leaving under power, check water cooling and oil pressure and give her a little touch ahead and astern to make sure all is O.K. with the reverse gear. One of the first times I was trusted with maneuvering a vessel of any size, I didn't make this last test, and I've never forgotten the embarrassment.

It was just after World War II, and I was a deckhand in a fishing trawler, or dragger. We were tied outside three or four other similar craft in the commercial fishing basin in Auckland, and since we were sailing that day, it was necessary to let go from where we were and nudge inside the other boats in order to load seven or eight tons of ice and various stores. Charlie, the skipper, deep in conversation with several other fishing captains on the wharf, had said to me over his shoulder, "Bring 'er in and stick 'er alongside." In feverish haste, in case he changed his mind, I scrambled down the old iron ladder, over boat after boat, until I arrived at ours.

She had a big, air-start, slow-revving diesel in her. Down in the engine room I first dipped the oil. Then I importantly pulled the little lever that gave her a shot of air and had the satisfaction of hearing the dependable, green-painted piece of machinery start up and tick over rhythmically.

Up on deck, and a glance over the side—circulating water O.K. Into the wheelhouse—oil pressure O.K. My two compatriots aboard, at a nod, let go the lines and heaved them aboard off the trawler alongside which we were berthed. I had handled her many times before under Charlie's supervision while away on trips, but today was different. Today I was in command!

Conditions were perfect. A moderate southwesterly wind blew us slowly sideways until we were separated by a few feet from the trawler we'd been tied to. The gang of fishing skippers on the wharf had all stopped talking and they were critically watching my moves. How could I miss? All the power in the world was thumping dependably away beneath my feet. The two men on deck, though still in their teens (I was their senior by about a year), were competent and could be relied upon to handle lines.

My right hand grasped the big gear lever projecting up into the wheelhouse from the engine room below; I gave it a mighty heave to put her into gear astern.

Nothing happened—nothing mechanical, that is. Physically, plenty happened. The gear lever, usually so stiff through its linkage to the reverse gear below, almost came away in my hand. Off balance, I spun around, tripped, and landed face first against the back of the wheelhouse. Eyes streaming, heart pounding (it had picked up a few revs), I headed for the engine room. What the hell! My bloody nose! The impact of my bugle being brought up short against the wheelhouse hadn't done me any good at all. My eyes were filled with water.

Down in the engine room, I blinked frantically to clear my vision, and the cause of why the ship failed to respond was obvious. Some shoreside engineers, working in the engine room the day before, had failed to connect up the long metal shaft from the gearbox lever to the one leading up through the wheelhouse floor. Meanwhile, we were drifting around inside the fishing basin, out of control, and under the critical gaze of as seasoned a bunch of sailors as it is possible to find.

And it was my fault—I was the one who had given the signal to let her go. What a curve—I've never forgotten it! I must have looked straight at that reverse gear lever when I started the engine, and I hadn't even noticed it was disconnected.

I will gloss over the rest of it—bolting all the various bits and pieces together with the help of the boys, up in the wheelhouse once more, gingerly putting her in gear ahead, shouldering inside the other boats to tie up and face the grins of every fisherman within sight.

Plan maneuvers ahead. If your intention is to dock, have it all figured out which side to you intend to lie alongside, so that fenders can be hung off in preparation and lines can be flaked out and ready. If it is not possible before approaching the dock to know if there is enough space to berth, or which side to it is going to be, make a dummy run. Eyeball the situation. Note the height of the dock, the space available to fit into, positions of piles or bollards to drop a line over, direction and strength of current (if any), direction and strength of wind—and whether or not there is anyone on the dock to take your lines. Then, having made your decision, stand off, prepare fenders and lines, and make your approach. Take no notice of onlookers waving you to come on in before you are ready. If you scratch up your boat (or someone else's) through acting hastily, you are the one who will be held responsible— not them.

Whenever possible, stem the wind or current when berthing. It is a whole lot easier than laying her alongside with the elements astern. If, however, you are coming in to dock with a strong current, and circumstances do not permit turning and stemming it, stop your vessel parallel to the intended dock site and about five or six feet out from it. The current, which will be trying to take the ship upriver, can now be used to back against. Work her stern against it, into the dock, run a quarter spring ashore, and let the stream lay her alongside.

(Before attempting this maneuver, know your vessel's capabilities under power. Some auxiliary sailboats, with low-powered engines and tiny propellers, don't back down too well, and, as a result, may have a hard time dealing with these conditions, especially if a wind is accompanying the current and is making itself felt in the rigging and, consequently, the steering of the ship.)

Pass or swing docklines ashore; don't throw them unless it is absolutely necessary. If you have to throw a line, bring the ship as close in to the dock as possible before giving the signal to heave it. A line thrown prematurely often falls into the water before reaching the dock. This, in addition to taking the shine off what could possibly be an efficient docking operation, can end up being embarrassing if the line gets under the vessel and around the propeller—disastrous stuff in front of a charter party!

If there is nobody on the dock to take a line, kick the stern in and land your mate. He, or she, can take a spring with him as he steps ashore. If wind and current are from ahead, ease up slowly and land someone off the port or starboard shoulder. A strong wind blowing off the dock can sometimes make it difficult to put a crew member ashore with a line. On a powerboat with a flying bridge, especially if the control station is located forward of amidships, the visibility afforded the helmsman usually permits him to land a person from over the bow with ease. On a lot of sailing auxiliaries and motorsailers, however, the helmsman is well aft in a cockpit, or inside a wheelhouse, and it sometimes can be difficult to judge the proximity of the ship to the dock when trying to land a crew member from the foredeck or off the end of the bowsprit. In such a case, I prefer to stop the boat five or six feet away from, and parallel to, the dock and then kick the stern in, so that the crew can step ashore with an after spring taken from the shoulder. The bow blows off with the wind, but this is of little consequence. As soon as the spring is fast aboard, she'll walk in sideways toward the wharf, with the engine in gear ahead.

Ships maneuver by the stern, and if you're standing aft at the controls, it is a lot easier to judge the distance of the stern from the dock rather than the bow, which may be 60 or 70 feet ahead.

In Pago Pago, Samoa, one black, squally night, we used the method just described when we had no option but to get alongside and tie up. The Pilot Book describes Pago Pago harbor as "the crater of an ancient volcano," and that's probably the truth of it. It is exceptionally deep, so the day we arrived, instead of anchoring, which we almost always do in every strange port, we allowed ourselves to be talked into picking up the only vacant mooring among a cluster of small craft owned mostly by local people.

Our first two or three days there were tranquil enough, but late one night (we were scheduled to leave the next day), it started to blow—and blow hard. By midnight, our anemometer was recording gusts of up to 45 knots, we were on a lee shore, and the "Rainmaker" mountain was supplying the wind with what seemed to be an unlimited amount of water. Seldom had we seen such rain.

Lying on a mooring that might or might not be any good, with our stern but a few feet away from a sloping rock embankment, was no place to be, so we started the engine, prepared lines and fenders, and steamed slowly upwind toward the big commercial wharf. We came to a stop with our starboard side a few feet away from the pilings. With the wheel hard a-port, and held there in a becket, I gave her a short, hard kick ahead; then astern; then repeated the procedure. Minine then stepped off an ice box on the starboard quarter to place the eye of an after spring, leading from our starboard shoulder, around a handy wharf bollard.

By now, the schooner was at an angle of about 45 degrees away from the piles. With the moderate gale blowing across the dock into the rigging, and tending to push her farther to leeward all the time, she responded to a slight port helm and half throttle in gear ahead by obediently coming slowly sideways toward the dock, with the 1¼-inch-diameter nylon spring bar taut. Once alongside, the engine was left in gear ahead at the same revs. I walked up forward, where Minine, a tiny figure crouched on the dock in the wind and driving rain, took the bow line, then the forespring, then the stern line.

We stopped the engine, dried off, and both turned in—me with a generous slug of rum coursing around inside (to help keep the damp out). We had just done an unremarkable job under conditions that none of us enjoys; neither we nor the ship had suffered a scratch, which of course is as it should be.

My only reason for recalling the incident is to drive home the simplicity of

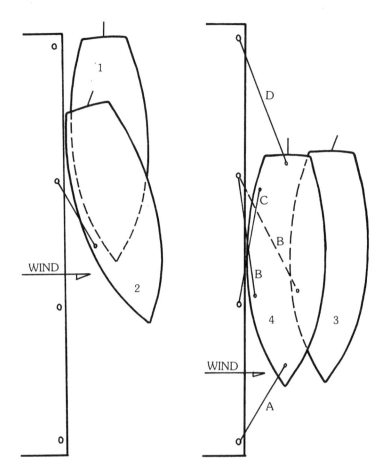

Docking with wind off under conditions where it is inconvenient or dangerous to land a crew member off the shoulder or bow. (1) Parallel approach. (2) Ship stopped, kick ahead with hard left rudder, kick astern and crew steps ashore with after spring from the shoulder. (3) Engine half ahead, slight left rudder. Revs and rudder angle often need adjusting (this can vary from ship to ship) so that the vessel will come slowly to, and parallel with, the dock. (4) Tie up alongside in usual manner. A = Bow line. B = After spring. C = Forespring. D = Stern line.

kicking in a ship's stern to put someone ashore. It was easy, dead easy—it almost always is—and that night, standing just a few feet from the point where my wife was able to step ashore, I had no qualms for her safety. To have put her safely over the bow, a bow 60 feet ahead of where I was standing at the wheel, and which I couldn't even see under the conditions prevailing, would have been impossible—for me, at any rate.

In situations where a wind is blowing *against* a dock, the first decision to arrive at is whether it is wise to lie alongside at all. A light wind in a sheltered boat harbor will not usually influence a skipper's judgment, but a fresh breeze with a sea to match, coming hard on the face of an unprotected wharf, is a different piece of cake altogether.

Have a good, long look at things in such a situation. Is it *really* necessary to lie alongside? Once there, could you get away again? Is there a chance you'll damage your vessel? If so, the hell with it. Do yourself (and your ship) a

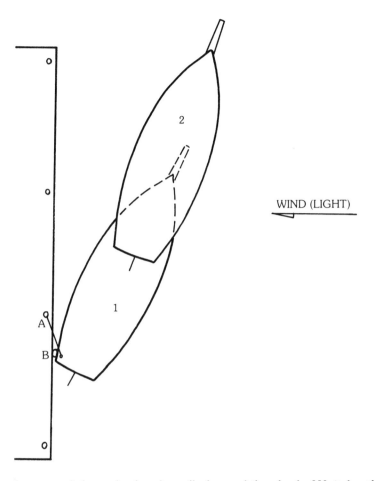

WIND (LIGHT)

Springing the bow out with a forespring led well aft when a light wind is holding the vessel against the dock. (A handy tactic for a boat with a bowsprit or pulpit that could be damaged by a maneuver that would require the bow to rest against the dock.) (1) Engine astern—rudder amidships. (2) Powering clear—rudder amidships. Caution: Right rudder will throw the ship's stern at the dock! A = Forespring. (This can be doubled, so that one end can be quickly released from aboard and hove around the dock bollard if there is no one ashore to let it go.) B = Fender.

favor and drop the hook well clear of the dock. Wait for the wind to go down or, if you're bound and determined to use the dock, slack away on your warp or cable once you're dug in, until your stern is close enough to get a line up. Or lie out at anchor and use your dinghy to load stores and transfer people. That, after all, is one reason why charter boats have efficient dinghies.

If you must dock with a light wind blowing on, stop your ship parallel to, and a few feet away from, the berth. The wind will put you alongside, and if the ship's fenders are sensibly arranged, or if she is equipped with an efficient guard, no damage should result.

Watch your bowsprit (if you have one) when springing her stern out to leave (see page 130). It could be damaged if the stern is taken out too far. A vessel with a bowsprit is sometimes difficult to get clear when a wind is holding her against a dock. As an alternative to springing the stern out with an after spring led from the bow, the bow may be worked out by going astern on a forespring made fast aboard well aft. Then, with rudder amidships, the ship powers ahead and clear.

Know your boat well before attempting this operation. Make sure there is a good, clear run ahead with nothing in the way; as soon as the engine is taken from astern, through neutral to ahead (and the spring let go and taken aboard), the wind will be trying to blow the bow back onto the dock.

To leave a dock when tied up on the lee side, simply start the engine, let go all lines and bring them aboard, and the wind will take the ship sideways out of the berth. In a situation where the wind, or other conditions, will not assist in leaving, work the stern or bow out with a spring, as previously described.

Pay attention to the range (rise and fall) of tide when tying up a ship. Lines secured tight and short at the top of high water can give the vessel a severe list and possibly place an unfair strain on cleats or bitts aboard as the tide falls. Whenever possible, in an area where the range of tide is extreme, tie up to a floating dock or pontoon. If such a facility is unavailable, use long spring, bow, and stern lines—or better still, anchor out.

Now and again, when tying up to a dock, pier, wharf, jetty (you name it), a ship will be higher than the bollards or posts she must drop a line over. Well-designed bollards with lugs cast into them can take a ship's line from almost any angle, but some cannot—in some instances, they are pieces of pipe or just wooden posts. If in any doubt about the ability of a line to stay on a dock bollard, take an extra turn of the bight of the eye around the bollard when placing the eye over it.

Never be too proud to bring out a chart and inspect it in front of charter guests. Some charter skippers recoil at the idea of this—they would claim that we are expected to *know*. The thing to remember here is that we are seamen first and charter captains second. If our chartering area is a small "milk-run," it is possible in time to know every rock and shoal to a hair. However, if the region we operate in is large, or the locale for a particular charter cruise is one that we haven't been in for a year or two, we should treat it as a brand-new area of operation by working from the charts, pilot books, and any dependable local "guide" publications available.

THE 'DON'TS'

After letting your mooring go, don't run over it and wind it around your propeller. The average charter party will be particularly hard to impress after such a start. Unless, of course, you can cap it off with something really spectacular, such as taking her out of the bay end-over-end for an encore!

When leaving a mooring, unplanned incidents are not confined to those who prefer to use their engine until clear enough of other boats, obstructions, or docks to "hoist the rag." I remember a 12-meter in St. Thomas sailing over her own dinghy and sinking it, outboard and all, when getting underway from a mooring. The dinghy was made fast to the buoy, and at the critical moment, just as a man forward was letting go, a puff of wind filled the mainsail. The mainsheet, which should have been left slack and free until the sloop drifted clear enough of the dinghy to sail off, was hove tight and belayed. The wind in the sail, instead of being harmlessly spilled, as would have been the case with a slack mainsheet, was immediately converted into power; this was transmitted to the hull in the flick of an eye, and she leaped forward over the top of the dinghy. Marvelous stuff to watch, this! Unless you're the guy who feels he must salvage the dinghy—in this case, me. Or, in turning, the big sloop misses your own ship by the thickness of a good coat of paint, causing you to fly below and check the level of the nearest rum bottle.

Don't run up to a dock without having lines and fenders ready. The sight of a crew member standing on deck, trying frantically to untangle a line as the boat nears a dock, will do nothing to contribute to the charterer's opinion of the standard of seamanship aboard your vessel.

Don't look around for someone to blame when you've just made a bad job of docking your ship. Sit down, take it easy, and, when you've cooled off, figure out what went wrong. In most cases you'll find that the only person you can sheet the blame home to is you, yourself.

Don't be ostentatious and berth your ship at speed. For continuity, this is something none of us can afford. The sight of a boat (any boat) charging up to a dock and coming to a stop with a great roaring of machinery and churning of water gives me goosebumps where no goosebumps have any right to be. For the day will come when the reversing equipment will fail. And let's not kid ourselves that this will happen late at night at a deserted dock, with nobody to see the show. No, the day the reverse gear fails, and our bow mounts the stern of the floating gin palace tied up ahead and we enter his cocktail party at a good 10 knots, will be a sunny afternoon, with the bay full of boats and the landing crawling with dockhoppers.

Don't shout! This, of course, does not apply to the incident just described—where a certain amount of noise is inescapable. I am referring to a normal docking, where we come in placidly, run a spring ashore, and lay her alongside. Yells and barked commands impress nobody—especially the mate who, in the middle of one of the skipper's imperious orders, might turn on her lord and master and loose off a broadside of her own. While this may be fascinating stuff to the onlookers, and give them a priceless glimpse of the trials and tribulations of life afloat—a glimpse that would seem to indicate that earth people (those who live in houses) are not the only ones subject to marital tiffs—it can hardly be calculated to endear the charter crew to their paying guests.

Don't drop your line over the other guy's on a pile or bollard; make it fast aboard, and leave it at that. If he wants to get underway in your absence, and finds that he can't—because your line is on top of his—he could get all bitter and twisted. And he might be bigger than you.

As mentioned earlier, to avoid striking a discordant note with the guy who got his loop over first, pass the eye of your line up through his, then drop it over the pile, bollard, or whatever point on the dock you are both using. If you're leaving before he is, release your line the same way, pull the eye up over the pile, and if it is held in a "nip" at one side by his, pull it free with a winch aboard your ship or jerk it loose with the weight of your vessel as you leave.

Don't anchor on top of the other fellow in a bay. If you swing too close or touch, you are the one who will have to move. Pick the spot where you intend to be, and then power or sail upwind or upstream a distance equal to the amount of anchor rode you consider will be necessary to hold in the depth of water and conditions prevailing. Drop the hook, give her scope, and if your eye is a good one (or if it isn't and you're lucky), you'll finish up just where you wanted to be.

Sometimes in a calm, crowded anchorage, yachts raft together. This, provided adequate fenders are used, can be a lot of fun. Don't expect the other guys to supply all the fenders. Carry a minimum of four good ones aboard your own ship.

And, while I am on the subject of fenders, make certain that none are left hanging over the side when underway. To have the gripping tale you're spinning the charter guests interrupted by another boat ranging alongside and a crew member with a grin yelling, "You're dragging a coupl'a fenders!" can put a dent in the most resilient of egos.

Don't create a wake in any area where it may inconvenience other people. To fully realize what a wake can do, it is almost necessary to be on the receiving end, such as 60 feet above the deck in a bosun's chair inspecting a masthead fitting, and have some clown roar through the anchorage at 20 miles an hour in a "fizzboat." The roll he sets up is bad enough at deck level; it can upset cups of coffee, bottles of beer, and do all sorts of unpleasant things. Aloft, however, swaying with the masthead three or four feet to one side and then the other, can make even the most tolerant of us think unkind thoughts about the gentleman's pedigree.

Slow down to "no-wake" when approaching an anchorage or marina. Sometimes a prominent notice will specify that five miles an hour, for example, is the speed limit. This should be strictly adhered to, and your speed should be regulated below this to ensure that you leave no wake. Watch out for the guy hanging from his masthead, or unloading stores from his dinghy, or over the side painting his hull. Sneak past him without creating a wash and you've every right to expect him to do the same for you.

146

Don't tie up to a dock, bring a fuel hose aboard, and merrily fill your water tanks with diesel. No matter how winning your personality, there's not a hope in the world of convincing your charter guests that a dash of fuel oil will improve the taste of their coffee. Mark the rims of all deck filler openings— water, gasoline, diesel, etc.— so that mistakes cannot be made. Don't mark the screw plugs. They could get mixed up, and you'd be back to square one. And don't take for granted that the hose, confidently handed aboard from the dock, will supply exactly the fuel you require. Some years ago, I gave a friend a hand to take the *Caravan,* a 50-foot motorsailer (sister to Irving Johnson's *Yankee*), across to Puerto Rico from the Virgin Islands. We made a night passage of it, and the next morning in San Juan decided to top up all tanks before going uptown to shop, the main purpose of our visit.

The dock attendant handed the diesel hose to my buddy ("Commodore" by nickname), who put it through the deck filler, gave the trigger a moment's pressure, stopped, and said, "Hey, this is gasoline—smell it!" It smelled like gas to me, so we brought up a cup from the pristine galley, half filled it, and sure enough, gasoline it was—coming from the diesel pump on the dock. The row this discovery sparked off was one of the really spectacular kind— violent oaths, clenched teeth, waving arms, everyone from the bellhop to the manager blaming each other, and the guy alongside in the big motor-cruiser (into whose diesel tanks the dock attendant had just pumped 1,500 gallons of gasoline) vowing and declaring he was, "gonna sue 'em!"

MISCELLANEOUS

The guy who knows it all has yet to be born. We never stop learning about the ships we sail in and about the sea itself. Get to know your boat and her habits to the best of your ability under sail or power, or both. But don't leave it at that. Keep trying to improve.

Know from the feel of the wind whether you should put in a reef before leaving the bay with a party aboard. It is usually easier to reef down before getting underway than when rolling around out there. If the horizon is visible from your anchorage, take a good look at it with the naked eye from the deck of your ship. Is it lumpy? If so, and especially if you plan a beat to windward with a party aboard, you could do a lot worse than tying or rolling in a reef before poking your nose out there.

Remember, the horizon is close, mighty close when viewed from the deck of the average sailboat. For those interested, the formula for computing the distance of the sea horizon in nautical miles is: Square root of the height of eye above sea level in feet, times 1.15. So from the deck of our vessel, with our eye nine feet above the ocean, we arrive at a square root of 3; when

147

multiplied by 1.15, it gives us 3.45. Our horizon then (it's a small world we live in) is in round figures, three and a half miles away. Closer than you thought, huh? Maybe, but far enough away for any lumps you can see on it (and I don't mean islands) to indicate that there's probably a bit of a sea running out there. So figure out how much rag the old girl should carry to be comfortable. Remember, you're not ocean racing—not this trip, anyhow. You are catering to a charter party, and you want them to come again.

The moment of truth for a charter skipper comes when he must handle his vessel under the eye of his paying guests. If he is new aboard—and let's assume that this is the case—he would do well to get in as much practice as possible beforehand.

Try her on every maneuver you can think of under sail or power where there is plenty of room. An ounce of practical experience here is worth a pound of theory or speculation. A vessel may be totally different to handle from what a skipper anticipated, no matter how long he's been at the game. If he's wise, he'll try to learn her little tricks before his charterers ever come down the gangplank.

Aboard a vessel that docks permanently at a marina and returns to her berth after every charter cruise, the necessity of carrying lines for the sole purpose of mooring does not generally apply. The lines in this case are left behind on the dock and pilings when the ship departs, and are handily brought aboard on her return.

A charter vessel that does not fall into this category—one that goes from port to port, bunkering, watering, and stocking up wherever she can—should carry permanent docking lines aboard. It is nice to know, when you're lining up your approach to tie alongside a dock that you've never seen before in your life, that your equipment to do the job is efficient and will not let you down.

Put a big spliced eye in one end of springs and bow and stern lines. A bowline knot tied in a line, and the loop then dropped over a bollard or pile, is acceptable practice aboard a vessel that docks only occasionally, but for permanence, a spliced eye is far more preferable. Besides its seamanlike appearance, as compared with a bowline, an eyesplice detracts little more than 10 percent from the breaking strain of rope, while the bowline knot almost halves it.

A neat palm-and-needle "sailmaker's" whipping looks, and is, a dependable way to terminate a line and hold it from raveling. A well-executed whipping of this type takes only a few minutes to do, and in five years it is still there.

Synthetic lines, which nearly all of us use these days, can have their ends melted and the fibers sealed together, thus preventing untwining or fraying into lubberly "Irish pennants." The sight of modern sailors dipping rope ends in a can of "instant whip" or fuzzing them up with a propane torch or electric soldering gun probably would make old shellbacks spin like pinwheels in their graves. But with small-diameter lines and lashings (while I am not strong on "instant whip"), the sealing of a rope end with heat has a lot to recommend it, tough as it may be on the sensibilities of old salts.

Lines above ⅜ inch in diameter are sometimes harder to finish in this manner without the glob of melted fibers appearing unsightly. However, with larger-diameter line, if a palm-and-needle whipping (using waxed Dacron thread or its equivalent) is stitched in near the end of a synthetic line—and the end itself is treated with a hot iron—the result can be both shippy and practical.

Before we finish with docking lines, guard them against chafe. A line, as it leads from a wharf bollard—especially if tied up in a berth normally used by freighters—can sometimes be damaged if it lies on a stringer between fender piles. The edge of the dock and the side of a rough piling are just two of the many things a line can chafe against. Over the years, we have tried various ways of keeping chafe from reaching a bow, stern, or spring line, and I am not referring solely to large charter yachts. In my little *White Squall*, we day-chartered out of Oranjestad, Aruba, and every time we tied up at the waterfront among the fruit boats from Venezuela to top up with water and take on stores, the concrete edge of the quay gave our lines a hard time.

The split-rubber chafe guards sold by marine stores are ideal around marinas, but in some of the ports we've been in, they would have a short life. The answer to all this grief (I'm repeating myself and I don't care) is to anchor out. It is then possible, with a dependable dinghy setup, to be spared the surveillance necessary to care for dock lines.

If, however, there is no other way but to lie alongside, attention must be given to the possibility of mooring lines becoming chafed. We have used the time-honored method of wrapping a burlap or jute gunny sack around the part of a line likely to be damaged, and using rope-yarn lashings to hold it there. We have also used heavy-wall plastic hose, and in my estimation, this is the best of all.

We purchased some 20 feet of this in Nuku Hiva, Marquesas Islands—of all places. It is about 1⅝ inches inside diameter, green in color, French made, and of excellent quality. We cut it into four five-foot lengths, drilled a ¼-inch hole a couple of inches from the end of each piece to take a lashing, and then threaded each of our 110-foot docking lines through a length of it. We slide it up a mooring line and hold it with the lashings in position covering the part of the line subject to chafe. While we have never been dock live-aboards (I figure if you want suburbia, you buy a house), we have lain alongside for a week or so now and again. At such times this tough plastic hose has taken everything thrown at it.

A couple of fender boards are worth carrying on a boat that must lie alongside piles and that is not equipped with a metal-covered guard or "belting."

Briefly, a fender board is a piece of lumber hung fore and aft over the side, with fenders between it and the ship's hull. Positioned correctly, so that a wharf pile bears on the piece of board between the two fenders, it completely protects the vessel from damage. An acceptable-size fender board for an average 50-footer would be two inches thick, eight inches wide, and eight feet long. The pennants used for hanging it over the side should be of a sturdy size (say, ½ inch in diameter) and each about eight feet in length. A pennant should pass through a hole drilled through the width of the fender board about four inches from the end. This way, it also is guaranteed freedom from chafe.

To introduce a bit of class into a fender board, while ensuring that after several seasons of use it will look much the same as the day it was made, fasten two pieces of half-round brass, for the full length of the board, close to the edges on the side that will bear against a pile or dock. Don't jazz it up too much with varnish and stuff, though, or it will look too good to use.

Have some way of holding the wheel or tiller so that the helm can be left in a desired position. This is particularly advantageous when docking shorthanded. After a spring is ashore, and the engine is left ticking over in gear ahead, the helm is adjusted to hold the ship parallel alongside, while the skipper takes his time walking around the deck tending the rest of the lines. A ship with a tiller can accomplish this simply by using tiller lines. Aboard a boat with a wheel, however—and most craft these days fall into this category—the problem of holding it in position is a little more complex.

On my 33-footer, I had a 3-inch-diameter bronze drum keyed on to the wheel shaft—and a brakeband (complete with lining) machined to fit around it. Pressure is applied by simply turning a knob on top of the wheelbox, causing the band to contract on the drum and so hold the wheel in any position. This system is common in vessels of all sizes and types.

Aboard White Squall II, all I have ever used is a becket, which is a line with an eye spliced in the end, its standing part made fast at deck level. We have one positioned each side of the wheel, and it is only necessary to drop the eye over a spoke to hold the wheel after the ship has been given the required amount of helm.

Don't use a clove hitch for anything but the lightest of jobs. Certainly never use this knot where it may be subject to a lot of strain, such as towing or making a dock line fast aboard in a breeze of wind. Every knot has its place, and for innocent little jobs, such as hanging a small coil of line off a stanchion, a clove hitch is fine. (A rolling hitch is better.) If you are caught with a tidal drop and a drum-tight bow line (or any other line) made fast aboard with a clove hitch, the only way to slacken it is with a knife or an axe.

Towboat hitch can never jam, and even a child can tie it or "slack away." (Photo by Ross Norgrove)

Use a towboat hitch (see photo). This can be tied by a child—and slacked by one, too, if necessary.

If you allow a drop of oil to fall into the water of most any marina, you will see the dockmaster react as if he'd suddenly had a wire brush drawn across an exposed nerve. So take great care when fueling that this just does not happen. Things are so organized in the average marina that from the moment the dock attendant hands his "non-drip" hose aboard to the time it is passed back, no liquid has gone anywhere but into the ship's tanks. It also means that our nice, dry, teak deck (which will soak up diesel with delight if given half a chance) is unmarked.

These facilities and standards, alas, do not exist in all ports. If your chartering life is one that takes you to various countries, it is almost inevitable that sooner or later you'll bunker some place where the people supplying the fuel are so cavalier in their attitude that they couldn't care less whether the diesel goes into the bay, over the deck, or down the hatch—just as long as you pay for it.

151

So, aspiring charter captain, be prepared. Before taking on fuel, scrub up a good froth with a liberal quantity of regular household detergent. Keep your deck wet and frothy while the fuel is coming aboard, and even if the hose fittings leak oil, the deck will be unmarked afterwards.

Carry every chart available of the area you charter in, or that you intend to charter in. Don't just take great pride in having them aboard; study them. Have in your mind anchorages, depths of water, outlying dangers, distances; and use the largest-scale chart of an area when navigating.

Be "in tune" with everything aboard your ship. It is possible, by constantly checking and attending to every contingency that arises, to know without consulting any list that it is time to end-for-end the mainsheet, check the stuffing box, go aloft in a chair and inspect every mast fitting, spread some burlap on deck and heave up the anchor cable for inspection, or change fuel filters. When you've reached this stage, it will probably mean that you've got a lot to attend to, but it will also mean that you are on the same wave band as your vessel. And it all comes under the heading of seamanship.

LICENSES

In some parts of the world, local law requires that the operator of a charter boat must be the holder of a license or certificate of competency (to give it another name) covering the type or size of vessel he (or she) is commanding.

This is usually not too difficult, and it should not be regarded by an intended charter captain as just another regulation to sidestep or ignore. It is ridiculous to buy a boat, equip her for chartering, and then break the law by trying to run her without a "ticket," which, if a man opens a few books and sticks his head in, he can earn without any trouble. Another thing—we've got to know all this stuff anyhow.

Rule 2a of the International Regulations For Preventing Collisions at Sea states: "Nothing in these rules shall exonerate any vessel, or the owner, master or crew thereof, from the consequences of any neglect to comply with these rules, or of the neglect of any precaution which may be required by the ordinary practice of seamen, or by the special circumstances of the case."

I was once handed a set of the Rules, or "Articles" as we called them, by an instructor at a school of navigation I was attending. Even though we were required to know them all by heart and by number, in the margin alongside 29 (now 2a in context) he had penciled the letters R.M.L.I.D., which I discovered means, "Read, Mark, Learn and Inwardly Digest."

So digest it. *Nothing* shall exonerate . . . any vessel . . . or owner . . . or master . . . *or crew!* All this means that it doesn't matter what type or size of craft you float around in, or whether you are in command or not, if you make a mistake, you're for the high jump. It is the old story—ignorance of a law is no excuse for breaking it.

The area you choose to charter in may have no license requirements. Fine, work there by all means, as free as the breeze. But whether you intend to sit for a license at some future date or not, bone up on your Collision Regulations. There are 38 of them, plus four annexes—and they apply to all of us.

Chapter Five

The Business Side

Within my experience, the charter boat most likely to show a good profit is the one owned and operated by a man-and-woman team who also live aboard and do their own maintenance.

They get it all ways. The boat is their home as well as their business, so their overhead is kept to a minimum. In almost every case they have pursued their hobby, so they are having fun while they work. In the "off season," the maintenance and mixing with other crews is a welcome change from the routine of chartering, and before they can get too grouchy over the work necessary to keep their ship a going concern, business again whisks them back to sea, where they make money.

A large number of charter parties consist of married couples or families, and they find it easy to relate to a couple running a ship. Women in a party seem to like a woman to be in the crew of the vessel. In most cases, it is the man in the family who has talked his mate into a vacation afloat, and although she may be anticipating her cruise with pleasure, the sight of another woman already aboard, completely at home in her environment, is reassuring.

Other types of chartering and different approaches to the game are mentioned further on in this chapter, but for the moment, we will deal with a typical case where a couple has bought a boat with the intention of living aboard and chartering her.

154

They are equipping their vessel for "The Game." She is a ketch of an average size of, say, 48 feet. They have decided on exactly the area in the world where they intend to work, and they have investigated and complied with any regulations concerning their chosen region.

This may be a well-kept secret. Or it may be the Seychelles, the San Blas Islands, Florida to the Bahamas, Dry Tortugas, Virgin Islands, Windward and Leeward Islands, the Maine coast, the Greek Islands, or Turkey and Yugoslavia. It could be Seattle or Vancouver to Alaska. They may intend to charter down to Baja from San Diego or Newport, from Tahiti to Bora-Bora and back, from Tonga and through the Fiji Islands, from New Caledonia to the Solomon Islands, to Sydney and up the Hawkesbury River, or through the Hauraki Gulf and the northern coastline of New Zealand.

They are preparing the ship and themselves for a sailing-business adventure. Let's make it a successful one!

BROCHURES

A good brochure is a must, and responsibility for supplying it falls in most cases on the boat owner. It is almost impossible without a brochure fairly to describe your ship when answering inquiries. Also, no charter brokers (agents) will handle bookings unless they have brochures of the vessels they represent to send out to potential charterers or for use in answering inquiries. A good brochure can make a big difference in how much business a vessel gets.

Before we take the plunge, however, and start dreaming up a brochure, let us see what happens at the other end of the line—the charterers' end.

Here we find, typically, two or three couples who, after much deliberation and consultation, have decided to share their next vacation. They will charter a boat. In answer to brokers' advertising, or our own, they write away and receive, in return, half a dozen brochures of different boats with a cruising resumé for each—also prices. It is right now, as they sit down to make their choice, that a good brochure is solid gold.

A brochure should, wherever possible, be in color. There should be many photos and little printing. Do not show pictures of your ship plowing along under clouds of canvas or in big seas. There are two reasons for this: First, you'll be expected to sail her like that all the time, and second, it can frighten some people. If that happens, you'll never get them aboard.

There should be a picture of the ship sailing sedately along, and if the background is picturesque, so much the better. Another shot should show her lying at anchor in a tranquil bay with the awning up. There should be a shot of the crew. There can be one or two deck scenes, with people sunning themselves at anchor and under sail. Eating it up—either on deck or below—should be portrayed, along with a few interior shots. A beach scene. A layout plan (cabins, bunks, galley, etc.) is a worthy inclusion, and where a vessel is confined to a specific locale for her chartering, a small map of the area (often reproduced on the back of a brochure) can help complete the picture for would-be guests.

The printed matter giving a description of the ship, her seaworthiness, and her crew should be kept short, with the emphasis on safety. Mention lifelines, harnesses for kids, radio (making it possible for guests to contact home if necessary), insurance. Instead of a long blurb about how clever you are and what you can do, make the brochure a little smaller, or stick in another couple of pictures. (Nobody will believe you, anyhow). A short account of the chartering area, and of typical activities while on board, will be well received, but don't go overboard and promise delights that you may be unable to fulfill. Remember, whatever you show or say in a brochure people will expect you to do.

GETTING INTO THE GAME

Write to charter brokers and send them your brochures and prices. If you're not sure how much to charge by the week (or day), or whether it should include food, liquor, and incidental expenses, or whether these should be an extra charge, ask around. Find out how much a boat comparable with your own is charging (and what it includes), and price yourself accordingly.

If yours is the only charter boat in the area, write to brokers or charter boats handling or working a similar region (write enough letters and someone will answer you), and use their replies as a guide. Choose your charter brokers carefully, however, when sending out brochures. Investigate their reputation wherever possible. A good broker is priceless, and an association with one who goes to the trouble of matching charter guests to the ship and the type of cruises you have to offer can be long and happy.

Usually a good broker will be able to tell you how much you can expect to receive and just what the charter price should cover. A point to bear in mind is that undercharging can sometimes lose a ship as much business as overcharging. (More of this and other aspects of charging later on.) A good broker can also advise on "seasonal" rates. Charter brokers with a world-wide clientele advertise in yachting and travel magazines. Write to several of them, then make up your mind what your rates will be. Remember, it's *your* boat!

In correspondence with a broker, describe fully the area you intend to charter in if it is not a well-known one. Give a rundown on its attractions and a typical itinerary. Provide all the information at your disposal regarding accommodation ashore for guests, either before or after their cruise, together with details about how to get there and about restaurants and duty-free shopping (if any). Give interested brokers a full account of yourself and your ship over and above the information shown in your brochure. Don't exaggerate or blow your own trumpet; a knowledgeable broker can pick out a phony ten thousand miles away. Play it straight with a broker, and you have the right to expect the same treatment from him (or her).

Make certain, through correspondence or through talking to brokers, that when charter guests eventually board your ship they know exactly what the charter price covers. Make sure that every broker with whom you correspond and to whom you send brochures has the same information on you and your ship. Don't give different prices to different brokers. To quote Jo Bliss (a top broker and old friend):

"The owners of the boats pay the commission to agents and are ethically supposed to quote the same price as we do. If we find one not following this practice, he's dropped from our books immediately. That's why we also say (to prospective charterers) that it costs no more to charter through a broker who can give you a candid opinion of the yacht and her crew."

Charter brokers' commissions vary, and they sometimes depend on what part of the world a vessel is operating in. Some brokers charge as little as 10 percent of the total charter fee, while others are as high as 20 percent. The usual brokerage commission, however, is 15 percent. Some charge their commission only on the basic boat cost, which is the total charter price less expenses (food, beverages, fuel, ship's laundry, ice, and port fees). Brokers situated in the heart of a chartering area sometimes handle bookings for other distant agents and split the commission. In such a case, a charter boat sometimes pays 5 percent above a usual commission of 15 percent, and the two brokers then divide it 10 and 10.

Brokers usually supply this kind of information in their initial correspondence. If they do not, ask for it and be certain you know what it is before agreeing to take any charters.

Legislation in some areas requires that charter brokers be licensed; some are even bonded. For the charter-boat skipper who has his life savings wrapped up in a boat and who is all fired up to do his best in the game, this represents protection. For although most brokers are dependable—and some have had years of experience—all it takes in certain localities is a typewriter, some stationery, and the price of an advertisement in a yachting magazine or the Yellow Pages for anyone to call himself a charter broker.

A good broker will want to meet you and, if possible, see your ship. If you are fortunate enough to experience this—and I strongly advise the aspiring charter captain to make every effort to bring about such a meeting—ask the broker all about his side of the business. What happens to the 50 percent deposit that the broker accepts from the charterer for a cruise on your ship? This can be $1,000 or $2,000 or more, depending on the size of the vessel and the length of the charter. Is it held in escrow or in a special trust account? It should be.

How soon before a charter do you get the deposit (less brokerage commission) to buy provisions? And have a look at their moves while on board. Do they know anything about boats? Some are very good, but others wouldn't know a good boat from a bathtub. By the same token, be prepared to cut the mustard yourself; you're probably on trial, too. Now is no time to fall down your own hatch, or have the outboard quit halfway between the landing and the ship and for the broker to discover that you can't row a dinghy.

While charter brokers (agents) have been established for some years now, and have carved a niche for themselves in the chartering scene, some of them have adopted a "holier-than-thou" attitude toward charter boats that is hard to understand. Crewed charter boats spearheaded the business and were making a good living as well as doing their own advertising and correspondence long before broker number one ever decided to get into the act and grab a piece of the charter fee as it went past.

Good brokers are an asset to the game and justify their existence by doing a competent job of matching inquirers' needs to boats, and vice versa. Those who genuinely do this earn their commission; any who don't, however (and this includes travel agents who sometimes handle bookings for charter boats), should sell their typewriters and cancel their advertisements.

You have as much right to inquire into the charter broker's side of the business as he has to inspect your vessel and ask questions regarding your cruise itinerary, feeding, and general entertainment of guests. It works both ways.

Don't ignore the fact that the investment you have in your ship is maybe 10 times as much (or more) as the broker has in his charter business. An inexperienced broker can double-book you (we've had this happen) or go bankrupt while holding your 50 percent of the charter fee, or even abscond with it. Brokers expect you to be available, competent, and trustworthy. Make every inquiry you can to satisfy yourself that *they* are, too.

Regarding an "exclusive," Evelyn Whitney (another top broker and old pal) says:

"The boat owner, whether he is to be the captain or not, should not give an exclusive to any one broker. This narrows the field for him and has proven to be an unwise move. Potential charter-boat owners often ask me to represent them exclusively. I always refuse. It puts restrictions on me that I

Heart of Edna *on her island-hopping charter run in the Pacific. (Photo by John Nicholls)*

don't care to have. I would then feel obliged to charter that particular boat first and foremost, compromising my integrity as a broker. My first aim should be to give the potential client the boat that is best for him and his party. Conversely, I never ask a boat owner to help subsidize my advertising by mentioning his boat or putting a picture of his boat in my ad. Again, this would obligate me to promote that boat over all others."

She goes on to say:

"Another 'touchy' aspect of broker-captain relations is the question of repeat business. There are skippers who tell their charterers to come back through them, that this will save them the broker's commission. There is no better way to alienate an active broker!"

As was mentioned earlier, play it straight with brokers and you have every right to expect the same treatment from them.

Some charter boats are listed with travel agents and are booked as part of a "package" deal. Airlines, hotels, taxis to and from the airport—everything is arranged for the client without his having the grief of coordinating the whole thing himself. Two boats currently getting their business this way are the 58-foot ketch *Danae III* and the 50-foot ketch *Heart of Edna. Danae III* works through a Newport, California, travel agency and is based at Ile Huahine, French Polynesia. Clients pay a set price per person, which includes everything except a few hotel meals. The cruises are in French Polynesia, and charter guests usually fly home from Bora-Bora.

Heart of Edna works through Australian and New Hebrides agencies and does cruises from New Caledonia through island groups almost to New Guinea. Cruises vary from two to three weeks, and guests board or leave the ship at islands and airports along the way. The package price includes everything except liquor.

Package deals are also being handled by a company in Louisiana that has offices in the British Virgin Islands. They currently offer "all-inclusive" Dalmatian cruises that end up in Greece. European-crewed charter boats are booked for the trips.

A "clearing agent" business, which is neither broker nor charter boat, is successfully operated by Ocean Enterprises Inc., in St. Thomas, Virgin Islands. The function of this company is to represent boats to brokers, and vice versa. They also collect deposits from brokers and handle bookings. Being situated on the spot, and being able to personally inspect boats and crews, Bob and Dorothy Smith can supply a broker (who may be thousands of miles away) with up-to-date information regarding a vessel, and by telex, cable, or phone, they can confirm her availability for specific dates.

From the broker's point of view, this takes all the speculation out of whether or not a boat is in ship-shape condition (as she will doubtless be shown in her brochure) and also if she is already booked. If for any reason she is unavailable, the clearing agent can recommend an alternative, in which again the broker can have confidence, for the simple reason that no company interested in business continuity can afford to recommend a "dud."

The benefit of all this to a charter skipper is:
(1) Under this system, he usually gets a lot of bookings. (2) To confirm a charter, the broker must forward the 50 percent deposit (less commission) to Ocean Enterprises, which puts it in a special account, so the skipper knows his money is safe and that he'll get it to use in provisioning his vessel 10 days before the charter is scheduled to commence.

There is, of course, a fee for this service. This is paid to the clearing agent by the charter boat (over and above the brokerage charge, which is commonly 15 percent). Ocean Enterprises' charges, as of this writing, are $10 per charter berth per month, which means, for example, that a six-passenger ship pays $60 per month for a six-month season. Off-season charges are the same only if the ship is booked.

A beneficial side effect of this operation to skippers who "play it straight" with each other is that there is no incentive for a vessel to try to attract business by offering a higher commission to brokers. All charters passing through clearing agents' hands are levied the same going commission.

Bob and Dorothy also operate ship-to-shore radio station W.A.H. They monitor channels 16, 25, and 28, plus AM frequencies—handling and answering telephone patching and periodic weather forecasts.

ADVERTISING AND HANDLING YOUR OWN BUSINESS

For those whose hackles rise at the thought of regimentation, or those whose natural bent is to go it alone and be grandly independent while at the same time keeping a larger slice of the cake than if they were shelling out commissions, go ahead and advertise yourself and handle your own business. In *White Squall II* we chartered 30 weeks a year, year after year, plus at least 20 weeks a year that we were too busy to handle and farmed out to other boats at 10 percent. Less than 5 percent of all our charters came through brokers.

Within my experience, charter brokers who do not insist that boats list with them on a sole agency (exclusive) basis are quite happy to deal with boats running their own advertisement.

For the charter-boat owner who decides to do this, my advice is to go carefully through yachting and travel magazines, preferably ones already catering to charter yachts, and then place your advertisement. It is not necessary to make a big splash. Your advertisement need not be a large one, for bona fide charterers read them all. However, it *must* be continuous and, once started, it should not change in size or format or be left out of an issue. Miss a month and your public will think you are out of business.

Answer inquiries immediately. Give the total price for the period in question, and then explain what it covers. Don't give a long spiel about sparkling sea, gorgeous sunsets, and then tell the inquirer the price at the end. It doesn't matter how much money the guy's got; he wants to know the price. Tell him that first, and then he'll read the rest of your stuff.

An answer to an inquiry (see Appendix II) should contain, in addition to the total price, all information regarding the deposit required for a reservation and when the balance is due. The balance is often paid by guests in cash or traveler's checks on boarding. Some vessels or agencies require it before the cruise commences, sometimes as much as 60 days before.

A client is required to send a deposit—often up to 50 percent of the total fee—to confirm a charter. On its receipt, the charter-boat owner or his representative sends two signed and witnessed agreements (see Appendix III). The charterer signs one, has it witnessed, and returns it. The other he keeps, and everyone knows where he stands. This contract is canceled and the deposit is refunded if the ship is not ready within 24 hours after the boarding date agreed upon.

If at any time the charterer decides to cancel his cruise, the deposit is only refundable if the boat can be rebooked for the period covered by the contract. This rule is practiced by many charter-boat owners and brokers, but it is by no means general.

One approach favored by certain brokers and boat owners is to refund the deposit in full if written notice to cancel is given not less than 60 days prior to the sailing date. Then the deposit is only refunded inside this limit if the charter dates can be resold. Another agent levies a fee of 50 percent of the deposit on any cancellation made between 30 and 60 days of departure. In cases where less than 30 days notice is given, full refund is made only if the period can be rebooked.

I know one charter skipper whose reaction to cancellation of a cruise he is unable to rebook is to keep the deposit but to make the ship available to the client for any (unbooked) period within a year. Another skipper returns the fee minus 25 percent, which he keeps for "processing."

Cancellations don't happen often. In fact, out of hundreds of charter trips, we've only had four cancellations. Three of these we were able to fill easily, and so return the deposit. The fourth was impossible to rebook; there just wasn't time. However, the guy pitched me such a terrible tale of woe that I gave him his money back, and I've always considered that I was the one who came out the winner. We've had only fun with charter parties, and I have an idea that guy would have broken our record. . . .

There is one golden rule that the charter-boat owner who distributes brochures among various brokers must adhere to, whether or not he also advertises privately. On confirmation of a charter from any source, he must immediately notify brokers so that they have an up-to-date picture on his bookings and available dates.

Another thing the boat owner (especially the absentee owner) must keep in mind if he wants to make money is that his boat is not in the business for the convenience of his family or friends. If he intends to charter on a serious basis, he must not block off time during peak periods, especially during the "season," for his friends. Brokers will expect him to be in business for business. If he is not available when the demand is highest, it is very likely they will forget him when business is less brisk.

CHARGES

Once again the question of how much to charge rears its head, and I can hear the aspiring charter skipper saying, "I still don't know how much to charge. I'm in an area where there are no charter brokers to ask. I don't know anyone to write to for an opinion. What do I do?"

You charge as much as the traffic can stand. This can vary tremendously with the type of operation you are running, the size and standard of your ship, and your clientele. If your customers are drawn solely from a local population who cannot (or will not) pay a charter price regarded as normal in a more tourist-oriented or affluent part of the world, this will greatly influence your charges. However, don't price yourself too low. You're not running a benevolent society; you're operating a charter boat, and you'll never make a go of it on breadline prices. Another thing: If you're too cheap, people will think you're no good or a fool, or that there is something wrong with your boat.

I've seen vessels arrive from time to time in the West Indies certain that they would become fully booked because they were prepared to go away for less money—sometimes $500 to $800 a week less than anyone else in the fleet. And they would sit in the bay month after month doing nothing, while most of us had as much business as we could handle. People are suspicious of a "too cheap" boat. Boats are not like hotels; hotels don't have to float. A charter boat drastically cheaper than its neighbor often does a freeze because people suspect its rates are in direct proportion to its dependability. Another reason for lack of business can be that charter brokers don't make as large a commission if they book it.

There is a popular belief among charter-boat operators starting up in an area that is little known and off the beaten track, that their price must be low or they will get no customers. This need not be so. If they have done their homework on the area, if they intend to serve good food, if they know that the sailing, the sights, and the anchorages are good, if there is access and people can get there—then they have every right to increase their price over a comparable boat working a "milk-run."

Running a first-class charter-boat operation in a remote area usually takes more money and effort than if the same ship were working a region that has every facility available. However, it has its compensations, not the least of which is uncrowded anchorages and relative freedom from rules and regulations.

The biggest trick is getting customers—customers prepared to pay top dollar for their cruise. If a boat has already been chartering in a busy area for a few years (and has been doing a good job), attracting business to a new locale presents little problem, as a proportion of her guests will follow her anywhere in the world. That I know.

For an unestablished boat starting up in an unknown area, bookings can be more difficult. But provided people can reach the site of embarkation without too much trouble, and fly home from the debarking point with equal ease, there is no reason why a well-run ship cannot charge a high price.

It is easy enough to discover who the top charter brokers in the world are. Look through the most popular yachting and travel magazines. Pick out a dozen or more charter brokers and write to them, sending the information already described. Write also to institutions doing oceanographic research. Send your proposed rate scale and what it covers, or ask their opinion—or

Eryx II, *83-foot schooner. $800 a day for six charter guests in French Polynesia. (Photo by Michel Feuga)*

both. Some boat owners interested in research advertise charter cruises in oceanographic magazines.

Having firmly decided what your price is going to be, send a hundred or so brochures to every agent who has indicated a desire to list you, and advertise yourself as well. In addition, give your brochures and rates to anyone else you can think of.

One factor that can prevent a vessel from reaching top-dollar listing is the dependability of the weather in her chartering area. This was referred to earlier on, but it is worth mentioning again, if only to drive home its importance. To be able to charge a high price, the weather *must* be good. Good weather is worth money and is one reason why charter boats often have two rates—a high one for the "season" and a lower one (sometimes much lower) for the "off-season."

Below are some of the ways of arriving at a weekly price for a crewed boat operating in a good chartering area (plenty of sunshine). All prices in these examples, including Income Statement, are in U.S. dollars. The prices must be regarded as hypothetical, but typical of what is charged by a well-found 48- to 50-foot auxiliary sailboat chartering in a reasonably priced (not high, not low) area. Charter prices, like a lot of things, change with the times and with inflation. To give the charter-boat owner a consistent level of return, they must be adjusted from time to time, along with the charges of airlines, hotels, and other businesses associated with the tourist trade. The prices given in the following examples are current, but they should be altered where circumstances or inflation make it necessary.

Various methods are used to arrive at an overall charter price. We will start with the basic boat rate, plus expenses (still favored by a lot of operators). Under this system, a breakdown of a $2,400 weekly price, with four guests and two crew, would be:

Basic boat price	$1,900.00
Expenses	500.00
Total charter fee	$2,400.00

Expenses of $12 per person per day, including crew, cover food, liquor, all other beverages, ice, ship's laundry (towels, sheets, etc.), fuel, water, port fees. This arrangement is realistic if it is possible to purchase liquor duty-free, if little fuel is used, and if port fees are not high.

Another way to charge for the same boat in an area where liquor is not duty-free and, possibly, where a local government has imposed a "head tax," is to specify a total price of $2,300 a week and have charterers pay for their liquor and any head tax levies as extras.

Another approach is to stick to the basic cost of $1,900 and charge everything as an extra. This involves a lot of toting up and splitting straws at the end of a trip—cost of food consumed, gallons of fuel used, and so on. I have always dodged this one.

Best of all is a total price—eat what you like, drink what you like. This resembles the basic-cost-plus-expenses exercise referred to in the first example, except that the charter boat does not need to justify a breakdown. It is also popular with brokers, who collect their commission on the total fee. Under the first system, they collect it only on the basic cost. Again, however, it is realistic only if liquor is duty-free.

Crewed boats catering to individuals—guests who board on a per capita basis—commonly write any head tax into the charter fee that each person pays on or before boarding, and then usually make a separate charge for drinks at the end of the cruise.

A cost that is generally an extra to be paid by guests is payment for telephone conversations. With many charterers, the main cost of a call from the ship to their home or office is billed to them through their credit card number. However, the local marine operator in the charter boat's area of operation usually levies a charge on the ship for each call as well. It is common practice for guests to pay this at the end of their cruise.

There are some charter boats whose clientele pay a basic fee per head on boarding, bring their own food, and cook it themselves. Such ships usually charge a lot less than others operating on an "all-found" basis. Their rates vary, but they are sometimes less than $20 a day per head. Often the reason for this arrangement, with its relatively low charge, is that the weather in the chartering region is unreliable; guests take the risk of bad weather for the entire trip. Usually they are also required to act as crew. All in all, it is hardly a setup on which a charter-boat skipper can expect to wax fat.

The amount (large or small) that a charter boat can ask for a cruise boils down to the ship's ease of access, comfort aboard, good food, and fine weather. There are other desirable ingredients, yes—as you will realize by now. A personable crew, a clean ship, an interesting itinerary . . . many things, and they all help, but the presence of each of the four main points is a must if a high price is to be charged—and maintained.

DEADHEADING

A cost to be considered, and one that can, and should, influence the overall charter price, is the amount of "deadheading" required. Deadheading, sailing back empty to the home port, or to another embarkation point to pick up a party, is normal business practice in the chartering game in many places. Vessels often charter "one way." A few examples are: Any of the U.S. west coast ports (San Francisco, Santa Barbara, Long Beach, San Diego), down to Baja, or even Acapulco, where the guests fly out; Grenada, via various West Indian islands to St. Thomas; Noumea to the Solomons or New Guinea (a long one); Tahiti to Bora-Bora; Florida to the Bahamas (a short enough jaunt, but the Gulf Stream can be rough either way).

On a trip such as this last one, a way to ensure that the guests arrive home with a smile on their faces, even if the ship is held up from returning by bad weather, is to have it all arranged for them to fly back and then deadhead back yourself. This saves the possibility of being weatherbound with a party who, after their charter time has run out, are eating their heads off at your expense and, because they're due back home, are getting more disillusioned with you and your boat as each day goes by.

It is usual either to make a separate charge for deadheading and add it to the charter fee, or calculate what it should be and work that into the overall price. Two examples are as follows:

(1) A charter boat based in the Virgin Islands is booked to pick up a party in Martinique (300 miles) and sail up the chain to drop them off in St. Thomas. The deadhead price, St. Thomas to Martinique, is calculated at three days (the time allowed to get there) at half the daily hire of the ship less expenses—in other words, half the basic price per day, which is added on to the charter fee. (Some boats charge the full basic price.)

(2) A charter boat, sailing in the most comfortable direction for guests

(usually downwind), picks up and drops off along a chain of islands or a coast. When she finally arrives at the last point where guests fly out (this may be after several months, and a couple of thousand miles or more), she deadheads back. A charge for this deadhead is calculated beforehand, and a proportion of it is applied to the charter price each party pays either before or after boarding the vessel.

Deadheading, instead of chartering the return voyage, is usual in cases where the passage back is likely to be a rough one and so cause seasickness among guests. If this happens, you'll never get them back—or their friends. The same, of course, applies in cases where a charter boat deadheads to an embarkation point.

The reason for charging is that deadheading takes time, which in any business represents money. It also takes effort and causes just as much (or more) wear and tear on the ship and her equipment as when a party is aboard, again justifying a fee. I remember when the *Thane* took Hugh Downs and his party on a charter from the Caribbean to Tahiti in the mid 1960s. The trip down was a sleigh ride, as it usually is, but the voyage back was something else, with a lot of wear and tear on both the ship and the crew.

ANSWERING INQUIRIES

A busy charter boat, doing many cruises and being advertised separately as well as listed with brokers, needs a responsible person ashore to answer inquiries. We have always been able to arrange this by paying a capable person by the hour for whatever time she spent on the job. In almost every case, our secretary has been the wife of a retired friend; she has also been "red hot" at answering inquiries.

Don't offer the position to anyone, however, just because he, or she, happens to be a pal, or simply because they can type. Whoever answers your inquiries must be good, very good. One woman we had was an ex-legal secretary; another had at one time written a newspaper column. Either of them could be relied upon to answer inquiries by return mail on the ship's own stationery.

Don't forget that when you receive an inquiry for a charter, it is a fair bet that three or four other boats have received the same letter. The reply, along with your brochure sent off by your secretary or "manager" (as one of my beauties styled herself), has to be up to the mark to win you the business. In addition to quoting the overall price, giving a rundown on what it covers and indicating the deposit, answer fully any questions the prospective charterer may have asked. Then give your own blurb—beautiful beaches, clear water . . . but don't lay it on too thick.

One thing I always insisted upon was that the inquirer be acquainted with the fact that we were very proud of our ship. I didn't want anyone to board my vessel thinking that I just regarded the whole thing as a job and the ship as something that we floated around in and worked on. I always hoped that prospective guests would get the message—that this wasn't just somewhere to hang your hat, or unpack your bag, like a hotel. This was different; this was a boat, *our* boat, and, by God, we were proud of her! I think it worked, too; we were never short of charters.

Leave instructions with your secretary to call a prospective guest long distance if she thinks it will clinch a charter. Or do it yourself by radio from the ship. Be a sport—a phone call costing $20 can sometimes make all the difference between gaining or losing a $3,000 charter.

Our secretary ashore always had plenty of ship's stationery on hand, plus a few dozen charter contracts I had already signed. On receipt of a deposit, she would fill out two contracts with all details relevant to the charter, witness both of them, and send them off to the charterer with a covering letter. He would sign one, have it witnessed, and return it, as has already been mentioned. She also notified all brokers we were listed with.

There is usually further correspondence with guests—how to get there, food dislikes or allergies, liquor or beverage preferences, what and what not to bring. The amount of contact with parties varies in most cases with the length (and cost) of the charter. With some groups, the exchange of letters is considerable.

Deposits are all banked in an account used solely for that purpose, and they are never touched until just before the charter or after it is completed. Keeping deposits intact is an absolute must, and to use this money for any other purpose but to provision for the charter to which it applies can be financial suicide. If the ship for any reason becomes unavailable, and the clients cannot be refunded their deposits, the whole chartering venture will end right there.

At the end of a charter cruise, when guests are leaving the ship, ask if they mind being referred to when you, or your representative, answer inquiries from the same state or the part of the world where they live. Keep a file of their names, addresses, and phone numbers. In your answer to a subsequent inquiry, you can then give the prospective charterer the number of an ex-charter guest to call to verify that your ship and your cruises are just as advertised. If you've given a guest a good time, he'll convince any inquirer who calls him. It is possible to get a lot of business this way.

Keep in touch with brokers who have you listed. Send them a note from time to time. Don't forget that you're way off over the horizon, out of sight. Keep them up to date with your movements. The boat that is ready, with a crew that is "on the ball," is the one that gets the business.

The same with ex-charter guests. Don't think that when they leave the ship, they will forget all about you. They all take photos, and we've yet to meet the gang who would refuse to send back copies of some of their best shots taken on the cruise. Send them a note thanking them. Then put the photos in a book and show them to other guests boarding your ship. They usually enter into the spirit of the thing and, on their return home, send photos, too. It is not much trouble to maintain contact this way, and when an ex-charter guest shows the photos to his buddies at home before he sends them to you (he'll only show the best ones), the advertising will do you no harm. Remember your ex-charterers at Christmas time, too; send them all a card. In addition to brochures, established charter skippers frequently have postcards printed of their boat, usually under sail. These are available to guests free during the cruise. Maps of the chartering area can also be provided. Guests trace their course from bay to bay; some take the maps home and frame them. It is all advertising.

The author and his wife, Minine, back in port after a charter cruise. (New Zealand Herald photo)

THE CHARTER GAME

The following is an income statement, based on the earnings over 25 weeks, of a top-condition 48- to 50-foot owner-operated-and-crewed auxiliary sailboat. The chartering area is the West Indies, and all figures are hypothetical but typical of what a well-found, conscientiously run and maintained craft can currently demand. The expenses she is likely to encounter are also listed. An explanation of the expense calculations follows the income statement. (All amounts are in U.S. dollars.)

Charter price is $2,400 per week, all found (food, drink, ship's laundry, fuel, ice), and the maximum number of charter guests is four.

Income Statement (One Year)

Charters: 25 weeks @ $2,400		$60,000
Expenses:		
Food and drink	$10,500	
Laundry (ship's)	375	
Ice	350	
Fuel	875	
Dockage	250	
Haulout	1,000	
Maintenance	2,000	
Insurance	2,700	
Advertising	1,000	
Audit and accountancy	300	
Motor vehicles or taxis	350	
Postage, stationery, cables	400	
Wages (secretarial)	2,000	
Commissions (10 weeks)	3,600	
Clearing agent	120	
	$25,820	$25,820
Net income (before tax) with 15 weeks charter from own advertising and 10 weeks from brokers		$34,180*

---

* This figure does not include depreciation of the vessel.

Explanation

$10,500 for food and drink: This is calculated at the rate of $10 per person per day including crew, e.g., four charter guests plus two crew times 10 = $60 a day, or $420 per week. 25 weeks = $10,500. In this example, liquor is available duty-free. In cases where liquor is not duty-free, it is seldom part of an all-inclusive price. It is more usual then for guests to pay a separate charge at the end of the trip for liquor consumed.

$375 for ship's laundry: $15 per week.

$350 for ice: $14 per week.

$875 for fuel: This is calculated at the rate of $30 per week for engine or generator fuel and $5 for stove fuel; it is, I consider, generous. However, fuel consumption can vary greatly from boat to boat. Some vessels use only a few gallons a week to generate power for batteries. Others, especially those with air conditioning and/or electric cooking, can exceed this figure.

$250 for dockage: This is calculated at $10 a day for the 25 times it will have been necessary to come alongside to take on fuel, water, and guests. We have always loaded stores by dinghy. The vessel that is forced by lack of anchoring room to lie at a dock when not on charter, or whose skipper may prefer to no matter what, will, of course, pay more than has been allowed here. In such a case, the figures must be adjusted accordingly.

$1,000 for haulout: This is an average price for a haul, scrub, two coats of good antifouling paint, zinc replacement, and inspection of underwater fittings. The cost is currently less in some areas; it may be more in others.

$2,000 for maintenance: This is the biggest imponderable of them all. It commonly depends upon the skipper's constant attention to his ship and her gear, plus his ability as a "Mr. Fixit," as to whether the yearly maintenance cost is double the amount allowed, or treble, or even more. If a sail has been unnecessarily exposed to chafe or a surfeit of sun, the repair is a maintenance charge. Fewer engine oil changes than the makers recommend, continuous use of a small auxiliary generator (especially if supplying electricity for air conditioning and/or cooking), allowing electrical equipment to get wet, overtightening a stern gland so that the packing "scores" the propeller shaft, neglecting to care for dinghy and outboard—all can result in large maintenance costs.

Then there is the possible breakdown of refrigeration or the stove, or the replacement of batteries or lifesaving equipment. Nothing lasts forever. Some of the gear we carry aboard our boats gives years of service, but no matter what brand name a piece of equipment (large or small) carries, if it is not given routine maintenance (which may only be regular inspection), one day it will quit—and its replacement or repair is a maintenance charge.

It may be said that the amount spent on maintenance depends upon the quality, age, and complexity of the equipment aboard a vessel, the material the ship is built with, and the amount of routine care and attention that is, or is not, lavished upon the unit as a whole.

This profit-and-loss exercise started with a 48- to 50-foot auxiliary sailboat in top condition, which meant a top price could be charged. It is reasonable, therefore, for the purpose of this example, to assume that her equipment is of good quality as well. We shall also assume that her owner-operator is maintenance-oriented and personally attends to the regular inspection and upkeep of gear aboard his vessel. The $2,000 maintenance figure is probably way above what the skipper would expect to incur in a normal year. However, since his ship is a workboat, there will be wear and tear, no matter how conscientiously he strives to keep it at bay. It can, and does, add up. I remember congratulating myself on spending only about $1,500 on maintenance in two years when, suddenly, the next year I had to pay out over $5,000 for a new auxiliary generator.

The $2,000 allowed for maintenance in this example should be considered an average sum (apart from haulouts) spent yearly on the vessel over the long haul.

$2,700 for insurance. See Appendix I.

$1,000 for advertising. This is to cover the cost of a small, continuous advertisement in a yachting magazine.

$300 for audit and accountancy. This assumes that the charter-boat owner/skipper keeps his own accurate accounting of income and expenses during the year and does not enlist the services of an accountant to do this. The figure shown is only for professional appraisal and presentation of an income statement, or for tax purposes.

$350 for motor vehicle expenses or taxis (to collect stores), and $400 for postage, stationery, and cables: these are average expenses and can vary a little from that shown, but not enough to make any great difference.

$2,000 for wages (secretarial) is the cost of a person ashore working part-time in answering inquiries, processing charter agreements, etc. This expense can be much smaller.

$3,600 for commissions. This is the amount paid to brokers on 10 weeks of charter at 15 percent. In this exercise we are assuming that the ship receives 15 weeks' bookings from her own advertising.

$120 for clearing agent. This represents the sum paid to the agent at the rate of $10 per charter berth per month, over a three-month period (or the 10 weeks of charter booked by brokers and coordinated by the clearing agent).

In a case where the 25 weeks of charter are all booked through brokers, the commission paid would be $9,000. The clearing agent's fee would also be increased to, say, $300. On the other hand, the amounts of $2,000 for secretarial wages, $1,000 for advertising, $400 for postage, $3,600 for commissions, and $120 for a clearing agent would not apply. The difference is as follows:

Broker's commission: 15% of $60,000		$9,000
Clearing agent		300
		$9,300
Commission and clearing agent	$3,720	
Secretarial fees	2,000	
Advertising	1,000	
Postage, stationery, cables	400	
	$7,120	$7,120
Difference		2,180
From previous income statement		34,180
Net income (before tax) after paying brokerage commission on 25 weeks		$32,000*

---

* Depreciation of the vessel not taken into account.

While the pre-tax profit shown is acceptable to many owner-skippers and their mates, who not uncommonly enjoy the romance of a chartering life for its own sake, it cannot be said to excite a person who expects to buy a boat, put someone else aboard to run it, and still make money. By the time an absentee owner has footed all the bills and paid his crew (at whatever rate is mutually agreed upon), he will not have much left over for himself. For all that, absentee ownership is popular among owners or companies seeking a tax shelter on the boat's expenses. They can use the ship from time to time themselves and have the satisfaction of knowing that she is "in commission" and being cared for by a professional crew.

It is possible, of course, to exceed 25 weeks of charter in a year. This depends upon the business available, the length of the chartering "season," and how hard the charter operator wants to work. It is possible in some areas to do 30 weeks or more, but over a period of time this can run the ship, the crew, and the skipper himself into the ground. It is important to realize that once maintenance on a ship is neglected—and this can happen if she's constantly out there working—all the profit of three or four years can be lost on resale or refurbishing. With 25 charter weeks a year, maintenance can be kept up and the life does not become monotonous. If there are charters you cannot handle or do not have time for, farm them out to other boats.

The break-even point in chartering is a frequent topic of discussion. An aspiring charter-boat captain/owner (for example) might typically be heard to say, "How many weeks must I charter my ship to live a full year and pay all expenses?"

THE CHARTER GAME

I say 10 weeks—unless there is a large, unexpected cost to be met, such as engine replacement or maintenance that keeps a vessel hauled out on an expensive slipway. Either of these can knock the stuffing out of any calculations. So can living high on the hog, or being tied up at a swanky dock all year. However, for those interested, I submit the following Income Statement based on 10 weeks of charter. Brokerage commission is paid on every charter, and the figures used are proportionately the same as in the other example—except maintenance, haulout, and insurance (which are calculated on a full year).

Income Statement

Charters: 10 weeks @ $2,400 $24,000

Expenses:

Food and drink	$4,200	
Laundry (ship's)	150	
Ice	140	
Fuel	350	
Dockage	100	
Haulout	1,000	
Maintenance	2,000	
Insurance	2,700	
Audit and accountancy	300	
Motor vehicle expenses, taxis	100	
Commissions	3,600	
Clearing agent (for 3 months)	120	
	$14,760	$14,760

Net income (before tax) $9,240*

---

* This figure does not include depreciation of the vessel.

Whether a couple who live aboard and do their own maintenance can exist for the rest of the year on the profit of 10 charter weeks depends entirely upon their commitments, their tax situation, and their standard of living. I know many cruising couples who get along fine on a lot less than $9,000 a year.

It must be understood that all costs used in the preceding examples are hypothetical, but they are, I feel, not generally undercalculated. The Income Statements shown are to be used as a guide only, because prices change year by year and are seldom the same in any two countries or, indeed, in different parts of the same country. Charter prices vary, too. For instance, it is often possible to command a charter fee up to 15 percent higher in the Mediterranean than in the Caribbean. Food in the Mediterranean also costs less, and it is generally less expensive to eat out. However, the season (May to October) is shorter. Tahiti-based boats usually have a higher price than their Caribbean counterparts. They have to charge more, as food, ship-chandlery, liquor, and just about every other sort of ship's stores costs more, due to the distance it has to travel to reach French Polynesia.

For all that, and for all the qualifying remarks I have found necessary to make when presenting the examples shown, I hope these figures will assist the aspiring charter captain (he can substitute his own figures where necessary) in doing his homework—and in deciding whether or not he can get out there and make it in the charter game.

During the course of a cruise, boats normally used for cruising now and again have a fling at chartering by picking up people in one country or group of islands and sailing on to drop them off in another. This may be an ocean passage of a thousand miles or more, or a short sail of only 50 miles (or less) to the intended embarkation point. It can be an excellent way of defraying expenses, it helps build up the cruising "kitty," and it is, I feel, something to be encouraged. I like to see a boat earning her keep by chartering in one form or another. That's the whole idea of this book. A word of warning, however, to the cruising man who plans to try this: Make sure that anyone you take from one country to another (no matter how short the distance) has airline or boat tickets that enable him to leave your boat once you arrive. Or have him deposit with you the cash for the passage back to his *own country*. If you don't do this, and if your passengers lack the funds or the visas, or both, to attend to it themselves, then you, as master of the vessel, are responsible for them after arrival. This usually means that you must either keep them aboard or pay their fare home yourself. I have two good friends who have had to do this—one in Tahiti and the other in Fiji.

HEADBOATS

"Headboats" vary in type and size, from motorboats shipping a gang away for fishing or sightseeing in home waters to sizable sailing craft taking 40 or more folk for a week or two among coastal or tropic islands. A headboat—so named because customers pay by the head (usually before they board)—is in most cases a bigger vessel, with a larger crew, than the average charter boat catering to parties who form their own group and who, within the limits set by the charter contract, have a say in where the ship goes.

Bareboats in Gorda Sound, British Virgin Islands. (Photo by Dave Ferneding)

Most of what is covered in this book applies as equally to a headboat as it does to the smaller-crewed charter boat. Give people a clean, efficiently handled ship to sail in, good food, plus a well-planned cruise itinerary, and you'll get them back.

BAREBOATS

The term "bareboat" applies to a vessel chartered by a person or group who either sail it themselves or employ someone other than the owner or owner's representative to do it for them. Bareboats range in size from small, open daysailers to fully found powerboats or auxiliaries of 80 (or more) feet dripping with chrome and nautical conveniences. For the experienced yachtsman who wishes to cruise for a few days or a week or two, doing his own navigating and cooking and making every decision necessary for a successful cruise, a wide variety of craft is now available to choose from. Some are to be found even in exotic, "remote" parts of the world.

Some companies have their own bareboat fleets and employ a womb-to-tomb arrangement whereby they provision the boats for charterers, pick them up at the airport, give them a book on where to anchor, rush out in a speedboat to assist them if they get into difficulties, put them up ashore (in accommodations also owned by the company), and finally wave them good-bye when they fly back home. These companies do their own advertising, booking, and maintaining of the boats.

Other companies handle privately owned boats and charter them out for their owners. For the owner of an auxiliary sailboat of, say, 30 feet who only uses his vessel occasionally on weekends, and whose cruising is limited to a

176

couple of weeks a year, the thought of her earning her keep and paying some (or all) of her own expenses can be attractive. His ship may, in addition, make a little extra to help with payments toward the capital cost and in a modest way provide him with a tax shelter.

In some parts of the world, and depending on the tax structure prevailing, if a person really makes a business of chartering his boat, expenses can be regarded as tax-deductible in proportion to the time the vessel is chartered and the owner is not using her. Depreciation can also be written off and, if the venture loses money, the loss is deductible from other income for tax purposes.

The owner of a vessel who wishes to bareboat her and at the same time avail himself of the maximum amount of tax shelter is well advised to consult an admiralty law firm to ensure that the moves he makes are the right ones. There is, for instance, only a thin line in some countries between legally bareboating and illegally carrying passengers for hire. Even the charterer is not exempt.

Under U.S. law, for example, if a boat is chartered "bare" by someone who wishes to take a gang of his buddies away, and one of them strolls aboard with a six-pack of beer (or anything else), this is regarded as a contribution to the costs. The ship is then placed in the category of a vessel carrying passengers for hire, and the charterer (who is the legal owner for the term of the charter) is placed outside the law unless both he and the vessel are licensed, which is seldom the case.

The law also states that while allowing the owner of a bareboat to furnish a master for the ship, the "owner surrenders the entire command and possession of the vessel and consequent control over its navigation to the charterer." To comply with the law, an owner must relinquish all care, custody, and control, and must turn his ship over to the charterer, lock, stock, and barrel. This means that any skipper he supplies cannot act as his representative.

It is not often, aboard the smaller (20 to 50 feet) bareboats, that a captain is hired; one of the most attractive features of this aspect of the game is the fact that for the term of the charter, the client is in command, standing on his own two feet and making the decisions. However, it does at times happen that a captain is required, especially with larger vessels handled by yacht management agencies. These agencies, handling pleasure boats of all sizes for owners, usually for the purpose of tax shelter, go in for bareboating in a big way. Some of them hire crews, supervise the ships' maintenance, and, through brokers, make the vessels available for bareboat charter.

To comply with current U.S. law, full control, possession, and navigation of the bareboat must be vested absolutely in the charterer, and the charterer must have full control over the discharge of the master, no matter who has hired him. The charterer must also be responsible for paying the master and crew. While the master must clearly be working for the client and not the owner during the term of the charter, there is a qualification limiting the charterer's control. This applies to situations in which, to comply with the client's wishes, the ship and/or her complement would, in the master's opinion, be placed in a hazardous position.

The law as to what does or does not constitute a bareboat charter is not as clearly defined in all countries. All that is needed in some areas to circumvent legislation concerning the carrying of passengers for hire is for an owner to charter his boat "bare" to a person or group with the (unwritten) understanding that he, or his representative, will go along for the ride—to take command.

For the private owner who works full time and wishes to bareboat charter his vessel, the going can be tough if he does not work through a broker. To handle the business himself, he will have to advertise, answer inquiries, and process charter agreements. He must attend to all mooring, maintenance, and provisioning (when required by the party). He must be prepared to test the person who will be handling the vessel and to familiarize the group with the controls and fittings aboard—stove, head, engine, etc. On her return from a charter, he must be on hand to inspect her thoroughly for damage, then rush around and clean her from stem to stern, all ready for her next venture into the world of commerce. He will also need increased insurance coverage, such as a rider clause on his existing policy covering damage done by a charterer to somebody else's property. While attending to this personally may present no problem, he might end up paying a higher premium than if he left it to a broker, who can often secure a more attractive rate through a group scheme.

If he has the time and inclination to do all this, fine—he'll save on commissions and labor. But the average boat owner is too busy. If he weren't, he'd be out sailing his boat, not chartering it. So he works through a broker.

The size of a broker's commission is usually in direct proportion to the amount of work he does. If the owner handles mooring expenses, there usually will be a reduction in the brokerage charge. If he cleans the boat himself after a charter or does any maintenance necessary, then such things help him retain a larger slice of the fee.

For a broker to take over the vessel completely, be responsible for every expense, and in some cases even guarantee a certain amount of business, commission can cost as much as 60 percent of the charter price. Thus, an owner with a weekly bareboat charge of $500 on his 30-footer ends up with $200. That, he may reckon, is still better than having her sit at the dock costing money.

Some brokers charge a flat commission rate of 15 percent on each charter they secure for the vessel. Every other expense is charged against the remaining 85 percent. The owner receives the balance. Another approach is for a broker to advertise a boat, answer inquiries, process the charter agreement (this includes collecting the total fee), and screen the charterers for competence—for 25 percent. The owner takes care of insurance, maintenance, and dockage.

The owner of a sailboat or powerboat who is contemplating placing her in an agent's hands for the purpose of charter is well advised to inquire about the standard of competence required of prospective charterers by the broker. Proof of sailing ability and overall seamanship by at least one member of a charter group should be to an acceptable standard before they are allowed to sail off with the boat. Some of the tactics favored by companies, brokers, or individuals handling bareboats in determining this factor follow:

(1) Proof of previous bareboating or chartering experience, or sailboat ownership.

(2) A certificate from a recognized sailing school.

(3) Proof of several years' experience in handling boats of a comparable size.

(4) A practical demonstration of the charterers' ability out on the water with a representative from the broker's office aboard.

Most agencies reserve the right to try out the charterer under sail if they have any doubts, or to put a skipper aboard (at the charterers' expense).

Brokers handling bareboats, or companies owning them, commonly provision the boats for charterers at an extra charge. This can be particularly attractive to clients who arrive aboard after a long trip from their homes. It means that, after familiarizing themselves with the vessel, they can sail away fully stocked for the cruise, rather than waste precious time shopping for provisions in a strange place, and possibly using a monetary system with which they are unacquainted.

Another score on which the boat owner must satisfy himself before leaving his ship in a broker's hands is the amount of refundable security deposit the charterer is required to place with the broker when completing the charter agreement. This deposit is to cover the cost of any damage (normal wear and tear excepted) caused to the boat by the charter group. Some brokers and chartering companies insist on a fixed sum to cover all sizes of boats they handle. Others—and this is the arrangement I prefer—demand that the security deposit be equal to the deductible written into the vessel's insurance policy.

Whichever way it is done, the security deposit is refunded in full if, upon completion of the charter, inspection shows that the ship is not damaged or any of her equipment lost or broken. The cost of any loss or damage is deducted from the deposit. The deposit is not returned if the cost of damage equals or exceeds it.

Some brokers, in stiff competition with others, ask for as little as $100 deposit against an insurance deductible of $500; the boat owner carries the $400 difference at his own risk. Whether or not an owner goes along with such a setup would, I imagine, depend upon the state of his nerves and also on how urgently he wanted his boat chartered out.

Another approach is for the charterer to deposit the full amount of the deductible with the broker and then insure the deposit for a relatively small amount. Thus a security deposit equivalent to a deductible of $500 may mean that he risks only a few dollars of his own money. This arrangement does not appeal to all bareboat owners. Some (including me when I owned a bareboat) feel that the chances of their boat being damaged by a guy who has only a few bucks to lose is greater than when she is chartered out to someone who has deposited a sizable amount out of his own pocket and who, as a consequence, has that much more reason to be careful.

For the purpose of inspection, and to safeguard both parties, a full inventory of the ship's equipment—tools, anchors, warps, dishes, knives, forks, flashlights, spares, every piece of gear carried aboard—should be sent to the client along with the charter agreement. Upon the client's arrival at the ship, he and the broker run through the list to verify the presence of every item, and also its condition. On the boat's return from the charter, a check can quickly show if anything is missing or damaged and, if so, the cost is deducted from the security deposit. It is fairest to both parties for the client and broker to do the checkouts together before sailing and on return. In the event that something is missing, it saves the client from feeling he has possibly been maligned and the broker from being uncertain whether the piece of equipment was aboard when the vessel sailed.

Damage to the boat above water is usually easy for a practiced eye to spot. Below-water damage, however, is a different matter, and there have been cases where a bareboat has hit a rock, reef, or underwater obstruction during her charter and has suffered damage to her underbody that has been not only undetected during her return inspection but also undeclared by the charterers, who have blithely pushed off home without saying a word. The best and quickest method of dealing with this possibility that I personally have encountered is one practiced by a Canadian bareboat company. They send down a scuba diver before and after each charter to check the vessel underwater. Thus damage (if any) incurred during the charter can be ascertained positively and the charterer held liable for the costs to the amount of his security deposit.

The owner of a bareboat who has placed her with a broker for charter is usually required to make his vessel available for a specific period, such as a "season." Brokers, especially those handling boats on an exclusive basis, often have a penalty clause in their agreement with an owner to the effect that any loss of business through cancellation brought about by the boat becoming unavailable (such as the owner going off on a cruise) calls for reimbursement from the owner with a proportion of the charter fee. This can be as high as 50 percent. The boat owner should have all this ironed out with the broker before committing his boat to charter. Any period during which he will require the vessel for his own use should be declared and clearly stated in the agreement.

It is common for brokers to insist that a boat placed with them for bareboat charter may not be sold without their permission before expiration of the agreement.

To confirm a reservation, it is usual for bareboat clients to deposit 50 percent of the charter price. The balance, plus security deposit, is due either beforehand (sometimes as much as 30 days) or on boarding. Again, no single rule applies, and procedure can vary from broker to broker. It is customary for many agents or companies to send a provisioning questionnaire to charterers before the balance is due, so they may indicate whether they will require the boat to be stocked in preparation for their cruise. The extra cost of provisions is added to the balance and is paid at the same time.

Cancellations for bareboat charters are treated similarly to those for crewed boats. A typical treatment of this problem, and one favored by a number of brokers, is to refund the deposit (less $20 handling fee) if written notice is received within 60 days of the charter date. If notification is less than 60 days, the deposit (less fee) is only refunded if the vessel can be re-chartered for the period.

The owner of a bareboat is often required to pay for a folder (mini-brochure) on his boat. This is commonly attended to by the brokers handling the chartering, and the price is deducted from the vessel's earnings.

Sail-together cruises are a feature in the program of some bareboat companies; they are ideal for the person who is experienced enough in his home waters but who hesitates to sail alone in an area he does not know. Usually a "sail-together-and-learn-to-cruise" party comprises several boats sailing a planned itinerary in a group, with an experienced skipper and crew in the lead boat keeping a weather eye on their flock.

There are several factors that the owner of a vessel should ponder before making her available for bareboat charter. A ship that requires constant maintenance may be unsuited for just that reason. Another boat may have equipment too complicated for clients quickly to familiarize themselves with and sail off on a cruise. Not all boats are suited for the bareboat game from either the owner's point of view or the client's.

The features a client typically looks for when chartering a boat are: a tight, safe craft; a snug, easy-to-handle rig; a dependable engine, preferably one that will start at the push of a button; four or more bunks; standing head-room; an enclosed head; a workable galley; a swimming ladder; a good dinghy. If the cruise is to be in the tropics, an easily erected awning is appreciated, as well as an efficient ice box.

The owner who bareboats his vessel must reconcile himself to the fact that his ship, which may occupy a place close to his heart, is now a workboat, earning her keep and collecting her share of wear and tear as a result. Some boats, unless owned by someone who has the time to attend to all main-tenance personally, can quickly develop a shopworn appearance if bare-boated, and rejuvenating them can eat up a large part of the profit. I had this experience with a sailboat I had built by the Cheoy Lee company in Hong Kong. The *Kiwi*, an Offshore 31 sloop, was shipped to Puerto Rico, where we rigged her, sailed her to the Virgin Islands, and put her into the bareboat game.

She was chartered for 17 weeks at $485 a week in her first year, but by the time I'd paid to have her beautiful teak brightwork restored to its original condition, stains removed from the teak decks, mast revarnished, plus every other attendant brokerage expense, there was only enough left over to make the bank payment. With that much business, a boat requiring less main-tenance would have made a modest profit, as well as contributing toward her capital cost.

Bareboating has changed drastically over the years. My introduction to this now well-established part of the chartering scene took place 25 years ago aboard a 34-foot auxiliary ketch on a gold-hunting expedition around the south end of New Zealand. My share of the gold (we didn't find any) was to be 25 percent for skippering the vessel.

By any standards, conditions were spartan. It rained day and night, and the decks leaked so badly we had to wear our foul-weather gear to bed. The reason the mattresses were not ruined is because we didn't have any. We slept on chicken wire that was stretched haphazardly over the bunks' framework.

Frank, one of the partners in the expedition, occupied the only dry spot aboard. That was on the floor between the bunks, and the only way he could use it was to lie there with a leg each side of the mainmast, his head a bare inch away from the engine.

The compass, which I had been assured was "spot on" before we left, showed 28 degrees easterly deviation on a nor'west heading. The galley was a little coal stove that belched enough smoke into the cabin to drive us all up on deck, no matter what the weather.

The *Halcyon* was our home for almost a month. She took us where we wanted to go and, leaking like a basket, managed, on the third attempt, to

Converted Baltic cargo schooner Lindo—*"head" charter boat and daysailer. (Photo by Dave Ferneding)*

bring us back. So ended my first bareboating experience. If I'd been asked, as we tied her up at the end of the trip, whether I'd ever do it again, my answer would have been, "No." But if I could have looked ahead and had a sneak view of some of the beauties available today and the way they are equipped, there is no doubt what my answer would be. For bareboating has changed—changed for the best.

DAY-CHARTERING

Day-charter boats (monohulls, catamarans, trimarans) taking a group aboard for a single day's sail are a common sight in many tourist-oriented regions. Chartering by the day is popular with those who do not have room to accommodate a charter party on a cruise or who prefer to have the ship to themselves at the end of the day and so avoid the responsibility of overnight passengers and the work of cooking and cleaning up.

For those who would like to day-charter their boat, it is often possible to arrange with a resort hotel to take its guests sailing, which benefits both the hotel and the vessel. This can be ideal for a couple on an extended cruise and looking for a chance to plump up the "kitty." It means that they can make money chartering their boat, without going to the expense of buying additional linen, cutlery, and all the rest of the paraphernalia necessary aboard a vessel taking overnight guests.

A typical setup with a hotel is for the hotel management to list a day's cruise in the sailboat among the activities available to guests. Charges vary, depending on what part of the world you are in and on the standard and type of vessel. It is seldom less than $20 per head, however, and this includes lunch. Drinks are usually extra. The hotel commonly takes a 15 percent commission on bookings if they supply their guests with a box lunch to take along, or 10 percent if the day boat supplies the food.

While all this is quite customary, it can, of course, vary. No hard-and-fast rule applies, and to the operator who finds an area where he can charter and where nobody wants a rake-off, all I can say is, "Bully for you, mate—but keep it to yourself!"

A typical day with a group aboard would be: Underway 10 A.M. Sail to a bay and anchor 12:30 P.M. Swim and/or snorkel off the boat or beach, a few drinks, lunch. Sit around, sunbathe, tell a few tall stories, or walk ashore to a point of interest. Sail back, timing return for around 5 P.M.

Some skippers don't like to mingle too much with guests, so it is up to the individual as to how he wants to play it. I personally enjoy shooting the breeze with guests—or anyone else, for that matter, now that I come to think of it. . . .

The attraction of working with a resort hotel, or hotels, taking their guests on an exclusive basis, is that a ready flow of clients is usually available. The advantage for the hotel is that the investment and responsibility of a boat and crew do not exist; a fully found vessel is at their beck and call, providing additional activity for guests at no cost to the hotel.

The purchaser of my 33-foot yawl tried another approach. Alan was owner and proprietor of a resort on the Virgin Island of Marina Cay, and for a couple of years, before he and Jean left on a world cruise in her, he day-chartered the little ship to his own guests. It is nice to see a boat paying her way, and it did my heart good, as we sailed around the islands on long-term charters in *White Squall II*, to cross tacks now and again with her little namesake—busily employed making a buck for her owner.

Some day boats get their business from the passing public, plucking their customers straight off the waterfront, so to speak, and pay commissions to nobody. Others work through brokers and keep busy that way. It depends on the area. A bustling tourist port, with good weather and nearby bays and islands to sail to, can keep several day boats occupied with all the business they need.

Day-chartering is completely different from the crewed type of enterprise. It is seldom possible to get to know your customers aboard a day boat. They no sooner arrive in the morning, it seems, than they're off and gone in the afternoon. A day-charter skipper must also learn to live with a short, ferryboat-type run. Day after day, this can become monotonous. We can't have it all ways: on a charter boat catering to overnight guests, who book months ahead for their cruise, we must feed, house, and take full responsibility for them day and night. Their decision to sail with us (as was mentioned earlier) has been no sudden whim; they have a fair idea of what is in store, and in most cases they are interested in us and our ship. During the charter, this can lead to genuine rapport and save the whole thing from becoming just another job.

If you're an aloof individual who prefers to keep apart, then most likely day-chartering will be your bag. If you're a garrulous sort of bird who likes to mix with people, your forte will most likely be the long-term charter. I've tried both, and in my book, the latter wins hands down.

MOTOR-YACHT CHARTERS

Almost everything covered in this book applies as equally to a motor yacht or motorsailer as it does to an auxiliary sailboat.

In some colder areas (the Canadian West Coast, Alaska, and the New Zealand fjords are typical), a charter cruise in a motor yacht or motorsailer with a large, comfortable wheelhouse can be more enticing than a trip on a conventional sailboat where guests, as a rule, are more exposed to the weather. However, aboard a vessel proceeding under power only for the entire voyage, there is always the question of how to entertain guests. This is the main problem in motorboat chartering; people become bored with just sitting and listening to a droning engine. Spectacular scenery helps, of course, and while it can aid a skipper in feeling that he is giving the gang their money's worth, there needs to be something else if he's going to get them, or their friends, back. The ultimate success of a long-term charter usually revolves around the food (*see* Chapter 4), but if that is all that is offered, along with an occasional glimpse of a snow-capped mountain through a wheelhouse window, few of the customers will yearn to return.

Aboard a sailboat operating in the tropics, there is seldom the problem of guests becoming disenchanted while underway, for a vessel that uses the wind to take her from A to B can provide her charter party with diversions in plenty as she sails. There is sail trimming, steering, sheets to tend as she beats up to anchor under the land, sails to furl, awnings to erect, preparing the ship for her next overnight stop—all activities directly related to the voyage. It doesn't really matter whether a guest throws himself whole-heartedly into this sort of routine or views it from a supine position in the sun (or shade). There has been plenty of interesting action, whether he's chosen to take part in it or not.

The motor-yacht charterer has no such entertainment as his ship proceeds, so to keep him happy and make him feel that he's getting more for his money than silence (once the engines are stopped), it is common for organized shoreside excursions to be incorporated as part of the cruise. Hunting parties, exploring expeditions, and barbecue picnics ashore are typical of the activities arranged, and if the whole thing is well planned, a motor yacht can keep busy.

In addition to every other expense covered in this book (except sails and rigging), whether or not she can be made to pay will depend upon the price and availability of fuel and the wear and tear on machinery. The aspiring charter operator of a motor yacht should have a good, long look at these factors when working out a charter price for guests, and before committing himself to the game.

SPORTFISHING

The main ingredient in any sportfishing venture is fish. A man can own the best-equipped sportfishing vessel afloat, and be capable of running it, but if there are no fish to take his bait (or lure) in the area he's chosen to work, he'll never make a cent. Fuel prices and the cost of engine maintenance are other important factors.

The outfitting of sportfishing boats and the techniques involved in hunting and landing the prey are adequately dealt with in other books written solely for that purpose. My advice to the reader who wants to try this part of the charter game is to study every piece of information on the subject he can lay his hands on—including the International Game Fish Association (I.G.F.A.) rules. The next move, unless he feels he is qualified to be a skipper, is to get a job as mate on a professional sportfisherman. A good mate is everything to a sportfishing captain. When a fish is finally alongside, it is the mate who gaffs, lands, and/or tags it. A mistake here can lose the fish—and, if the fisherman is accumulating points for competition, lose them as well. A mate must be able to make up baits, look after and overhaul fishing gear, deal with any fish brought aboard or hove up alongside on the gin pole, and keep a clean ship. If you can make it as a mate, you just might become a competent skipper.

A first-class professional captain-and-mate sportfishing team can, between them—and without touching the line (that's against the rules)—be responsible for a rank amateur bringing in a sizable fish.

A few years ago I met a middle-aged couple, whom I shall call Bill and Mary, in Acapulco. They were from New York, and in the shade of the yacht club bar over margaritas, they proudly showed me a photo taken the day before. It was a picture of Mary, who was standing, rod in hand, alongside a large sailfish she had caught from a local sportfishing boat. Not only was this

The mate who can gaff a fish without losing it and get it aboard without fuss or bother is solid gold to a sportfishing captain. (Photo by Dade Thornton and Bailey Bobbitt)

the first time that Mary had fished; she had never been aboard a boat before.
All of which means, of course, that somewhere along the Acapulco waterfront was a top-notch captain-and-mate sportfishing team.

As for the economics of a sportfishing operation, some make it and some
starve. A sportfisherman, especially if based in a "seasonal" area, can quickly
have the odds stacked against him. An absence of fish, plus a consistent run
of bad weather, is a tough combination to fight and still yield a profit. And this
can happen.

The edge for consistently making money, in my opinion, is with the crewed
auxiliary sailboat. A chartering sailboat can duck and dodge her way from
bay to bay during bad weather and, if forced by conditions to lie at anchor,
she can often content her party with an expedition ashore. A sportfishing
vessel cannot do that. She is chartered to catch fish, and to do that, she has
to be out there. A short fishing season, coupled with consistently bad
weather that causes clients to cancel or not book at all, can quickly make
sportfishing a marginal business. It follows, then, that if the first ingredient for
a successful operation is fish, the second is weather and a long season. The
more days a sportfishing boat can spend on the job, the more money she'll
make, for she is paid by the day. Some skippers working an area that
provides a relatively short season of 140 days also hold down another job.
Others, operating in a more equable region, crack 200 days and leave it at
that. I have known Virgin Island sportfishing boats to exceed 300 days a year.

THE CHARTER GAME

In common with day boats, sportfishermen frequently draw their clients from hotels. Some boats are owned by hotel chains. The option of a day's, or sometimes half a day's fishing is listed by the hotel, along with other activities for guests, who usually have priority over clients drawn from an outside source. Other vessels work through agents, get their customers through game-fishing clubs, or, again in the manner of day boats, work off the waterfront.

We often worked with sportfishermen when chartering in the Virgin Islands. Typically, a party would request in advance that a day's sportfishing be incorporated into their charter cruise. We would arrange the booking, keep in touch by radio with the fisherman, and, on the day in question, be anchored in a bay convenient for him to pick up his customers. During the day we would continue with our own program (it was seldom that the entire party wanted to fish), and late afternoon would see us anchored in a cove close to the sportfisherman's course to his home base, so that, with a minimum of trouble, he could land our gang back aboard. The fishing trip was always regarded as an extra over and above our total charter fee, and the fisherman was paid directly by our party.

I have heard sportfishermen assert that the game these days is not as good as it was before long-ranging foreign commercial fishing boats started catching "sport" fish to eat. Be that as it may, and while I don't doubt that now and again a marlin or swordfish capable of playing havoc with a sportfisherman's adrenalin is caught for commercial purposes, I have only seen this once— and by someone to whom no sportfisherman worth his salt would begrudge the catch.

It was early one morning, off the isthmus between Tahiti-iti and Tahiti. We were trolling about a mile outside the reef in Ed's (a friend's) sportfishing boat. All hands were watching the bait being towed astern. The horizon was clean—except for a little dot, which, as we turned to go back over the course again, steadily got bigger.

It turned out to be a canoe—an outrigger some 20 feet long. Seated aft, and paddling industriously, was a brawny Tahitian wearing a broad smile and little else. He had every reason to smile. Lying across his frail craft—its tail on the outrigger and body on the center of the canoe's slim hull—was a blue marlin. It was 250 pounds if it was an ounce, and as we slowed down to range closer and marvel, his hand plunged down into the canoe.

It emerged again with a tangled mass of line and a large hook, which was waved triumphantly above his head—his fishing gear. Back into the canoe went his precious equipment (how the devil he ever caught a marlin with it, I'll never know), and away he went, paddling strongly toward a gap in the smoky line of reef ahead.

His tactics in hooking and landing his prize wouldn't have earned him point number one in any I.G.F.A. competition, but I have a feeling that wouldn't have worried our hero at all. Come nightfall, he would be the man of the hour at the village kai kai—and you could bet your last coconut on that!

WATER SKIING

Water-ski boats—small, open craft usually driven by powerful outboards—are frequently owned by waterfront hotels in resort areas and used for guests' recreation. Others, privately owned, pick up business from the passing public at beach resorts, or work through hotels, or sometimes brokers, to whom they pay commission.

At first glance, it might seem that the operator of a water-ski boat has a dream job, one without worry or responsibility. In fact, the exact opposite applies. A ski boat can be a lethal machine capable of slicing open the head of a swimmer, sending out a wake that can cause moored craft to roll badly enough to injure someone aboard and even inflict injury on its own customers. I have a friend who can testify firsthand to that.

Boris was water skiing in the Bay of Islands, Suva, and in trying a spectacular "cut" over one side of the wake, misjudged, released the ski rope, and ended up in the water. All of which can be a lot of fun and is something that has happened to most of us who have had a fling at the sport. In this case, however, when the boat turned back to pick him up, it dragged the ski rope over where he was floating. Boris reached out to grab it, a half hitch in the line neatly settled over his thumb, and, after a few seconds that he prefers not to recall, took half of it away.

The operator of a ski boat has a lot of responsibility riding with him when he opens up the throttle and starts towing people around. Here are some of the "dos" and "don'ts":

Make sure every skier wears a flotation belt.

Take it easy with beginners. Don't pull around in too tight a curve so that they're forced to let go and end up in the mangroves, or in shallow water, where they may land on a bed of sea urchins or a pile of rocks.

Don't run over a "ditched" skier on your way back to pick him up.

Don't run over the ski rope and get it around your propeller.

Don't go tearing in at speed toward a skier in the water. If you haven't room to turn in a wide, slow arc and approach him from downwind, haul your ski rope aboard, maneuver your boat carefully around, and nudge up to him dead slow.

Don't water ski close to anchored or moored boats. The roll that your wake sets up is the reason why a large section of the cruising gang loves water skiers about as much as a dog loves a cat.

THE CHARTER GAME

Ideally, a secluded estuary or bay, or best of all, an allotted water-skiing area, is what the ski-boat operator should look for. Here he can ply his trade without distraction, secure in the knowledge that not only is he giving his clients their money's worth but his popularity is intact as well. Ski boats should carry another person as well as the driver, as it is difficult for a driver to watch a skier and the water ahead at the same time. In some parts of the world, legislation requires that ski boats have two persons aboard for this reason.

GLASS-BOTTOM BOATS

Glass-bottom boats are not charter boats in the strict sense. The reason for their inclusion in this book is that, in addition to being an important part of the floating tourist scene, they can also be moneymakers.

The basic elements necessary for a successful glass-bottom boat enterprise are: clear, preferably sheltered water; interesting underwater sights—such as coral, fishes, a wreck, or better yet, all three; a base for operating where there is customer potential. Regarding this last element, a busy tourist port in the tropics, or even a large hotel, can often justify a venture into the glass-bottom boat game.

Glass-bottom boats get their clients from hotels, the passing tourist stream, and travel agents. It is common for a glass-bottom boat trip—ranging from a few hours to a full day—to be arranged by an agent as part of a package deal with airlines, hotels, and, frequently, cruise ship companies. In this manner, a boat can sometimes be booked months ahead.

A glass-bottom boat, with her precious glass covered over inside, can also be used for another facet of the tourist game, the moonlight cruise.

For the uninitiated, the glass bottom—through which they can spy on the underwater world (without getting wet)—is a piece of plate glass set in the bottom of the boat and surrounded by a trunk inside. The size of the glass depends on the vessel. A 22-foot boat might, typically, have a piece of glass five feet long and 14 inches wide. A 64-footer carrying 100 passengers—such as the *Coral See II*, which Colin, a friend, owns and operates in Suva, Fiji—has 24 feet of glass, 18 inches wide, for surveying the depths. The glass is set in the bottom in four six-foot lengths and is ⅝ inch thick. The top of the inside trunk—which should always rise well above the load waterline in case of accidental glass fracture—forms the table for buffet luncheons.

A running commentary on sights over a loudspeaker system, a diver from the boat who can be watched feeding fishes through the glass, entertainment and/or a picnic ashore on an island—all are part of the glass-bottom boat scene.

Aboard Coral See II, *64-foot glass-bottom boat licensed to carry 100 passengers, Suva, Fiji. Glass bottom through which passengers see underwater sights . . . .*

. . . . is concealed by flush hatch covers for a buffet luncheon. (Photos by Colin White)

DIVING CHARTERS

Diving charters, involving the use of scuba (self-contained underwater breathing apparatus), have a large following in many parts of the globe. It can almost be said that wherever there is water there is diving, or, if the sport hasn't reached there yet, it will one day. With more and more people becoming interested in giving and taking courses and attaining qualified diver status, the necessity for new, interesting locations underwater to dive on, explore, and photograph will, perhaps, always exist.

To devote anything less than a full book to this magnificent pastime would seem to do it an injustice. However (and as a convert of many years standing, I could never do this), space, plus the purpose of this book, dictates that I concentrate on the chartering aspect.

While most of us prefer to dive in warm tropic water, in many cases without a wet suit, it is an undeniable fact that life and sights beneath the surface in many temperate regions attract large numbers of divers.

A scuba-diving operation is one section of the chartering game that appears less dependent on fine, warm weather than any other. In some colder climes, provided that the underwater world is interesting, scuba continues long after winter has caused other types of chartering to bog down. Dive boats can operate and make money under conditions where other charter boats couldn't make a dime. The reason for this is that the average diver's interest is centered on what is happening below the surface, not on what the weather or scenery is like on top. Clad in his wet suit and well insulated against the cold, he can slip over the side of a vessel that's rolling her scuppers under to enter a tranquil, well-ordered world. On the surface, the conditions and temperature may be such that any other type of charterer would want his money back, but to the real dyed-in-the-wool, gung-ho diver, weather is just incidental stuff, to be endured so that he may indulge his first love of diving.

A wide variety of vessels cater to scuba divers. Often it is only a small outboard-powered boat, which doubles as a ski boat, that is used to take divers from a hotel or diving camp to a nearby underwater site. Larger vessels (usually powerboats) cruise with divers aboard and offer the same facilities and services as long-term charter boats. Procedures for the stocking up, anchoring, general seamanship, maintenance, and treatment of guests covered in this book apply as equally to these larger boats as to any other craft in the charter game. Such vessels usually carry a large compressor for charging bottles; some dive boats even have a decompression chamber.

Some auxiliary sailboats cater to divers during a regular charter cruise. Dave, a professional instructor, and Rozzy (old friends) have done so for years in the Mediterranean and West Indies on the 47-foot ketch *Parandah*—

Steel catamaran diving boat Whai, *Whitianga, New Zealand. (*Waikato Times *photo)*

also in the West Indies in the ketches *Summer Wind* (77 feet) and *Glen-Mac* (50 feet). Guests intersperse their diving with sailing and sightseeing. This can be popular with clients who don't want to dive to the exclusion of everything else. A word of warning, though, to the sailboat owner who would do this: diving parties can be tough on a boat, and their equipment takes up quite a lot of room aboard. Scuba tanks dumped on teak decks or hatches can really mark them up.

A not-unusual dive-boat operation on the other side of the world is that of the 44-foot catamaran *Whai.* Working in a temperate climate, and exceeding 200 days of diving a year, she takes clients from Whitianga, New Zealand, to dive around the Mercury Islands. Her operators have a dive shop ashore that handles bookings and sells diving gear, as well as hiring out bottles and equipment to clients taking a trip on the boat.

Diving clubs are responsible for supplying a lot of business to charter boats employed in the scuba game. This, in general, is good, as it more or less guarantees that everybody coming aboard is an experienced diver. Other parties make up their own groups. Some well-heeled adherents of the sport travel all over the world to charter a boat and dive. In all cases—no matter how short or how long a distance they have come or who they are— the responsibility for their safety rests with the charter skipper. He must be able to take care of his party in the water. Anyone can say he is a diver. Some members of diving parties are qualified; some are not. The person in charge of divers (usually the skipper) should be an experienced, fully licensed diver capable of putting unqualified divers through their paces. He should watch the moves of all the divers in his party. If he has taken their money, they are his responsibility.

Something worth mentioning here is the charging of bottles aboard while on a diving cruise. Nothing disturbs a quiet bay more than a dive boat with a compressor going half the night. Carry as large a unit as possible so that this part of the business may be attended to quickly, and with the least inconvenience to others.

Regarding the economics of diving charters: the range of vessels catering to divers is so varied and the locations so different that only the most basic rules can be touched upon as a guide to pricing—again, without dedicating an entire book to the subject. But one thing is obvious: the owner of a dive boat can go broke as quickly as the operator of any other type of charter boat if he doesn't price his services realistically. I have come across more than a few diving operators hovering on the brink of bankruptcy, and the

Large (8.5 cubic feet per minute) compressor on the stern of the 50-footer Glen-Mac. *The engine is a 12 hp Lister diesel. Compressor is fitted with 25-foot filler hose and 4-tank manifold. Eight tanks can be filled in one hour without taking them from the dinghy. Note plastic intake hose led well up to windward. (Photo by Dave Ferneding)*

Scuba bottles stowed in teak cradles on deck of sailing charter boat Glen-Mac. *(Photo by Dave Ferneding)*

general answer to my queries of "Why?" has been, "We can't charge any more—divers won't come out with us if we do!" To which I say, raise the prices anyhow—high enough to give a reasonable return on your investment and labor (it may mean that you must improve your services also)—or get out of the game.

If you're only taking divers out for a few hours at a time in a rubber dinghy or motorized raft, your charges need not be high, because—let's face it— you're not really supplying much and your investment is not great. However, if you're in pretty deep financially, and your ship supplies accommodations and services comparable with those of a good, crewed charter boat, you *must* charge. You'll be outward bound as a diving operator if you don't! I consider that diving charges should be in direct proportion to services offered, which go hand in glove with the effort it takes to supply them and the size of the investment involved.

Chartering, it will be seen, is the same as any other business. Some do well, some break even, some go broke. The difference with a crewed, owner-operated sailing charter yacht as a commercial venture over a bareboat, ski boat, glass-bottom boat, and most sportfishing and scuba operations is that your charter boat is your home and so obviates the necessity of maintaining a domicile ashore. If you should decide to change your base of operations, you sail there in your own house. It can be an ideal business for the couple with a yen to live aboard and have their boat pay the way. Another factor in favor of the sailing charter boat is that any escalation in the price of fuel is not a major consideration.

195

Chapter Six

Giving the Customers
and Yourself a Good Time

A charter-boat captain should never lose sight of the fact that he is in the game because he wants to be. This is one of the glamour occupations, and there are not many of them. The whole idea of being afloat permanently and of being paid to take people sailing is that you want to be free, be away from the rat race, and be your own boss, doing just that.

Pick the place in the world where you want to charter carefully and, having made your choice, give it all you've got. The area (if you've done your homework properly) will be interesting, have good anchorages, a climate that suits you, and be far enough off the beaten track for your customers to want to return, and for you to want to stay.

As mentioned before, read up on the region you are chartering in. Do some research through books and papers that record the history of the area. Bone up on the local tales, both historic and modern, that people living in the region can supply. All this can and should be enjoyable. Don't approach this facet of the charter business with an attitude of, "Oh, I suppose I've got to know it." If you don't do the research and accumulate a fund of anecdotes and facts to retell to charter parties, you'll still make out, but you can lose on the feeling that comes from earning your bread in the same waters as perhaps a notorious freebooter did (in a different manner) a few hundred years before. Or not be able to marvel, as you sail in the lee of Guadeloupe (or get becalmed in the lee), that but for the result of the famous naval battle that took place there so long ago, the world might be apportioned differently.

To some, this may seem like kids' stuff, but not to me, no sir! Whether Drake ever sat on a hill in St. Thomas and spied on the Spanish fleet is debatable, but the seat up there marking the spot is good enough for me. And when we sailed by Tofua in the Tonga Islands with a party aboard, all hands knew to a hair (as a result of my spying in a book below before coming on deck to announce it airily) the exact moment we sailed over the spot where the mutiny on H.M.S. *Bounty* took place. . . .

For the average charter party, this is all an enjoyable part of the game. Incidentally, in delving into the antics of some of our predecessors, I have found that far from having to add a few embellishments to liven up the tales, it has often been necessary to leave out some of the more lurid parts to make them palatable!

Check into likely points of interest ashore, too. An old castle, an abandoned mill, a hill from where spectacular views may be enjoyed (and photographed), interesting flora, fauna—all add spice to a cruise.

Participate in all this yourself. Enthusiasm is contagious—if you like it, they'll like it. Don't forget, you're showing them your world, your life, and you've every right to be proud of it. You are one of the guys who has made the break. Some of the people you take away would give their eye teeth to be able to do what you are doing.

Some parties like to dress up and dine ashore now and again during a cruise, so keep suitable hotels or restaurants in mind as the trip progresses. Know something about them, such as type of food, prices, and quality. And the food *must* be good. Dinner ashore is a guaranteed morale booster for the ship's cook. For one precious night, she (or he) is out of the "barrel" and off with the crowd, and it never fails to go over big. The way I have always played it financially is: if I suggest we all go ashore and eat, I pay. If they want to take us ashore for dinner, fine—they pay.

We have never encouraged segregation, such as having the party eat separately from us aboard the ship, so we have never had a gang that headed off ashore to eat by themselves. However, this does happen on some of the larger vessels that are run by a paid crew and are not owner-operated. I don't believe it contributes to a relaxed, happy atmosphere, though. I remember one family who came with us on a cruise in the Virgins after chartering a 96-footer "down islands" the year before. They luxuriated in the freedom: the kids took the wheel and gave a hand with the sails, and all were especially happy about the fact that they weren't expected to call me Captain.

Lunch ashore at a restaurant, often after a morning sail, can suit both party and crew. While the guests poke around the village or town, and perhaps make a few purchases, it is possible to shop for provisions, shoot

THE CHARTER GAME

the breeze with other charter crews, and all meet for a few cold ones before eating.

In order to continue enjoying yourself at the charter game, and also to be able to show returning customers fresh sights, try to visit new places whenever possible. Learn your chartering region inside out. This may take years in some places, but it is a surefire way to appreciate the territory and so prevent life from becoming monotonous.

While a lot of people enjoy participating in sailing the ship, the planning of each day's activities can also attract a fair amount of interest.

Whenever the occasion warrants it, spread out a chart of the cruising area for all hands to pore over and see what is going on. Explain alternative routes and anchorages. This is always well received. Whether it is really understood doesn't matter; the sense of participation is what counts. For the benefit of those whose knowledge of chartwork is rudimentary or non-existent, explain a few of the elemental facts. Show them how to measure distance off the latitude scale at each side of the chart, how to lay off a course, how to take a running fix.

Now and again, people who are taking a navigation course ashore will come away on a trip. We have often had the experience of watching amateur Magellans scurry between deck and chart table, taking bearings and plotting

White Squall II *taking it easy under awnings behind Wandingi Islet in the Fiji Islands. (Photo by Ross Norgrove)*

positions—great stuff! One gang I remember in particular comprised three couples. Each owned a motor-cruiser on Lake Erie, and the men were all taking an advanced course in celestial navigation. They got in a lot of practice with my sextant that trip when underway, and they were able to discover firsthand that the only really difficult part of navigation can be the taking of an accurate sight.

Dinghy excursions—up a river, exploring an inlet, or to a coral reef to snorkel over or just gaze at through a lookbucket—can be enjoyed by charter party and crew alike. An exhilarating sail is what we all sign on for, and it is something from which each of us, in varying degrees, gets pleasure. However, an interesting dinghy trip, with a few "cold ones" stashed away in an ice chest to fortify the troops as we go along, has a lot to recommend it and represents the other side of the coin.

The knowledge that there are creeks, bays, or reefs within his cruising area that can be used for this kind of entertainment gives a charter skipper another string for his bow. If the weather kicks up outside, prior knowledge that he can take his guests on a dinghy excursion with maybe a picnic thrown in—and without leaving the bay—will often keep everyone happy and save a few of them from tossing their cookies as well.

On a rainy day, try to do the same things you would have done if it were fine. If you had planned on sailing into a bay, taking the dinghy ashore, and climbing a hill to inspect an old fort, then do just that, rain or no rain. Sitting around aboard ship is no good either for you or your guests. If some of the gang want to stay in the ship and play gin rummy (or whatever), fine, but it is seldom that they all do. So pile the energetic folk into the dinghy and take them on a trip. You'll all feel better for it.

Trolling from the dinghy for surface fish can be a lot of fun, too. In fact, I think we have caught more fish this way over the years than by any other method or from any other boat, including *White Squall II.* Our system is to tow a silver "spoon" or feather "jig" about 50 yards astern of the dinghy. We use a three-foot wire trace and an 80-pound breaking strain monofilament line. Once the lure is out and we are trolling slowly along, I pass a bight of the line through an eye bolt inside the dinghy transom and place it over the stern anchor cleat. Minine, sitting on the middle thwart, holds the part of the line leading inboard from the eye bolt. We have found this more efficient than a fishing pole or than making the line fast directly to the cleat, for when a fish hits, the line renders just a little through the eye bolt, round the cleat, and so to her hand—and he's hooked. Minine grabs the line over the transom, and as I turn the dinghy slowly toward the side where the fish is, without slackening speed and still keeping strain on the line, she brings him in hand over hand. Not very sporting, perhaps, but highly effective!

Bonefishing has a large following among anglers, and adherents to this

Awnings, backgammon, cold drinks . . . all part of the charter scene. (Photo by Dave Ferneding)

sport will often be among a charter group. Look around for bonefishing flats within your chartering area. Know where to take your bonefishing buffs. For bait, you can use hermit crabs, but best of all are the little white-opaque "ghost" crabs that live in sand. Dig up some with your hands and take them along on your next expedition. They'll tickle the taste buds of the fussiest bonefish! Don't kill the bonefish when you catch them; let them go so they can fight again. They may be full of bones and no good to eat, but, pound for pound, they're the gamest sport fish in the world.

While on the subject of using the dinghy for excursions and fishing trips, don't forget to carry plenty of outboard gas.

Birthdays and anniversaries of the guests are often celebrated when away on a cruise. Be prepared by having champagne, candles, and paper hats aboard. These events can give everyone enjoyment. And don't forget your own special occasions, either; the charter group will usually join in!

If you advertise yourself as a sailboat, then sail! Don't just steam from bay to bay with an awning up, unless your party specifically requests it or unless there is a deadline you must meet, and existing conditions, such as a calm or a strong headwind, make the assistance of an engine desirable.

Regarding calms, some people don't mind them. I've seen charter parties lie around the decks sunning themselves, with the sea as flat as a board. The ship may be hardly moving, but if those sails are up, they are happy.

And that's the whole thing right there—keeping a happy ship. As I have stressed throughout this book, give them what they came to get, and there is no way you can miss being successful. It is possible for a charter skipper to feel at times that he is living a dream, to marvel, while his vessel slides along in a moderate sea, that he's actually getting paid to do this! He is entitled to the feeling, and so is his crew, just as long as they know they are giving the charter party a fair deal—in other words, once again, a clean, well-run ship, good food, and an interesting cruise.

Try to leave your ship in a safe place and take a vacation away in the "off" season. If you've been working solidly at the game, the break will prevent you from becoming stale, for even paradise can pall on us human beings. After the vacation, if you have been to one or two cities, you'll be so glad to get back aboard that you'll wonder why you ever left the boat.

An aspiring charter captain can draw consolation from the fact that we've all had to do it the first time. There is no substitute for the first charter. After you've done one, you're home and free. They are all easier after that. And don't think that your ex-charter guests will forget you, that they will not remember, a year or two after their cruise, the glimpse they have had of the life you lead, or their experiences aboard your ship. There is real satisfaction in being able to give people a memorable vacation—and to enjoy yourself at the same time.

Appendix I
Charter People and Insurance

by Henry F. Milstrey
Director, Edinburgh Insurance Company Limited
Road Town
Tortola, British Virgin Islands

Here in the Virgin Islands, amidst what many believe to be just about the finest sailing area in the world, chartering has become more than a way of life. It is a local industry and governments are now aware of its presence. Ordinances governing licensing, conduct, taxation, etc., have taken away much of the glamour and adventure that had existed for a number of years. The enchantment of sailing through the Islands, the fine weather and sea conditions, uncrowded anchorages—these are perennial.

But, the old happy-go-lucky, great adventurers are fast disappearing and are being replaced by charter-people who are at least aware of the logistics of the business, including insurance. As an insurance underwriter, heavily involved in yacht insurance, for both private and charter use, I may pass on a few bits of information for the potential charter-skipper.

For the protection of his business property, the charter-skipper should insure his yacht against loss or damages to the Hull, Machinery, Equipment, etc., by an All-Risk Policy. Premium rates will vary in accordance with the age of the vessel, type of construction, condition, area to be navigated, use, etc. In certain instances, the Insurer will require a survey, the cost of which must be borne by the vessel. The premium rate will be affected by the amount of the deductible, i.e., the higher the deductible, the lower the rate. (A typical example will follow below.)

We now come to what has become in these recent years the most important section of the charter policy, Protection and Indemnity. This covers the vessel against claims for Bodily Injury and Property Damage. Today, it is not unusual to be faced suddenly with a claim of six figures for a simple fracture of the arm, etc. The public, including charterers, has evidently found the ultimate get-rich-quick schemes in insurance claims. In the writer's opinion, it would be extremely unwise for a charter-skipper to carry P and I with a Combined Single Limit of less than $300,000. This means that each accident or occurrence, be it Bodily Injury or Property Damage (or a combination of both) is covered up to the insured limit. Medical Payments with a limit of $1,000 are usually included in the P and I premium.

To illustrate all the above, let us create a hypothetical example of insurance costs and requirements, for coverages in this area of the Caribbean.

THE CHARTER GAME

The risk: A 48′ stock molded fiberglass auxiliary ketch with diesel power. Built 1970 by a reputable builder, with all standard ancillaries, safety equipment, a competent, licensed skipper with adequate experience in the area plus a satisfactory condition survey made by a recognized independent surveyor within three years. The navigating area, whilst on charter, to be the U.S. Virgin Islands and the British Virgin Islands, or held covered at a rate to be arranged. (This means, e.g., that if the vessel has a charter for a single voyage "down islands," an endorsement giving this extension of the navigating limits would be attached to the Policy and an additional premium, based upon the duration, distance, or any other circumstances of the voyage, would be charged.) It should be noted that the original navigating limits are quite standard in this area of the Caribbean and this is well accepted by the charter operators. It should also be noted that the U.S. Coast Guard sets a limit of six passengers on any vessel, be it U.S. flag or other, chartering out of U.S. Territorial Waters. It is common practice for larger charter vessels (such as *White Squall II*, when the Great Old Man was chartering here) to put six passengers on board at St. Thomas, U.S.V.I., and transport the balance of his charter party via ferry or airplane to Tortola in the British Virgin Islands where they would go on board. Upon completion of the charter, it would be legal to return the entire party to any U.S. port. As in other parts of the world, entry fees are charged, and in the B.V.I., for example, a "head tax" is charged upon exit.

For the purpose of our typical quotation, we will assume that the vessel accommodates six in the charter party. The crew consists of two, the skipper and one other, split-tail or macho. Now, the quotation, as we would offer it:

Insured	Captain X	
Address	Homeport, St. Thomas, U.S.V.I.	
Effective	Twelve (12) months at June 1, 1977, Noon L.S.T. upon the 48′ auxiliary ketch *Fairwind*	
Hull, Machinery, Equipment, etc.	Valued $90,000 (market value)	
Deductible	$1,000 each and every claim except Total Loss.	
Rate	2½% (assuming satisfactory survey)	
Premium		$2,250
Protection & Indemnity	with limits of $300,000 each and every occurrence	450 C.S.L.
Medical Payments	with limits of $1,000 each accident	included
	TOTAL	$2,700
		Cancelling Returns Only.

Special Conditions:

Permission granted to Charter with a maximum of six passengers and with the Owner or the Owner's professional, licensed skipper in charge whilst on Charter.

Navigation Limits:

U.S. Virgin Islands and British Virgin Islands or held covered at a rate to be arranged.

Warranted:

Vessel's dinghy 11′ Avon inflatable, with 12 h.p. Johnson outboard, total value $1,200, included in policy and premium with a deductible of $125 each and every claim except Total Loss.

Information, not Warranty:

Vessel built 1970, by Blank Yachts, Inc., Camden, Maine, of fiberglass construction and powered by a Blank 65 h.p. diesel engine.

N.B. Standard Endorsements would include: Cancellation Clause, Seaworthiness Clause (only required for Cruising Yachts), Loss Payee Endorsement (where required).

It should be noted that the above comprises "ballpark" figures and each potential risk would be rated on its own merits and appraisal.

Appendix II
Typical Reply to a Charter Inquiry

Auxiliary Ketch *Fairwind*
Someport
September 7, 19—

Mr. S. Jones
Any Street
Darien, Conn.

Dear Mr. Jones:

Thank you for your letter of September 2 addressed to George Blank, captain of *Fairwind*. He will be delighted to hear from a friend of Tom Brown, whose charter last year he spoke of with pleasure.

I note your request for *Fairwind*'s charter cost per week for a party of four, also available dates early April. We will deal with the weekly rate first, which is as follows: Total price for one week, four guests, two crew, is $2,400.00. This is an "all-found" cost, including food, beverages (liquor, beer, wines, sodas), fuel, ice, ship's laundry, incidental port fees—everything except tobacco.

A deposit of half the charter fee is required to make a reservation firm. On receipt of this, I will send you two signed and witnessed copies of our standard charter agreement. One you keep, the other you complete and return, along with a list of any food dislikes or allergies—also beverage preferences.

As of this date, *Fairwind* is free from April 3 through 20, so I will tentatively book you for April 4 through 11, pending receipt of your deposit. As we cannot hold dates without a deposit, I urge you to send this as soon as possible in case someone confirms this period before you.

Fairwind, as you can see from the accompanying brochure, is a safe, comfortable boat, with private accommodation for two couples below, and plenty of lounging room on deck. Crew's quarters are separate. Cruises have the accent on sailing to remote islands and bays, swimming, snorkeling, delicious food, informality, and fun.

George and Betty Blank are very proud of their ship, and delight to show charter guests her paces under sail. They are out on charter at the moment, but on their return (three days), will read your letter along with the rest of the mail.

They'll look forward to welcoming you aboard.

Sincerely,

(Mrs.) John R. Blow,
for Capt. George Blank

Appendix III
Charter Contract

This charter contract has been in use aboard *White Squall II* for fourteen years. Any extra provisions, such as charges for deadheading (we had a 1,300-mile deadhead on one occasion in the Pacific), are written on the reverse side as an addendum and are signed and witnessed by both parties.

Charter Contract: _____ September 15th, 19-- _____ _____ "FAIRWIND" _____
                              DATE   BOAT

between ___ G. BLANK ___ and ___ S. JONES ___ ___ DARIEN, CONN. ___
        CAPTAIN/OWNER   CHARTERER   ADDRESS

from ___ NOON ___ ___ APRIL 4th,19-- ___ to ___ NOON ___ ___ APRIL 11th, 19-- ___
         TIME   DATE   TIME   DATE

Contract cancelled if Boat not ready by ___ NOON APRIL 5th. ___ .
                                                DATE

___ $2,400.00 ___ ___ $1,200.00 ___ ___ $1,200.00 ___ ~~plus expenses incurred~~
   AMOUNT CHARTER   DEPOSIT   BALANCE DUE CASH OR
                                          TRAVELERS CHECKS ON BOARDING

$ ___ NIL ___ ___ ~~per person per day including certain area~~. Maximum charter guests ___ 4 ___
        AMOUNT

___ ISLANDS ___ ___ SOMEPORT ___ ___ SOMEPORT ___
   CRUISING AREA   PORT OF BOARDING   PORT OF RELEASE

General:

The captain is competent, not only coastwise, but in deep sea navigation. The captain shall handle clearance and the normal running of the yacht. The captain shall be responsible for the safe navigation of the vessel, and the Charterer shall abide by his judgment as to sailing, weather, anchorages and pertinent matters.

Should the yacht, during the period of this charter party, be lost, stranded or disabled by act of God, fire, perils of the sea or other unavoidable accident, rendering her unfit for the use or purpose of this charter, and not brought about by act or fault of the Charterer, charter hire shall cease from the time thereof and neither of the parties shall be liable for any loss, damage, expense or inconvenience resulting therefrom.

The Charterer agrees not to assign this agreement, or sub-charter the yacht without the prior consent of the Owner.

The charterer agrees to be responsible for and to replace or make good any injury to the yacht, her furnishings and equipment, caused by himself or by any of his party, and to return the yacht in the same condition as received, less ordinary wear and tear. The yacht shall be surrendered free from any indebtedness that may have been incurred for account of or by order of the Charterer.

The Charterer agrees that this yacht shall be employed exclusively as a pleasure vessel for the sole and proper use of himself, his family, guests, and servants during the term of this charter.

The owner shall, for his own protection, keep the yacht fully insured against fire, marine and collision risks with protection and indemnity at his own expense for the period of this Agreement. In case of any accident or disaster, the charterer shall give immediate notification to the owner of same.

To the true and faithful performance of the foregoing agreement the said parties hereto bind themselves, their heirs, executors, administrators and assigns, each to the other.

IN WITNESS WHEREOF, the parties hereto have set their hands.

_____   _____
           WITNESS   OWNER

_____   _____
           WITNESS   CHARTERER

_____
            DATE

Index

THE CHARTER GAME